ALI BABA
AND THE
FORTY THIEVES
AND OTHER
STORIES

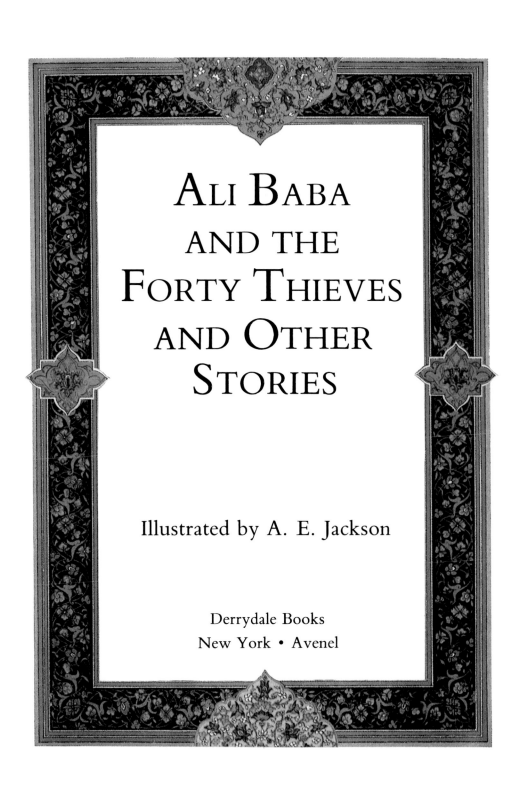

ALI BABA
AND THE
FORTY THIEVES
AND OTHER
STORIES

Illustrated by A. E. Jackson

Derrydale Books
New York • Avenel

Published by Derrydale Books,
distributed by Random House Value Publishing, Inc.,
40 Engelhard Avenue,
Avenel, New Jersey 07001

Random House
New York • Toronto • London • Sydney • Auckland

Designed by Liz Trovato

Printed and bound in Singapore

Library of Congress Cataloging-in-Publication Data
Arabian nights. English. Selections. 1994
Ali Baba and the forty thieves / illustrated by A.E. Jackson.
p. c.m.
Contents: Ali Baba — Sinbad the sailor — The enchanted horse.
ISBN 0-517-10178-5
[1. Fairy tales. 2. Folklore, Arab.] I. Jackson, A.E., ill.
II. Title.
PZ8.A4 1994
[398.21]—dc20   94-5148
                                 CIP
                                 AC

1 2 3 4 5 6 7 8

Contents

Introduction

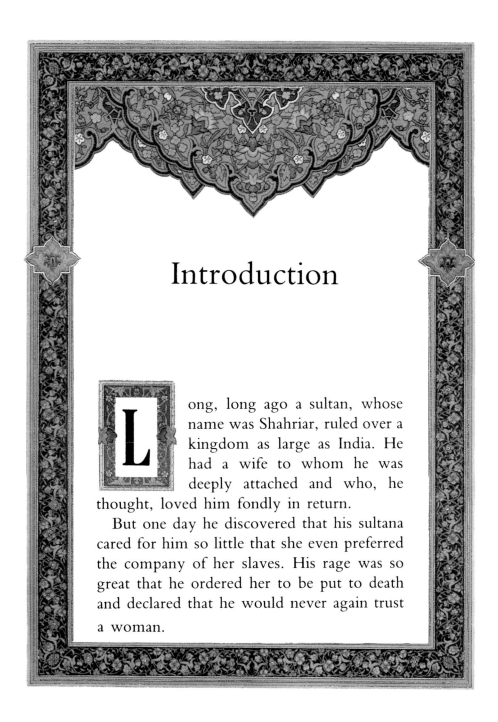

Long, long ago a sultan, whose name was Shahriar, ruled over a kingdom as large as India. He had a wife to whom he was deeply attached and who, he thought, loved him fondly in return.

But one day he discovered that his sultana cared for him so little that she even preferred the company of her slaves. His rage was so great that he ordered her to be put to death and declared that he would never again trust a woman.

Consequently, since the sultan did not care to remain single, he married a new wife every day, and had her put to death the following morning.

Now the grand vizier—that is to say, prime minister—had a beautiful daughter whose name was Sheherazade. In addition to being very beautiful she was very accomplished. She also had an amazing memory and never forgot anything she had read or heard. In fact, she possessed almost every virtue, and was the apple of her father's eye.

One day, when the grand vizier was looking extremely worried because so few suitable young ladies were left for the sultan to marry, his daughter, Sheherazade, came to him and said, "My father, I have a favor to ask."

"Ask, my child," he replied, "and if the request is reasonable, which, coming from you, it is sure to be, you may consider it granted."

"Then, my dear father," said Sheherazade, "let *me* be the sultan's next wife."

The grand vizier was at first struck dumb and breathless with horror. When he had recovered, he did his best to persuade his daughter to change her mind. But Sheherazade persisted and begged and coaxed the poor man until, much against his will, he agreed that she should have her way.

Even the sultan himself was surprised when the grand vizier proposed the match; for, as he plainly told his minister, his daughter must not expect to escape the fate which had befallen all the wives who had preceded her.

The grand vizier, with tears in his eyes, replied that both he and his daughter were well aware of this, but that they would, nevertheless, regard the temporary alliance as a great honor.

"In that case," said the sultan, "the marriage can take place tomorrow."

8

So, Sheherazade, gorgeously arrayed, was led to the palace and the marriage took place.

Now, as before mentioned, Sheherazade was extremely beautiful, and the sultan was quite charmed with her, and felt almost sorry that he would have to order her to be put to death in the usual way.

The day was just beginning to break when Sheherazade said, "I wonder if His Imperial Highness would allow me to relate one of my stories? Please let me tell one more tale before my lips are closed forever."

"What is that?" asked the sultan sleepily. "Let you tell a story? Why, certainly."

 10

At first he did not pay very much attention to the tale. But, as it went on, he became so enthralled that he felt he simply *must* hear the end. So, since it was time for him to rise and attend to affairs of state, he decided to put off the execution of Sheherazade for another twenty-four hours, or more if required.

The story of "Ali Baba and the Forty Thieves," and the others that follow, were among the tales told by Sheherazade during the "thousand and one nights," for each successive night brought a story as wonderful as those that had gone before. The sultan eventually fell in love with the fair storyteller and had not the heart to kill her. And everyone will agree that, had he done so, he would have been not only a very wicked but a very foolish man.

 11

Ali Baba
and the Forty Thieves

In a town in Persia there lived two brothers, one named Cassim, the other Ali Baba. When their father died, what little property he had was equally divided between his two sons. Cassim, however, married the daughter of a rich merchant and soon became the owner of a fine shop and several pieces of land. Consequently, through no effort of his own, he became one of the richest merchants in the town.

Ali Baba, on the other hand, married a woman he loved, who was as poor as himself, and had to eke out a living by cutting wood in a neighboring forest, loading it on his three donkeys, which were his only possession, and selling it about the town.

One day Ali Baba went to the forest and had almost finished cutting as much wood as his donkeys could carry when he saw coming toward him a large company of horsemen. He feared from their appearance that they might be robbers. He was a cautious man, so he climbed a tree that grew at the foot of a large rock and hid himself among the branches, where he could see without being seen.

Almost immediately it became evident that this very rock was the destination toward which the troop was bound. When they arrived each man alighted instantly from his horse, tethered it, and removed a sack that seemed by its weight and form to be filled with gold. There could no longer be any doubt that they were robbers. Ali Baba counted forty of them.

Just as he had done so, the man nearest to him, who seemed to be their leader, advanced toward the rock, and in a low but distinct voice uttered two words, "Open, Sesame!" Immediately the rock opened like a door, the leader and his men passed in, and the rock closed behind them.

For a long time Ali Baba waited. He didn't dare to descend from his hiding place lest they come out and catch him in the act. At last, when the waiting had grown almost unbearable, his patience was rewarded. The door in the rock opened, and out came the forty men, their captain leading them. When the last of them was through, the leader said, "Shut, Sesame!" and immediately the face of the rock closed together as before. Then they all mounted their horses and rode away.

As soon as he felt sure that they were not returning, Ali Baba came down from the tree and made his way to that part of the rock where he had seen the captain and his men enter. He remembered

the words the captain had said and wondered what would happen if he said them. "Open, Sesame!" he exclaimed, and the rock suddenly flew open.

Ali Baba, who had expected to find only a dark and gloomy cave, was astonished to see a large, spacious, well-lighted vaulted room, dug out of the rock and so high that he could not touch the ceiling with his hand. Light came in from an opening at the top of the rock. He saw in it a large quantity of provisions, numerous bales of rich merchandise, a store of silks and brocades, and, besides all this, great quantities of coins, both silver and gold, some piled in heaps and the rest stored in large leather bags placed one on top of another.

Ali Baba did not hesitate for a moment, but entered the cave. As soon as he was in, the door closed behind him. But, since he knew the magic words by which to open it, this did not worry him. He paid no attention to the silver, but went directly for the gold coins, and particularly the portion that was in the bags. Having collected as much as he thought he could carry, he went out in search of his donkeys, which he had left to look after themselves when he climbed the tree. They had strayed some way, but he brought them close to the opening in the rock. He loaded them with the sacks of gold and covered the sacks with wood so that they might not be seen. Then he closed the rock by saying the magic words he had learned, and departed for the town, a well-satisfied man.

When he got home he drove his donkeys into a small court. Shutting the gates carefully, he took off the wood that covered the bags and carried them in to his wife. She, discovering them to be full of gold, was afraid that her husband had stolen them and began sorrowfully to reproach him. Ali Baba soon put her mind at rest and, having poured all the gold into a great heap upon the floor, he sat down at her side to consider how wonderful it looked.

Soon his wife began counting the gold piece by piece. Ali Baba let her go on for a while, then he began laughing. "Wife," he said,

"you will never finish it that way. The best thing to do is to dig a hole and bury it, then we shall be sure that it is not slipping through our fingers."

"That will do well enough," said his wife, "but it would be better first to know how much gold is here. While you dig the hole I will go to Cassim's and borrow a measure small enough to give us an exact reckoning."

"Do as you will," answered her husband, "but see that you keep the thing secret."

Off went Ali Baba's wife to her brother-in-law's house. Cassim was away from home, so she asked his wife to lend her a small measure. This set the sister-in-law wondering. Knowing Ali Baba's poverty she was all the more curious to find out what kind of grain would require so small a measure. So before bringing it she covered the bottom with lard, and giving it to Ali Baba's wife told her to be sure to be quick in returning it. Ali Baba's wife agreed and made haste to get home; there finding the hole dug for its reception, she started to measure the gold into it. First she set the measure upon the heap, then she filled it, then she carried it to the hole; and so she continued until the last measure was counted. Then, leaving Ali Baba to finish the burying, she carried back the measure with all haste to her sister-in-law.

No sooner was her back turned than Cassim's wife looked at the bottom of the measure, and there to her astonishment she saw sticking to the lard a gold coin. "What!" she exclaimed, "has Ali Baba such an abundance of gold that he measures it instead of counting it? If that is so, how in the world did he get it?"

The moment her husband, Cassim, entered the house his wife flew to him and said, "Cassim, you think you are rich, but Ali Baba has infinitely more wealth; he does not count his gold as you do, he measures it." Cassim demanded an explanation, and his wife showed him the piece of gold she had found sticking to the bottom of the measure.

16

Far from feeling any pleasure at his brother's good fortune, Cassim was extremely jealous. The next morning, before sunrise, he went to Ali Baba with the intention of solving the mystery.

"Oh, Ali Baba," he said, "you are very reserved in your affairs. You pretend to be poor and yet you have so much money that you must measure it."

"Oh, my brother," replied Ali Baba, "I do not understand. Please explain what you mean."

"Do not pretend ignorance," answered Cassim, and he showed Ali Baba the piece of gold his wife had given him. "How many pieces have you like this that my wife found sticking to the bottom of the measure that your wife borrowed yesterday?"

17

Ali Baba, realizing that further concealment was useless, told his brother exactly what had happened and offered him an equal share of the treasure.

"That is the least that I have the right to expect," answered Cassim haughtily. "But you must also tell me exactly where the treasure lies so I may, if necessary, test the truth of your story. Otherwise I shall find it my duty to denounce you to the authorities."

Ali Baba, having a clear conscience, had little fear of Cassim's threats. But out of pure good nature he gave him all the information he desired, not forgetting to instruct him in the words that would permit him to get into the cave and out again.

Cassim, who had thus got all he had come for, lost no time in putting his own plan into execution. Intent on possessing all the treasures that yet remained he set off the next morning before day-break, taking with him ten mules laden with empty crates. When he arrived at the rock, he remembered the words his brother had taught him. No sooner was "Open, Sesame!" said that the door in the rock opened wide for him to pass through. And when he had entered, it shut behind him.

If the simple soul of Ali Baba had found delight in the riches of the cavern, greater still was the exultation of a greedy nature like Cassim's. Drunk with the wealth that lay before his eyes, all he could think of was gathering with all speed as much treasure as the ten mules could carry. Finally, having exhausted himself with heavy labor and greedy excitement, he suddenly found on returning to the door that he had forgotten the magic words.

"Open, Barley!" he said, but the door did not bulge an inch. He then named the various other kinds of grain, all but the right one, but the door did not move.

The more he tried to remember the word *sesame,* the more he failed. He threw to the ground the sacks he had collected, and paced

backward and forward in a frenzy of terror. The riches that surrounded him no longer had any attraction for him.

Toward noon the robbers returned, and saw, standing about the rock, the ten mules laden with crates. They were greatly surprised, and began to search with suspicion among the surrounding crannies and undergrowth. Finding no one there, they drew their swords and advanced cautiously toward the cave.

Cassim, who from within had heard the trampling of horses, now had no doubt that the robbers were back and that they would kill him. Resolved however to make one last effort at escape, he stood ready by the door. No sooner had the opening word been uttered than he ran forward with such violence that he threw the captain to the ground. But his attempt was in vain. Before he could break through he was mercilessly killed by the swords of the robber band.

When the robbers entered the cave they immediately found the sacks of gold that Cassim had left near the entrance, and replaced them. But they did not notice the absence of those taken by Ali Baba. They were, however, puzzled as to the means by which Cassim had managed to enter the cave. To scare off anyone else who might dare to enter, they cut the body of the unfortunate Cassim into quarters, and placed them near the door.

Then they mounted their horses, and set off to commit more robberies.

Meanwhile, Cassim's wife had grown very uneasy at her husband's failure to return. Finally, at nightfall, unable to endure further suspense, she ran to Ali Baba, told him of his brother's secret expedition, and begged him to go out instantly in search of him.

Ali Baba had too kind a heart to refuse her. Taking with him his three donkeys he set out immediately for the forest. Since the road was familiar to him he soon found his way to the door of the cave. When he saw there the traces of blood he became filled with misgiving, but no sooner had he entered than his worst fears were

realized. Nevertheless, brotherly love and respect gave him courage. Gathering together the severed remains and wrapping them
gently, he placed them upon one of the donkeys and concealed
them with wood. Then thinking that he deserved some payment for
his trouble he loaded the two remaining donkeys with sacks of
gold, and, covering them with wood as he had on the first occasion, he made his way back to town while it was yet early.

Leaving his wife to take care of the treasure borne by the two donkeys, Ali Baba led the third to his sister-in-law's house. Knocking quietly so that none of the neighbors might hear, he was presently admitted by Morgiana, a female slave whose intelligence and discretion had long been known to him.

"Morgiana," he said, "there's trouble on the back of that donkey. Can you keep a secret?"

Morgiana's nod satisfied him better than any oath.

"Well," he said, "your master's body lies there, and our business now is to bury him honorably as though he had died a natural death. Go and tell your mistress that I want to speak to her."

When Ali Baba's sister-in-law came to him in great anxiety, he first made her promise to listen calmly to the story he had to tell, and then related all that had happened. "Sister," he added, "you must control your grief and do your crying later. We must contrive to bury my brother as though he had died a natural death. I have an idea which, I think, with the help of Morgiana, can be carried out."

At this, Cassim's widow allowed her sobs to subside, for she was not without common sense, and listened while Ali Baba coached Morgiana in the part she was to play.

Accordingly, Morgiana assumed a woeful expression and went to the shop of the nearest apothecary, where she asked for a particular medicine which was supposed to cure the most serious ailments.

On the following day Morgiana again went to the apothecary and, with tears in her eyes, asked for an essence that was customarily administered only when the patient was reduced to the last extremity and no other remedy had been left untried.

"Alas!" she cried, as she received it from the apothecary, "I fear this remedy will be of no more use than the other, and I shall lose my beloved master!"

Since Ali Baba and his wife were seen going to and from the house of Cassim in the course of the day, with very long faces, no one was surprised when, toward evening, the piercing cries of the widow and Morgiana announced his death. And when a sound of wailing arose within the house all the neighbors concluded without further question that Cassim had died a natural and honorable death.

But Morgiana had now a still more difficult task to perform, it being necessary for the funeral that the body be made in some way presentable. Very early the next morning she went to the shop of an old cobbler who lived some distance off. Coming up to him, she wished him good day and put a piece of gold in his hand.

Baba Mustapha, a man well known throughout the city, was by nature of a gay turn of mind, and had always something laughable to say. He examined the piece of money, and seeing that it was gold, said, "This is good wage; what is to be done? I am ready to do your bidding."

"Baba Mustapha," said Morgiana to him, "take all your materials for sewing, and come with me. But I insist on this condition, that you let me cover your eyes until we have reached our destination."

Baba Mustapha began to object. "Oh, ho!" said he, "you want me to do something against my conscience or my honor."

But Morgiana interrupted him by putting another piece of gold in his hand. "Allah forbid," she said, "that I should require you to do anything that would hurt your conscience or stain your honor. Come with me and fear nothing."

Baba Mustapha allowed himself to be led by Morgiana, who bound a handkerchief over his eyes, and brought him to Cassim's house. She did not remove the bandage until he was in the room where the remains were placed. Then, taking off the covering, she said, "Baba Mustapha. I have brought you here so that you may sew these four quarters together. Lose no time. And when you have finished I will give you another piece of gold."

When Baba Mustapha had completed his gruesome task, Morgiana bound his eyes again, and, after giving him the third piece of money, according to her promise, and begging him to keep her secret, she conducted him to the place where she had first put on the handkerchief. Here she uncovered his eyes, and left him to return to his house, watching him, however, until he was out of sight, lest he have the curiosity to return and follow her.

Then the body of the unfortunate Cassim was washed, perfumed, wrapped in an elegant shroud, and buried with due ceremony.

The widow remained at home to lament and weep with the women of the neighborhood, who, according to custom, had repaired to her house during the ceremony. But Morgiana followed the coffin, weeping and tearing her hair.

Ali Baba had a son who had served his apprenticeship with a merchant of good repute. He now put the young man in charge of the shop that had belonged to Cassim, while he himself moved with his belongings to his late brother's house, which was larger and more commodious than his own.

Leaving Ali Baba to enjoy his good fortune, we will now return to the forty thieves. On returning to the cave they were amazed and

alarmed to find the body of Cassim gone, together with a large portion of their treasure.

"We have been discovered," said the captain, "and if we are not very careful, we shall lose all the riches we have gathered with so much trouble and work. All we know is that the thief whom we surprised when he was going to make his escape knew the secret of opening the door. But evidently he was not the only one. Another must have the same knowledge. And, since we have no reason to suppose that more than two people are acquainted with the secret, having destroyed one, we must not allow the other to escape. What say you, my brave comrades?"

The other thirty-nine robbers agreed that it would be advisable to give up every other enterprise, and occupy themselves solely with this affair until they had succeeded.

"Then," resumed the captain, "the first thing to be done is that one of you who is bold, courageous, and cunning should go to the city, unarmed and in the dress of a traveler, and employ all his art to discover if the death we inflicted on the culprit we destroyed is being talked about. Then he must find out who this man was, and where he lived. But, to prevent his bringing us a false report, which might occasion our total ruin, I propose that the one selected to perform the task shall consent to the penalty of death in case of failure."

Without waiting until his companions should speak, one of the robbers said, "I agree to those terms. If I should fail, you will, at least, remember that I displayed both courage and readiness in my offer to serve the troop."

Amid the commendations of the captain and his companions, the robber disguised himself in such a way that no one could have suspected him of being what he was. He set off at night, and entering the city just as day was dawning, went toward the public bazaar, where he saw only one shop open. It was the shop of Baba Mustapha.

The merry cobbler was seated on his stool ready to begin work. The robber went up to him and wished him a good morning, saying, "My good man, you rise early to your work. Does not so dull a light strain your eyes?"

"Not so much as you might think," answered Baba Mustapha. "Why, it was only the other day that at this same hour I saw well enough to stitch up a dead body in a place where it was certainly no lighter."

"Stitch up a dead body!" cried the robber, in pretended amazement, concealing his joy at this sudden intelligence. "Surely you mean in its shroud, for how else can a dead body be stitched?"

"No, no," said Mustapha. "What I say I mean. But since it is a secret, I can tell you no more."

The robber drew out a piece of gold. "Come," he said, "tell me nothing you do not care to. Only show me the house where lay the body that you stitched."

Baba Mustapha eyed the gold longingly. "Would that I could," he replied. "But alas! I went to it blindfolded."

"Well," said the robber, "I have heard that a blind man remembers his road. Perhaps, though seeing you might lose it, blindfolded you might find it again."

Tempted by the offer of yet another piece of gold, Baba Mustapha was soon persuaded to make the attempt. "It was here that I started," he said, showing the spot, "and I turned as you see me now." The robber then put a handkerchief over his eyes and walked beside him through the streets, partly guiding and partly being led, until of his own accord Baba Mustapha stopped. "It was here," he said. "The door by which I went in should now lie to the right." And he had in fact come exactly opposite the house which had once been Cassim's and where Ali Baba now dwelt.

The robber marked the door with a piece of chalk that he had brought for the purpose. He removed the handkerchief from Mustapha's eyes and left him to his own devices, then returned with

all possible speed to the cave where his comrades were awaiting him.

Soon after the robber and cobbler had parted, Morgiana happened to go out on an errand, and as she returned she noticed the mark upon the door.

This, she thought, is not as it should be. Either some trick is intended, or there is evil brewing for my master's house. Taking a piece of chalk she put a similar mark upon the five or six doors lying to right and left. And having done this she went home with her mind satisfied, saying nothing.

In the meantime the robbers had learned from their companion about the success of his venture. Greatly elated at the thought of the vengeance so soon to be theirs, they formed a plan for entering the city in a manner that should arouse no suspicion among the inhabitants. Passing in by twos and threes, and by different routes, they met at the marketplace at an appointed time while the captain and the robber who had acted as spy made their way alone to the street where the marked door was to be found.

Presently, just as they had expected, they saw a door with the mark on it.

"That is it!" said the robber, but as they continued walking to avoid suspicion, they came upon another marked door and another, until they had passed six in succession. So alike were the marks that the spy, though he swore he had made only one, could not tell which it was.

The captain was very annoyed, but there was nothing to do but return to the forest, where the unlucky robber had his head cut off as the penalty for his failure.

In spite of this, another robber, who flattered himself with hopes of greater success, asked to be allowed to see what he could do. Permission was granted, so he went to the city, bribed Baba Mustapha with more gold, and the cobbler, with his eyes bound, went

through the same performance and led him to the house of Ali Baba.

The thief marked the door with red chalk in a place where it would be less noticed, thinking this would be a surer method of distinguishing it. But a short time afterward Morgiana went out, as on the preceding day, and on her return the red mark did not escape her sharp eyes. She immediately made a similar mark on all the neighboring doors.

When he returned to his companions in the forest, the thief boasted of the precautions he had taken to distinguish the house of Ali Baba, to which he offered to lead the captain without fail. But the result was the same. A whole row of front doors marked with red chalk met the captain's irritated eye; and the second robber lost *his* head.

This reduced the forty thieves to thirty-eight, and the captain decided to undertake the task himself. He returned to the city and, with the assistance of Baba Mustapha, found Ali Baba's house. But, having no faith in chalk marks, he imprinted the place thoroughly on his memory, looking at it so attentively that he was certain he could not mistake it.

He then returned to the forest, and when he had reached the cave said, "Comrades, I know with certainty the house of the culprit who is to experience our revenge, and I have planned an excellent way of dealing with him."

He then ordered them to divide into small parties, which were to go into the neighboring towns and villages and there buy nineteen mules and thirty-eight large leather jars for carrying oil. One of the jars must be full, and all the others empty.

In the course of two or three days the thieves completed their purchases to the captain's satisfaction. He made one of the men, thoroughly armed, enter each jar. He then closed the jars, so that they appeared to be full of oil, leaving, however, a sufficient space to admit air for the men to breathe. And, the better to carry out the

deception, he rubbed the outside of each jar with oil, which he took from the full one.

Thus prepared, the mules were laden with the thirty-seven robbers, each concealed in a jar, and with the jar that was filled with oil. Then the captain, disguised as an oil merchant, took the road to the city, where the whole procession arrived about an hour after sunset.

The captain went straight to the house of Ali Baba, intending to knock and request shelter for the night for himself and his mules. He was, however, spared the trouble of knocking, for he found Ali Baba at the door, enjoying the fresh air after supper. Addressing him in tones of respect, the captain said, "Sir, I have brought my oil a great distance to sell tomorrow in the market. And at this late hour, being a stranger, I do not know where to seek shelter. If it is not troubling you too much, allow me to stable my beasts here for the night."

The captain's voice was now so changed from its accustomed tone of command that Ali Baba, although he had heard it before, did not recognize it. Not only did he grant the stranger's request for bare accommodation, but as soon as the unloading and stabling of the mules had been accomplished, he invited him to stay not in the outer court but in the house as his guest. The captain, whose plans this proposal somewhat disarranged, tried to excuse himself. But since Ali Baba would take no refusal he was forced at last to yield, and to submit with apparent pleasure to some entertainment, which the hospitality of his host extended to a late hour.

When they were about to retire for the night, Ali Baba went into the kitchen to speak to Morgiana. The captain of the robbers, on the pretext of going to look after his mules, slipped out into the yard where the oil jars were standing in line. Passing from jar to jar he whispered into each, "When you hear a handful of pebbles fall from the window of the room where I am lodged, cut your way out of the jar and make ready, for the time will have come." He

then returned to the house, where Morgiana came with a light and conducted him to his chamber.

Now Ali Baba, before going to bed, had said to Morgiana, "To-morrow at dawn I am going to the baths. Let my bathing linen be put ready, and see that the cook has some good broth prepared for me when I return." Having therefore led the guest up to his room, Morgiana returned to the kitchen and ordered Abdallah the cook to put on the pot for the broth. Suddenly, while Morgiana was skim-ming it, the lamp went out, and, on searching, she found there was no more oil in the house. At so late an hour no shop would be open, yet somehow the broth had to be made, and that could not be done without a light.

"As for that," said Abdallah, seeing her perplexity, "why trouble yourself? There is plenty of oil out in the yard."

"Why, to be sure!" said Morgiana, and sending Abdallah to bed so that he might be up in time to wake his master in the morning, she took the oil can herself and went out into the court. As she approached the jar which stood nearest, she heard a voice within say, "Is it time?"

To one of Morgiana's intelligence an oil jar that spoke was an object of even more suspicion than a chalk mark on a door. In an instant she realized what danger for her master and his family might lie concealed around her. Understanding well enough that an oil jar that asked a question required an answer, she replied quick as thought and without the least sign of perturbation, "Not yet, but presently." And thus she passed from jar to jar, thirty-seven in all, giving the same answer, until she came to the one which contained the oil.

The situation was now clear to her. Aware of the source from which her master had acquired his wealth, she guessed at once that, in extending shelter to the oil merchant, Ali Baba had actually admitted to his house the robber captain and his band. She imme-diately knew what she had to do. Having filled the oil can she

returned to the kitchen. There she lighted the lamp, and then, taking a large kettle, went back once more to the jar that contained the oil. Filling the kettle she carried it back to the kitchen, and putting under it a great fire of wood had soon brought it to the boil. Then lifting it once more, she went out into the yard and poured into each jar in turn a sufficient quantity of the boiling oil to scald its occupant to death.

She then returned to the kitchen and, having made Ali Baba's broth, put out the fire, blew out the lamp, and sat down by the window to watch.

Before long the captain of the robbers awoke from the short sleep he had allowed himself. Finding that all was silent in the house, he rose softly and opened the window. Below stood the oil jars. Gently into their midst he threw the handful of pebbles agreed on as a signal. But from the oil jars there came no answer. He threw a second and a third time. Though he could hear the pebbles falling among the jars, there followed only the silence of the dead. Wondering whether his band had fled, leaving him in the lurch, or whether they were all asleep, he grew uneasy, and descending in haste, he made his way into the court. As he approached the first jar a smell of burning and hot oil assailed his nostrils, and looking within he beheld the dead body of his comrade.

In every jar the same sight presented itself until he came to the one that contained the oil. There, in what was missing, the means and manner of his companions' death were made clear to him. Aghast at the discovery and awake to the danger that now threatened him, he did not delay an instant, but forcing the garden gate open, and from there climbing from wall to wall, he made his escape out of the city.

When Morgiana, who had remained on the watch all this time, was assured of his final departure, she got her master's bath linen ready and went to bed well satisfied with her day's work.

The next morning Ali Baba, awakened by his slave, went to the

baths before daybreak. On his return he was greatly surprised to find that the merchant was gone, leaving his mules and oil jars behind him. He asked Morgiana the reason.

"You will find the reason," said she, "if you look into the first jar you come to."

Ali Baba did so, and, seeing a man, started back with a cry.

"Do not be afraid," said Morgiana, "he is dead and harmless. And so are all the others whom you will find if you look further."

As Ali Baba went from one jar to another, finding always the same sight of horror within, his knees trembled under him. When he came at last to the one empty oil jar, he stood for a time motionless, turning upon Morgiana eyes of wonder and inquiry. "And what," he said then, "has become of the merchant?"

"To tell you that," said Morgiana, "will be to tell you the whole story. You will be better able to hear it if you have your broth first."

But Ali Baba's curiosity was far too great. He would not be kept waiting. So without further delay Morgiana told him everything, so far as she knew it, from beginning to end. And by her intelligent putting of one thing against another, she left him at last in no possible doubt as to the source and nature of the conspiracy that her quick wits had so happily defeated.

"And now, dear master," she said in conclusion, "continue to be on your guard, for though all these are dead, one remains alive. And he, if I am not mistaken, is the captain of the band, and for that reason is the more formidable and the more likely to cherish the hope of vengeance."

When Morgiana had finished speaking Ali Baba realized that he owed to her not merely the protection of his property, but life itself. He was full of gratitude. "Do not doubt," he said "that before I die I will reward you as you deserve. And as an immediate proof, from this moment I give you your liberty."

This token of his approval filled Morgiana's heart with delight,

but she had no intention of leaving so kind a master, even had she been sure that all danger was now over. The immediate question that presented itself was how to dispose of the bodies.

Luckily, at the far end of the garden there stood a thick grove of trees. Under these Ali Baba was able to dig a large trench without attracting the notice of his neighbors. Here the remains of the thirty-seven robbers were laid side by side, the trench was filled again, and the ground made level. As for the mules, since Ali Baba had no use for them, he sent them, one or two at a time, to the market to be sold.

Meanwhile the robber captain had fled back to the forest. Entering the cave he was overcome by its gloom and loneliness. "Alas!" he cried, "my comrades, partners in my adventures, sharers of my fortune, how shall I endure to live without you? Why did I lead you to a fate where bravery was of no avail, and where death turned you into objects of ridicule? Surely had you died sword in hand my sorrow would be less bitter! And now what remains for me but to take vengeance for your death and to prove, by achieving it without aid, that I was worthy to be the captain of such a band!"

Thus decided, at an early hour the next day, he assumed a disguise suitable to his purpose, and going to the town took lodging in an inn. Entering into conversation with his host he inquired whether anything of interest had happened recently in the town. But the other man, though full of gossip, had nothing to tell him concerning the matter in which he was most interested, for Ali Baba, having to conceal from all the source of his wealth, had also to be silent as to the dangers in which it involved him.

The captain then inquired where there was a shop for rent. Hearing of one that suited him, he came to terms with the owner, and before long had furnished it with all kinds of rich stuffs and carpets and jewelry which he brought gradually and with great secrecy from the cave.

This shop happened to be opposite the one that had belonged to

Cassim and was now occupied by the son of Ali Baba. Before long the son and the newcomer, who had assumed the name of Cogia Houssain, became acquainted. Since the youth had good looks, kind manners, and a sociable disposition, it was not long before they became close friends.

Cogia Houssain did all he could to seal the pretended friendship, particularly since it had not taken him long to discover how the young man and Ali Baba were related. So, plying him constantly with small presents and acts of hospitality, he forced on him the obligation of making some return.

Ali Baba's son, however, had not at his lodging sufficent accommodation for entertainment. He therefore told his father of the difficulty in which Cogia Houssain's favors had placed him. Ali Baba with great willingness at once offered to arrange matters. "My son," he said, "tomorrow being a holiday, all shops will be closed. After dinner invite Cogia Houssain to walk with you and as you return bring him this way and beg him to come in. That will be better than a formal invitation, and Morgiana shall have supper prepared for you."

This proposal was exactly what Ali Baba's son could have wished. The next day he brought Cogia Houssain to the door as if by accident, and stopping, invited him to enter.

Cogia Houssain, who saw that he was getting just what he wanted, began by showing pretended reluctance, but Ali Baba himself came to the door, urged him in the most kindly manner to enter, and before long had led him to the table where food stood prepared.

But then an unforeseen difficulty arose. Wicked though he might be the robber captain was not so impious as to eat the salt of the man he intended to kill. He therefore began to excuse himself with many apologies. When Ali Baba sought to know the reason, "Sir," he said, "I am sure that if you knew the cause of my resolution you would approve of it. Suffice it to say that I have made it a rule to eat of no dish that has salt in it. How then can I sit down at your table if I must reject everything that is set before me?"

"If that is your scruple," said Ali Baba, "it shall soon be satisfied," and he sent orders to the kitchen that no salt was to be put into any of the dishes to be served to the newly arrived guest.

"Thus," he said to Cogia Houssain, "I shall still have the honor, to which I have looked forward, of returning to you under my own roof the hospitality you have shown my son."

Morgiana, who was just about to serve supper, received the order with some discontent. "Who," she said, "is this difficult person who refuses to eat salt? He must be a curiosity worth looking at." So when the saltless courses were ready to be set upon the table, she herself helped to carry in the dishes. No sooner had she set eyes on Cogia Houssain than she recognized him in spite of his disguise. Observing his movements with great attention she saw that he had a dagger concealed beneath his robe.

"Ah!" she said to herself, "here is reason enough! For who will eat salt with the man he means to murder? But he shall not murder my master if I can prevent it."

Now Morgiana knew that the most favorable opportunity for the robber captain to carry out his plan would be after the food had been withdrawn, and when Ali Baba and his son and guest were alone together drinking their wine. This was indeed the very plan that Cogia Houssain had made. Going out quickly, Morgiana dressed herself as a dancer, assuming the appropriate headdress and mask. Then she fastened a silver girdle about her waist, and hung upon it a dagger of the same material. Thus equipped, she said to Abdallah the cook, "Take your tabor and let us go in and give an entertainment in honor of our master's guest."

So Abdallah took his tabor, and played Morgiana into the hall. As soon as she had entered she made a low curtsy, and stood awaiting orders. Then Ali Baba, seeing that she wished to perform in his guest's honor, said kindly, "Come in, Morgiana, and show Cogia Houssain what you can do."

Immediately Abdallah began to beat upon his tabor and sing an air for Morgiana to dance to. And she, advancing with much grace, began to move through several figures, performing them with the ease and facility that none but the most highly practiced can attain.

Then, for the last figure of all, she drew out the dagger and, holding it in her hand, danced a dance that excelled all that had preceded it in the surprise and change and quickness and dexterity of its movements. Now she presented the dagger at her own breast, now

at one of the onlookers; but always in the act of striking she drew back. Finally, as though out of breath, she snatched his instrument from Abdallah with her left hand, and, still holding the dagger in her right, advanced the hollow of her tabor toward her master, as is the custom of dancers when claiming their fee. Ali Baba threw in a piece of gold. His son did the same. Then advancing it in the same manner toward Cogia Houssain, who was feeling for his purse she struck under it, and before he knew had plunged her dagger deep into his heart.

Ali Baba and his son, seeing their guest fall dead, cried out in horror. "Wretch!" exclaimed Ali Baba, "what ruin and shame have you brought on us?"

"No," answered Morgiana, "it is not your ruin but your life that I have saved. Look closely at this man who refused to eat salt with you!" So saying, she tore off the dead robber's disguise, showing the dagger concealed below, and the face which her master now recognized for the first time.

Ali Baba's gratitude to Morgiana for preserving his life a second time knew no bounds. He took her in his arms and embraced her as a daughter. "Now," he said, "the time has come when I must fulfill my debt and how better can I do it than by marrying you to my son?" This proposition, far from proving unwelcome to the young man, did but confirm an inclination already formed. A few days later the nuptials were celebrated with great joy and solemnity, and the union thus auspiciously commenced was productive of as much happiness as lies within the power of mortals to secure.

As for the robbers' cave, it remained the secret possession of Ali Baba and his posterity; and using their good fortune with equity and moderation, they rose to high office in the city and were held in great honor by all who knew them.

The
Enchanted Horse

Once upon a time there was a King of Persia named Sabur. He had one son and one daughter. The son, Feroze-shah, was the apple of his father's eye, and, indeed, he was the handsomest, bravest, and most amiable prince in all the world.

On the first day of the year, which was observed as a festival, the king always held a public audience at which he received gifts and congratulations, and bestowed pardons and rewards.

On one of these occasions, a Hindu presented himself before the king with a magnificent horse made of ebony and inlaid with ivory. This horse was so beautifully sculpted that it almost seemed alive.

The king was delighted with it and immediately offered to buy it.

But the Hindu, prostrating himself before the king, explained that this was an enchanted horse, which would carry its rider wherever he wished to go, in the shortest possible time. He added that he was willing to part with the horse on only one condition. But, before stating that condition, he would give an exhibition of the horse's powers.

"Then mount," said the king, "and bring me a branch of the palm tree which grows at the foot of yonder hill." And he pointed to a hill about three leagues away.

The Hindu mounted and, turning a peg on the right side of the horse's neck, was instantly borne upward and carried through the air at a great height and with the speed of lightning, to the amazement of all beholders.

In less than a quarter of an hour he was back with the palm branch, which, on dismounting, he laid at the feet of the king. The king's desire to possess this magic steed was now increased a hundred times, and he offered to pay whatever sum the other demanded.

"Sire," replied the Hindu, "there is only one thing I will take in exchange for this horse, which, as your Majesty perceives, is one of the wonders of the world."

"What is that?" inquired the king. "Name it and it is yours."

"The hand of the princess, your daughter," was the reply, which excited the ridicule of all who heard—for the Hindu was not only unpleasant in appearance, but was at least twice the age of the king. And the princess, who was only fifteen, was as beautiful as she was charming.

Prince Feroze-shah, who stood beside the King, his father, was extremely indignant.

"I hope, my father," he said, "that you will not hesitate to refuse such an insolent demand."

"My son," replied the king, who had a craving for anything that was rare and curious, "I have no intention of granting the request. But, perhaps, he is not serious in making it, and would accept the weight of the horse in gold. In any case, suppose you mount the horse yourself and give me your opinion of it."

The prince was all too willing to agree and the Hindu ran to assist him. But the prince mounted without his help and as soon as he had his feet in the stirrups, without waiting for instructions, he turned the peg as he had seen the other do. Instantly, the horse rose in the air, as swift as an arrow, and in a few moments both horse and rider were out of sight.

The Hindu, alarmed at what had happened, prostrated himself before the king, who was angry and distressed at the disappearance of his son.

"Your Majesty must admit that I was blameless," he said. "The prince gave me no time to utter a word, or to point out to him a second peg by which the horse is controlled and made to descend. It can also be guided by means of the bridle. But it is possible that the prince may discover this for himself."

"Your own life shall answer for that of my son," said the king. "And until he returns, or I hear some tidings of him, you shall be put in prison and fed on bread and water."

Meanwhile, the prince was being carried so rapidly through the air that in less than an hour he was out of sight of the earth. He then thought it was time to return. He pulled the bridle and grabbed the peg with which he had started the horse. He turned the peg the opposite way. When he found that this had no effect, but that the horse continued to ascend, he became alarmed. He continued to turn the peg one way and another, but without arresting the horse's

ascent. It seemed as though, in time, he would be burnt up by the sun. Then, to his great joy and relief, he discovered another, smaller peg behind the horse's other ear. Turning this, his upward flight was instantly checked and he began to descend, but at a much slower rate.

The sun was already setting. It grew dark rapidly as he drew near the earth, so that he was unable to discover what was beneath him—whether a city, a desert, a plain, or a mountain top. It was equally possible that the horse might plunge with him into a lake or a river, or even into the sea. Consequently, when at the dead of night the horse at last came to a stop, and the prince felt solid ground beneath his feet, he was inexpressibly relieved. He was also agreeably surprised to find himself on the terrace of a magnificent palace, gleaming with white marble.

He was faint and hungry, having eaten nothing since the early morning, and at first could scarcely stand. But, leaving the horse, he groped his way along until he came to a staircase, which he found led downward. At the foot of the stairs there was a half-open door, through which a ray of light shone.

Descending as noiselessly as possible, the prince paused at the door and, listening, heard the loud breathing of sleepers within. He advanced cautiously, and by the light of a lamp saw that the sleepers were guards. Their naked sabers lay beside them, and he realized that this was the guard chamber of some royal personage.

Proceeding on tiptoe, the prince crossed the room, without waking any of the sleepers, to a curtained archway. Raising the curtain, he saw a magnificent chamber with a raised couch in the center. Around the sides of the chamber were low couches on which a number of female servants were sleeping. The prince crept softly toward the center couch, and saw the most beautiful princess in the world sleeping on her silken pillows, her hair spread round her like a veil.

 48

Falling on his knees, he remained entranced by her loveliness until the power of his gaze penetrated her closed eyelids, and, opening her eyes, she saw the handsomest prince in the world regarding her in an ecstasy of admiration.

She showed the greatest surprise, but not the least sign of fear. The prince ventured to address her in the most respectful manner.

"Beautiful Princess," he said, "you see at your feet the Prince of Persia, brought here by what he now regards as a most happy and fortunate adventure, and who implores your aid and protection."

"Prince," she replied, "the kingdom of Bengal, in which you now are, will afford you all the hospitality and assistance you may require. My father, the Rajah, built this palace not far from his capital for the sake of the country air. Of this place I am absolute mistress and I bid you welcome. At the same time, though I much desire to know by what means you have arrived here from such a far country as Persia, and by what magic you have evaded the vigilance of my guards, I am convinced that you must be in need of rest and refreshment. I will, therefore, direct my attendants to show you to an apartment where you may obtain both before answering any of the questions which I am dying to put."

Her attendants, though naturally surprised at the sight of the prince in their midst, at once carried out her commands. He was conducted to a handsome room, where, after he had been given the refreshment of which he was so much in need, he slept soundly until morning.

The princess took great pains with her toilet the next day, and changed her mind so often as to what she would wear, and, generally, gave so much trouble to her attendants that they plainly perceived what a favorable impression the stranger must have produced.

When her mirror assured her that never had she appeared so charming, she sent for the prince and expressed a desire to hear

what strange adventure had caused his sudden appearance of the night before.

The prince was only too pleased to relate the story of the enchanted horse and all that had befallen him since he had mounted it. He concluded by thanking her for the kind and hospitable manner in which she had received him. Then he declared that it would now be his reluctant duty to return without delay, and relieve the anxiety of his father.

The princess urged him to stay a short time longer, as her guest, to see a little of the kingdom of Bengal, where he had so unexpectedly arrived and of which he would then be better able to give an account of his return to Persia.

The prince could hardly refuse such a request from such a charming princess. And so he put off his return from day to day and from week to week, while the princess entertained him with feasts, concerts, hunting parties, and every other form of amusement she could think of. In this way, the time flew so fast that the prince was surprised and ashamed when one day he realized that two months had passed, during which time his father must have either suffered the greatest possible anxiety, or else have concluded that his son was dead. Not another day would he consent to remain at the palace. And yet, he asked, how could he tear himself away from his adorable princess?

The princess made no reply to this, beyond casting down her eyes and blushing. In spite of this, the prince went on to ask whether he might dare to hope that she would return to Persia with him?

Without uttering a word, she gave the prince to understand that she had not the least objection to this arrangement, although she afterward admitted a little nervousness in case the enchanted horse might refuse to carry a double burden. But the prince easily reassured her. He also declared that, with the experience he had gained

on his journey, he was now quite capable of managing and guiding the horse as he desired.

The princess thereupon consented to fly with him. She arranged matters so that no one should have the slightest suspicion of their intentions.

Very early the next day, when all the other inhabitants of the place were still sleeping, she stole from her room to the terrace, where both the horse and the prince awaited her.

The prince turned the horse toward Persia and, having first mounted himself, helped the princess to mount behind him. Then, when she was safely settled, with both her arms around his waist, he turned the peg, and the horse mounted into the air.

It flew as rapidly with two riders as with one. In little more than two hours Prince Feroze-shah could distinguish the domes and minarets of the city of Shiraz, from which he had flown on the first day of the New Year.

He thought it better not to fly directly to the palace, and so they alighted at a summer palace, just outside the walls. Here he left the princess while he went to break the happy news of his return to his father. Leaving the enchanted steed behind, he obtained another horse, on which he rode; and, being recognized as he passed through the streets, was welcomed with shouts of joy by the people.

The news of his return preceded him, and he was received by the king, his father, with tears of joy. In as few words as possible, the prince gave an account of all that had befallen him, including his sensations during the flight, his arrival at the palace of the princess, and all the kindness and hospitality that had been shown to him since.

"If," replied the king, "there were any way by which I could show my gratitude to this lady, I would do it even if it cost me half of my kingdom."

"My father," replied Prince Feroze-shah, "you have only to con-

sent to my marriage to this charming princess to assure the happiness of both of us. Indeed, I felt so sure of your consent that I persuaded her to accompany me on my return flight. She is now waiting for me at the summer palace. Allow me to return and assure her that you will gladly welcome her as a daughter."

"Son," replied the king, "I not only consent most heartily, but will myself accompany you there and escort her with due honor to my palace, where the marriage shall be celebrated this very day."

The king then ordered that the Hindu should be brought from the prison, where he had been confined for the last two months, and set before him.

When this had been done, he said, "I swore that your life should answer that of my son. Thanks be to God, he has now returned in safety. Go, take your enchanted horse, and never let me see your face again."

The Hindu had already learned, from those who had been sent to release him, of the return of the prince from a far country, accompanied by a princess who was reported to be of great beauty. He also knew that she was at the summer palace awaiting the prince. The king had ordered him to take his horse and depart and he now saw a means by which to obey the king and, at the same time, revenge himself upon the monarch as well as upon the prince, to whom he also owed a grudge.

Consequently, while a procession, with musicians to accompany it, was being arranged, and a magnificent litter was prepared for the princess, and while the king was putting on his grandest robes and a feast was being hastily set out, the Hindu, without losing an instant, started off for the summer palace. He reached it before the procession had begun to move on its slow and ceremonious way.

He soon learned the whereabouts of the princess and, appearing before her, announced that he came from the Prince of Persia, to bring her on the enchanted horse into the presence of the king, who with his court and all the inhabitants of the city had assembled in

the great square of the palace to view the marvel of her flight through the air.

The princess did not hesitate for a moment, but mounted at once: The Hindu placed himself before her, with many protestations of respect, turned the peg, and the horse soared upward.

At this moment, the king, the prince, and the entire court were about halfway to the summer palace. Hearing a mocking laugh that seemed to come from overhead, the prince glanced up. To his great surprise and distress he saw the enchanted horse bearing the princess and the Hindu high above the heads of the procession, which, on hearing the prince's cry of anguish, came to a dead stop.

The king also saw and recognized the Hindu, and, furious at this insult to his dignity, hurled curses upon him as horse and riders rapidly dwindled to a speck in the sky.

The courtiers and other members of the procession added their voices and produced such a clamor that it was heard all over the city. But the grief of Prince Feroze-shah was beyond words.

He returned to the palace, where for a time he shut himself up and refused to see anyone or take any food. Then, realizing the uselessness of this behavior, he obtained the habit of a holy man through a trustworthy servant, for he had formed a plan to disguise himself, and set out and search for his beloved princess until he had found her, or had perished in the attempt. He did not know which way to go, but he trusted Providence to direct him. So, furnishing himself with sufficient money and jewels to last a considerable period, he quietly left his father's palace without telling anyone of his purpose.

Meanwhile, the princess, as soon as she found that instead of being taken to her prince, she was being torn from him, had wept and begged her captor to restore her to her dear Feroze-shah. It was impossible to escape except by throwing herself from the horse's back, and this she was afraid to do.

After a flight that lasted through the night, she found herself

early next morning in the kingdom of Cashmere. The Hindu had descended in a wood outside the walls of the capital city and the Princess now had a chance of getting help. In spite of all his efforts to prevent her, she cried as loudly as she could, in the hope that someone would hear her and come to her assistance.

It happened, very fortunately, that the sultan of that country was returning from a hunting expedition; he passed within earshot of her cries, and went to her rescue.

He saw the Hindu struggling with the princess, whom, in trying to stifle her voice, he had half suffocated, and demanded who he was, and why he was ill-treating the lady.

The Hindu, ignorant of the rank of the inquirer, replied insolently, "She is my wife and I shall treat her as I please. It is no one's business to interfere."

But the princess cried, "Do not believe him. I am a Princess of Bengal and was about to be married to the Prince of Persia when this wicked person, whom I believe to be a magician, lied to me and carried me off on the horse you see yonder, which is enchanted. Whoever you are, have compassion on me and save me from this wicked man."

She had no need to urge the sultan further. Her beauty, dignity, and evident distress were all in her favor. Convinced of the truth of her appeal, and enraged by the insolence of the Hindu, the sultan made a sign to his guards, who at once surrounded the now terrified Hindu, and put an end to his prayers for mercy by cutting off his head.

The sultan then conducted the princess to his palace, where she was sumptuously lodged, and received all the respect due to her beauty and high rank.

The princess was overjoyed at her escape and hoped that the sultan would immediately take steps to return her to the Prince of Persia. But she was bitterly disappointed, for the sultan, charmed by her appearance and manner, had resolved to marry her himself.

At the break of day she was awakened by the beating of drums, the blowing of trumpets, and other sounds of general rejoicing that had been commanded in honor of the occasion.

Later, when the sultan came to inquire about the health of the princess, she asked the meaning of all these festive sounds. When she was told that they were part of the festivities in honor of her own marriage, she was struck speechless with dismay. And when the sultan went on to ask her agreement to what had already been arranged, she fainted away—which the Sultan took to be the effect of extreme joy.

When the princess came to herself, to gain time she resolved to feign madness. This she did by tearing her clothes and her hair, biting her cushions, and rolling on the floor. She even pretended to attack the sultan with her fingernails, and alarmed him so much that he left her presence hurriedly, and went to give orders to stop the drums beating and the blowing of the trumpets and to postpone all further preparations for the marriage.

Several times during the day he sent a servant to inquire if the strange and violent attack which had so suddenly seized the princess had passed off or lessened. But each time he was told there was no improvement and whatever change there might be was for the worse.

The next day, since the princess still talked and acted very violently, the sultan sent his own physicians, as well as those most famous in the city, to visit her and report upon the case. But she not only refused to allow them to feel her pulse or examine her tongue, but would not even let them approach her. They came away looking very wise, but shaking their heads and declaring that the case was hopeless and that if they could not cure her nobody could. In spite of this, the sultan sent far and wide for other physicians, who came, looked at the princess (who became more violent at each visit), shook their heads, prescribed medicines for her, and went away looking wiser than ever.

He even sent messengers to other kingdoms, offering generous rewards and great honor to anyone who could cure the princess of her malady. But the result was always the same, and the sultan began to despair, for all this only made him more and more anxious to marry the princess.

Meanwhile, Prince Feroze-shah, disguised as a holy man and plunged in grief, was wandering about the country looking for his lost princess. He traveled from province to province and from town to town, inquiring everywhere if anyone had seen or heard anything of an enchanted horse that could fly through the air, and describing its two riders. The result was that most of those he met and spoke with thought he was out of his mind and, because he was handsome and amiable, pitied him.

At last, as he was making his usual inquiries in a city of Hindustan, he heard the people talking of a certain Princess of Bengal, who was to have been married to the Sultan of Cashmere had she not become violently mad on the marriage day.

At this—for him it seemed that there could be only one Princess of Bengal—the prince at once set out for the kingdom of Cashmere.

Arriving at the capital, after many days, he took a humble lodging at an inn where all the talk was of the mysterious mad princess with whom the sultan was so much in love.

Mention was also made of the Hindu and his well-merited fate. The enchanted horse, it was reported, had been placed among the royal treasures. All these circumstances convinced the Prince of Persia that his lost princess was found at last. The only difficulty was to get to see her. And even this was not a difficulty for long.

The crowd of physicians who had visited and prescribed in vain for their fair patient, great as it had been, was exaggerated by the gossips of the city. It seemed to the prince that it would be the easiest thing in the world to add himself to the number.

His beard had grown to quite a respectable length during his travels and gave him a look of age and wisdom. Thus, he had only

to exchange the clothes of a holy man for those of a physician to be received with civility and respect at the palace of the sultan.

"I have come to cure the princess," he declared. "Many have tried and failed. If I do not succeed you may cut off my head."

Some time had elapsed since any new physician had appeared at the palace and the sultan had begun to give up hope of the princess's recovery. He immediately gave orders that this new physician, who showed so much faith in his healing powers, should be admitted to his presence. He then informed him that, since the Princess of Bengal could not endure the sight of a physician, he would have to be content with a view of his patient through a lattice in an adjoining chamber to that which she occupied.

In this way, Prince Feroze-shah again caught sight of his beloved princess after their long separation. She was sitting in a despondent attitude, and singing, with tears in her eyes, a mournful melody in which she lamented her sad fate in being separated from all she loved. It brought tears to his own eyes and he determined to restore her to health and happiness at any cost.

With this intention, he told the sultan that he now quite understood the nature of the complaint from which the princess was suffering, and that he would undertake to cure her. But, he added, it was absolutely necessary to speak with her in private. If he were allowed to do so, he was convinced that he could overcome the violent dislike that she showed to any physician who approached her.

The sultan was much cheered by this and ordered that the new physician should be ushered into the presence of the princess without delay.

As soon as the princess caught sight of what she took to be yet another tiresome physician come to prescribe for her affected madness, she began to go through her usual performance of threatening to attack with teeth and fingernails anyone who attempted to come near enough to feel her pulse, or examine her eyes and skin.

But the prince, disregarding this, went straight to her, and, bending in salutation, said in a low tone, for fear of listeners, "Oh, my Princess, let your beautiful eyes pierce my disguise and see, in the pretended physician, the Prince of Persia, your faithful Feroze-shah, who has sought you in sorrow which is now turned into joy."

At the sound of the well-known voice, the Princess almost fainted with rapture and relief. But, since the prince warned her that it was possible that they might be under observation, she made an effort to appear calm. At the same time the Prince of Persia, while briefly acquainting her with his own doings and adventures, and listening to the princess's story, took care to feel her pulse and behave in every way like the physician he was impersonating.

He asked her if she knew what had become of the enchanted horse, by which he hoped they might both make their escape. But she could not tell him anything about it. Then, when a plan had been arranged between them, the prince, thinking it unwise to pay too long a visit, left his patient and went to make his report to the sultan.

The sultan was delighted to hear that a change for the better had already take place, and promised the new physician a great reward if he succeeded in entirely restoring the princess to health. The next day the sultan paid the princess a visit. And when the lady, instead of biting the cushions and threatening to tear his beard out by the roots, received him in a most gracious and charming manner, he came away with the conviction that the prince was the greatest physician in the world. He even wished to have the preparations for the marriage resumed where they had broken off. But the prince declared that the princess was not yet so perfectly restored as he would wish. He asked from what country she had come and by what means she had traveled to Cashmere. The sultan at once obliged him with the entire story of the Hindu and the enchanted horse, as far as he knew it.

Although the sultan was unacquainted with the use and management of the horse, he had ordered it to be kept in his treasury, as an object of curiosity and value.

Hearing this, the pretend physician stroked his beard and assumed an expression of profound wisdom.

"Sire," he said, "I am inclined to think that the principal cause of the trouble is this very horse itself. The princess, having ridden upon the horse, which, as your Majesty knows, is enchanted, has herself been affected by the enchantment. In order, then, that the improvement which I have been so fortunate as to effect in her condition may continue and be made lasting, it is necessary that I should use a certain incense, the burning of which will disenchant the horse, and so complete the cure of the princess. If Your Majesty wishes to see a wonderful sight, and give a great surprise and marvelous entertainment to the people of the city, you will have the enchanted horse brought tomorrow to the great square before the palace, and leave the rest to me."

The sultan signified his willingness to carry out to the letter the directions of this newest and greatest of physicians, and asked if the princess should be present on the occasion.

"Most certainly," was the reply. "Let the lady be arrayed as a bride and adorned with jewels to set off her beauty to the greatest advantage."

Thus, early the next day, the enchanted horse was, by order of the sultan, brought with great ceremony and beating of drums to the square in front of the palace.

The news had spread through the city that a rare sight was to be provided, and so great a crowd assembled in the square that the sultan's guards had all they could do to keep a space clear around the horse.

A gallery had been erected to accommodate the sultan and his court. At the proper moment, the Princess of Bengal, accompanied

by a band of ladies of high rank who had been chosen for this service, approached the horse, and was assisted to mount. The supposed physician then had a number of braziers of lighted charcoal placed at regular intervals around the horse. Into these braziers he now solemnly cast handfuls of incense. With downcast eyes, hands crossed on his breast, and muttering strange words which much impressed the hearers, he paced three times around the horse, within the circle made by the braziers, which now began to give off thick clouds of perfumed smoke.

In a few seconds these clouds became so thick that neither horse nor rider was visible. At this moment, for which he had been waiting, the prince jumped nimbly up behind the princess and, stretching out his hand, turned the right-hand peg.

Instantly, the horse rose into the air, and, as the spectators gaped after it, the following words floated down and reached the ear of the sultan, who was just beginning to surmise that something was wrong.

"The next time the Sultan of Cashmere thinks of marrying a princess who has come to him for protection, let him make sure that he has the lady's consent."

In this way was the Princess of Bengal rescued from the palace of the Sultan of Cashmere, and brought the same day to Shiraz, the capital of Persia, where the return of the missing prince and the lost princess was greeted with general joy by high and low.

The King of Persia at once sent an ambassador to the father of the princess, who had for months been mourning the mysterious disappearance of his daughter, to request his consent to her marriage with Prince Feroze-shah. When that was given, the marriage was celebrated with much magnificence, and the Prince and Princess of Persia lived in honor and happiness for many years.

A. E. JACKSON

Sindbad the
Sailor

L ong, long ago, there lived in Baghdad a poor porter named Hindbad. One day during the violent heat of summer, when he was carrying a heavy load from one end of the city to the other, he came to a street where the pavement was sprinkled with rosewater in front of a large mansion; from the windows came not only sounds of melody but—which to Hindbad seemed a hundred times better—delicious smells of cooking. A grand feast was in progress, he concluded, and wondered who was the fortunate person to whom the house belonged. He therefore ventured to put the question to some handsomely dressed servants who were standing at the door.

"Are you an inhabitant of Baghdad and do not know that this is the residence of Sindbad the sailor, that famous voyager who has roamed over all the seas under the sun?"

The porter, who had heard of the immense riches of Sindbad, could not help comparing the situation of this man with his own poverty-stricken condition, and exclaimed in a loud voice, "Almighty Creator of all things, deign to consider the difference there is between Sindbad and myself. I suffer daily a thousand ills, and have the greatest difficulty in supplying my family with bad barley bread, while the fortunate Sindbad enjoys every pleasure. What has he done to obtain so happy a destiny, or what crime has been mine to merit a fate so hard?"

He was still thinking about this when a servant came toward him from the house, and said, "Come, follow me. My master, Sindbad, wishes to speak with you."

Remembering the words he had uttered, Hindbad feared that Sindbad intended to reprimand him and therefore tried to excuse himself by declaring that he could not leave his load in the middle of the street. But the servant assured him that it would be taken care of, and insisted so much that the porter could not very well refuse.

He was led into a spacious room where a number of people were seated around a table covered with all kinds of luxuries. In the principal seat sat a grave and venerable personage, whose long white beard hung down to his breast. This person was Sindbad, to whom the porter made obeisance with fear and trembling. Sindbad desired him to approach, and seating him at his right hand, to his surprise and embarrassment, helped him to the choicest dishes and fine wine.

Toward the end of the repast, Sindbad inquired the name and profession of his guest.

"Sir," replied the porter, "my name is Hindbad."

"I am happy to see you," said Sindbad, "and I should like you to repeat the words I overheard you utter a little while ago in the street."

At this Hindbad hung his head, and replied, "Sir, I must admit that I uttered some indiscreet words, which I beg you to pardon."

"Oh," resumed Sindbad, "do not imagine I am so unjust as to have any resentment on that account. But I must undeceive you on one point. You appear to suppose that the riches and comforts I enjoy have been obtained without labor or trouble. You are mistaken. Before attaining my present position, I have endured the greatest mental and bodily sufferings you can possibly imagine. Perhaps you have heard only a confused account of my adventures in the seven voyages I have made, and as an opportunity now offers, I will relate to you and the rest of this honorable company some dangers I have encountered. Listen then to the history of my first voyage."

THE FIRST VOYAGE

I squandered the greater part of the fortune I inherited from my father in youthful dissipation. But I saw my folly, and resolved to collect the small remains of my inheritance and use it profitably in trade. This I did, and then went to Basra, where I embarked with several merchants in a vessel that had been equipped at our joint expense.

We set sail, and steered toward the Indies, by the Persian Gulf, touching at several islands, where we sold or exchanged our merchandise. One day, we were unexpectedly becalmed before a small green island. The captain gave permission to those passengers who wished to go ashore, and I was one. But while we were enjoying ourselves, the island suddenly trembled, and we felt a severe shock.

Those who had remained in the ship immediately called to us to reembark, or we should perish. What we supposed to be an island was really the back of a great whale. The most active of the party jumped into the boat, while others threw themselves into the water, to swim to the ship. As for me, I was still on the island, or, more properly speaking, on the whale, when it dived below the surface, and I had only time to seize a piece of wood, which had been brought to make a fire with, when the monster disappeared beneath the waves. Meanwhile, the captain, anxious to avail himself of a fair

breeze that had sprung up, set sail with those who had reached his vessel and left me to the mercy of the waves. I remained in this deplorable situation the whole of that day and the following night. The next morning I had neither strength nor hope left. But when I was at my last gasp a breaker happily threw me onto an island.

Much weakened by fatigue, I crept about in search of some herb or fruit that might satisfy my hunger. I found some and had also the good luck to discover a stream of excellent water. Feeling much stronger, I began to explore the island and entered a beautiful plain, where I saw some fine horses grazing. While I was admiring them, a man appeared who asked me who I was. I related my adventure to him, whereupon he led me into a cave where I found some other persons, who were no less astonished to see me than I was to meet them.

I ate some food that they offered me and upon my asking them what they did there, they replied that they were grooms to the king of that island, and the horses were brought there once a year for the sake of the excellent pasturage. They told me that the morrow was the day fixed for their departure, and if I had been one day later I must certainly have perished; because they lived so far off that it would have been impossible for me to have found my way without a guide.

The next day they returned, with the horses, to the capital of the island, and I accompanied them. On our arrival the king, to whom I related my story, gave orders that I should be taken care of and supplied with everything I might want.

Since I was a merchant, I associated with persons of my own profession in the hope of meeting someone with whom I could return to Baghdad; for the capital is situated on the seacoast and has a beautiful port, where vessels from all parts of the world daily arrive.

As I was standing one day near the port, I saw a ship come toward the land. When the crew had cast anchor, they began to

unload its goods. Happening to cast my eyes on some of the packages, I saw my name written on them, and recognized them as those which I had put aboard the ship in which I left Basra. I also recognized the captain and asked him to whom those parcels belonged.

"I had on board with me," replied he, "a merchant of Baghdad, named Sindbad. One day, when we were near an island, or at least what appeared to be one, he went ashore with some other passengers. But this supposed island was nothing but an enormous whale that had fallen asleep on the surface of the water. The monster no sooner felt the heat of a fire they lighted on its back to cook their provisions, than it began to move and flounce about in the sea. Most of the persons who were on it were drowned, and the unfortunate Sindbad was one of the number. These parcels belonged to him. I have resolved to sell them so that if I meet with any of his family I may be able to pay to them the profit I shall have made."

"Captain," I then said. "I am the Sindbad you supposed dead, but who is still alive. These parcels are my property."

When the captain heard what I had to say he exclaimed, "That is impossible. With my own eyes I saw Sindbad perish. The passengers I had on board were also witnesses to his death. And now you have the insolence to say that *you* are that same Sindbad? At first sight you appeared a man of probity and honor. Yet you are not a man of probity and honor. You are not above telling an outrageous falsehood to take possession of merchandise that does not belong to you."

"Have patience," I replied, "and listen to what I have to say."

I then related how I had been saved and by what lucky accident I found myself in this part of the country.

The captain was rather surprised at first, but was soon convinced that I was not an imposter. Then, embracing me, he exclaimed, "Heaven be praised that you have escaped. Here are your goods.

Take them, for they are yours." I thanked him, and selected the most precious and valuable things in my bales as presents for the king, to whom I related the manner in which I had recovered my property. The king accepted the presents, and gave me others of far greater value. I then reembarked on the same vessel in which I had first set out, having first exchanged what merchandise remainded for aloes, sandalwood, camphor, nutmeg, cloves, pepper, ginger, and other products of the country.

We touched at several islands and at last landed at Basra, from where I came here. And, as I had realized about a hundred thousand gold pieces as the result of my voyage, I determined to forget the hardships I had endured, and to enjoy the pleasures of life.

Having thus concluded the story of his first voyage, Sindbad ordered a purse containing a hundred gold pieces to be brought him. He gave it to the porter, saying, "Take this, Hindbad. Return to your home and come again tomorrow to hear the continuation of my story."

The porter returned home and the account he gave of his adventure to his wife and family made them call down many blessings on the head of Sindbad.

On the following day, Hindbad dressed himself in his best clothes and went to the house of Sindbad, who received him in a friendly manner. As soon as the guests had all arrived the feast was served. When it was over, Sindbad said, "My friends, I will now give you an account of my second voyage."

THE SECOND VOYAGE

As I told you yesterday, I had decided to pass the rest of my days in peace in Baghdad. But the desire to travel returned, so I brought some goods and set sail with other merchants to seek fortune.

We went from island to island, bartering our goods very profitably. One day, we landed on an island that was covered with a variety of fruit trees, but we could not discover any habitation or the trace of a single human being. While some of my companions were amusing themselves by gathering fruits and flowers, I sat under some trees and fell asleep. I cannot say how long I slept, but when I rose to look for my companions they were all gone. And I could only just make out the shape of the vessel in full sail, at such a distance that I soon lost sight of it.

After some moments of despair, I climbed a high tree to look about me. As I gazed around, my eye was caught by a large white spot in the distance. I climbed down quickly, and, making my way toward the object, found it to be a ball of enormous size. When I got near enough to touch it, I found it was soft and so smooth that any attempt to climb it would have been fruitless.

The sun was then almost setting and suddenly it seemed to be obscured, as by a cloud. I was surprised at this change, but then my amazement increased, when I realized that it had been caused by a

bird of the most extraordinary size, which was flying toward me. I remembered having heard sailors speak of a bird called a roc, and I concluded that the great white ball that had drawn my attention must be the egg of this bird. I was not mistaken. Soon afterward the bird lighted on the white ball and seated itself upon it. When I saw this huge fowl coming, I drew closer to the egg, so that I had one of the bird's claws just before me. This claw was as big as the trunk of a large tree.

I tied myself to the claw with the linen of my turban, hoping that the roc, when it took flight the next morning, would carry me off that desert island. My plan succeeded. At break of day the roc flew away, and bore me to such a height that I could no longer see the earth. Then the bird descended with such rapidity that I almost lost my senses. When the roc alighted, I quickly untied the knot that bound me to its claw. I had scarcely released myself when it darted at a serpent of immeasurable length. Then, seizing the snake in its beak, the bird flew away.

The place in which the roc left me was a deep valley, surrounded on all sides by mountains of such height that their summits were lost in the clouds, and so steep that there was no possibility of climbing them.

As I walked through this valley, I noticed that it was strewn with diamonds, some of which were of astonishing size. I amused myself for some time by examining them, but I soon saw far away some objects that destroyed my pleasure, and caused me great fear. These were a great number of enormous serpents. To escape from them I went into a cave, the entrance of which I closed with a stone. There I ate what remained of the provisions I had brought from the ship. All night I could hear the terrible hissing of the serpents. They went to their lairs at sunrise, and trembling, I left my cave and may truly say that I walked a long time on diamonds without feeling the least desire to possess them. At last, I sat down and fell asleep, for I had not once closed my eyes during the previous night. I had

scarcely begun to doze when the noise of something falling awoke me. It was a large piece of fresh meat. At the same moment I saw a number of other pieces rolling down the rocks from above.

I had always disbelieved the accounts I had heard from seamen and others about the Valley of Diamonds, and of the means by which merchants procured these precious gems. I now knew it to be true. The method is this: the merchants go to the mountains that surround the valley, cut large pieces of meat, and throw them down. The diamonds on which the lumps of meat fall stick to them. The eagles, which are larger and stronger in that country than in any other, seize these pieces of meat and carry them to their young at the top of the rocks. The merchants then run to the eagles' nests, oblige the birds to retreat, and then take the diamonds that have stuck to the pieces of meat.

I had begun to look on this valley as my tomb, but now felt a little hope. I collected the largest diamonds I could find and with these filled the leather bag in which I had carried my provisions. I then took one of the largest pieces of meat, tied it tightly around me with my turban, and laid myself on the ground.

I had not been long in this position before the eagles began to descend. Each seized a piece of meat, with which it flew away. One of the strongest darted on the piece to which I was attached, and carried me up with it to its nest. The merchants then began their cries to frighten away the eagles. When the birds had left, one of the merchants approached, and was surprised and alarmed at seeing me. He soon, however, recovered from his fear, and began to quarrel with me for trespassing on what he called his property.

"You will speak to me with pity instead of anger," I said, "when you learn by what means I reached this place. Console yourself. For I have diamonds for you as well as for myself. And my diamonds are more valuable than those of all the other merchants together."

Saying this, I showed him the stones I had collected. I had scarcely finished speaking when the other merchants, seeing me,

crowded round with great astonishment. Their wonder was even greater when I told my tale and showed my diamonds, which they declared to be unequaled in size and quality.

Everyone was content with his share of the diamonds that I distributed among them. The next day we set out, traveling over high mountains that were infested by large serpents. We had the good fortune to escape them. We reached the nearest port, where I exchanged some of my diamonds for valuable merchandise. And at last, after having touched at several ports, we reached Basra, from where I returned to Baghdad.

When Sindbad finished relating this story of his second voyage, he again ordered a hundred pieces of gold to be given to Hindbad, whom he invited to come on the morrow, when, after the usual feast, he began to tell the story of his third voyage.

THE THIRD VOYAGE

I soon forgot the dangers I had encountered on my two voyages, and, tired of doing nothing, again set sail with merchandise from Basra.

After a long voyage, during which we touched at several ports, we were overtaken by a violent tempest. The storm continued for several days and drove us near an island where we were compelled to cast anchor, although it was inhabited by a savage community of Pigmies. Their number was so great that the captain warned us to make no resistance, or they would swarm upon us like locusts and kill us. This information, which alarmed us very much, proved only too true. Very soon we saw advancing a multitude of hideous savages, entirely covered with red hair and about two feet high. They threw themselves into the sea, swam to the ship, and soon came swarming on the deck.

Unfurling the sails, they cut the cable, and after dragging the ship ashore, obliged us to disembark.

We left the shore and, penetrating into the island, found some fruits and herbs which we ate in fear and trembling. As we walked, we saw in the distance a great building, toward which we walked. It was a large and lofty palace, with folding gates of ebony that we pushed open. We entered the courtyard, and saw, facing us, a vast

apartment with a vestibule, on one side of which was a large heap
of human bones, while on the opposite side appeared a number of
spits for roasting.

The sun was setting and while we were still paralyzed with horror, the door of the apartment suddenly opened with a loud noise,
and there entered a man of frightful aspect, as tall as a large palm
tree. In the middle of his forehead gleamed a single eye, red and
fiery as a burning coal. His front teeth were long and sharp and
projected from his mouth, which was as wide as that of a horse. His
ears resembled those of an elephant and covered his shoulders, and
his long and curved nails were like the talons of an immense bird.
At the sight of him we almost lost our senses. And when, after
closely examining us, he seized me and began to pinch me all over,
I thought I was as good as dead. Fortunately, he found me too
skinny, so, dropping me, he seized the captain, who was the fattest
of the party, and spitting him like a sparrow, he roasted and ate him
for his supper. He then went to sleep, snoring louder than thunder.

He did not wake until the next morning, but we passed the night
in the most agonizing suspense. When daylight returned the giant
awoke, and went away, leaving us in the palace.

We tried to escape, but could find no way out. Toward evening
the giant returned and supped upon another of my unfortunate
companions. He then slept, snored, and departed, as before, at daybreak.

Our situation was so hopeless that some were on the point of
throwing themselves into the sea. But I dissuaded them, as I had a
plan which I proceeded to describe to them.

"My friends," I said, "you know that there is a great deal of
wood on the seashore. Let us build some rafts and then take the
first opportunity to execute my plan." My advice was approved by
all and we immediately built some rafts, each large enough to carry
three people. We carefully hid the rafts.

When the giant returned, another of our party was sacrificed. But

we soon had revenge for his cruelty. As soon as we heard him snore, I and nine of the most courageous among us each took a spit, and, making the points red hot, thrust them into his eye and blinded him.

The pain made the giant groan hideously. He threw his arms about in an attempt to catch us, but we were able to avoid him. At last he found the door and went out, bellowing with pain.

We immediately ran to the shore where our rafts were hidden, but we had to wait until daybreak before embarking.

The sun had scarcely risen, however, when, to our horror, we saw our cruel enemy, led by two giants nearly as huge as himself, and accompanied by several others, coming toward us.

We immediately ran to our rafts and rowed away as fast as possible. The giants, seeing this, picked up some huge stones, and, wading into the sea to their waists, hurled them at the rafts. They sank all but the one I was on. Thus I and two companions were the only men who escaped.

We rowed with all our strength and were soon beyond reach of the stones. We got to the open sea, where we tossed about for a day and a night. We then had the good fortune to be thrown onto an island where we found some excellent fruit, and soon recovered some of our exhausted strength.

When night came, we went to sleep on the seashore, but were soon awakened by the noise made by the hissing of an enormous serpent, which devoured one of my companions before he had time to escape.

My other comrade and I took flight. We saw a very high tree and climbed it, hoping to spend the next night there in safety. The hissing of the serpent again warned us of its approach, and, twining itself round the trunk, it swallowed my unfortunate companion, who was on a lower branch than myself, and then retired.

I remained in the tree until daybreak, when I descended, more dead than alive.

Toward evening, I collected a great quantity of wood and furze, an exceedingly spiny plant. Tying it in bundles, I placed it in a circle around the tree. Then, tying another bundle on my head, I sat down within the circle. The serpent returned with the intention of devouring me but, though he watched and waited the whole night, was prevented from approaching me by the prickly rampart I had created. He left at sunrise. I felt that death would be preferable to

another night of horror and so I ran toward the sea. But just as I **was about to dive** into the waves, I saw a ship at a distance. I called out with all my strength and unfolded and waved my turban to attract the attention of those on board. It did so and the captain sent a boat to get me.

Everyone on board was amazed at the story of my marvelous escape and treated me with the greatest kindness and generosity.

One day, the captain called me and said, "Brother, I have in my possession some goods that belonged to a merchant who was a passenger on my ship. Since he is dead, I am going to have them valued, that I may give an account of them to the heirs of this man, whose name was Sindbad. In this task I shall be glad of your assistance."

I looked at the captain in amazement and recognized him as the one who on my second voyage had left me asleep on the island.

Both of us were changed in appearance, which accounted for neither at first recognizing the other. But, when I declared myself, he remembered me and begged my forgiveness for the error by which I had been abandoned. "God be praised for your escape," he cried. "Here are your goods, which I have stored with care and now have the greatest pleasure in returning to you."

And so, at last, with all this additional wealth, I landed at Basra and came from there to Baghdad.

Sindbad thus finished the tale of his third voyage. Again he gave Hindbad a hundred gold pieces, inviting him to the usual repast on the morrow, when he continued the story of his adventures.

THE FOURTH VOYAGE

In spite of the terrible dangers I had encountered on my third voyage, it was not long before I tired of the land and again set sail with merchandise, as before.

All went well until one day we met with a sudden squall and were driven onto a sandbank, where the boat went to pieces and a number of the crew perished.

I and some others had the good fortune to get hold of a plank on which we drifted to an island where we found fruit and fresh water. We refreshed ourselves and then lay down to sleep.

The next morning, when the sun had risen, we left the shore and, walking inland, saw some dwellings toward which we made our way.

But the inhabitants took us prisoner and made all but myself eat of a certain herb.

I refused, since I suspected some evil purpose. I was right, for my companions soon became lightheaded, and did not know what they said or did.

Then a meal of rice cooked in coconut oil was offered us. I ate sparingly, but the others devoured it ravenously. This rice was to fatten us, for we had the terrible misfortune to have fallen into the

hands of cannibals, who intended to feast on us when we were in good condition.

And so, one by one, my poor companions, who had lost their senses and could not foresee their fate, were devoured. I, who ate next to nothing, became thinner and less palatable each day.

In the meantime, I was allowed a great deal of liberty. One day I took the opportunity to escape. I walked for seven days, taking care to avoid those places that appeared to be inhabited, and living on coconuts, which gave me both drink and food.

On the eighth day I came to the seashore, where I saw some people gathering pepper, which grew plentifully in that place. As soon as I approached them, they asked me in Arabic where I came from.

Delighted to hear my native language once more, I readily satisfied their curiosity. When they left I went with them to the island from which they had come. I was presented to their king, who was astonished at the story of my adventures and treated me with such kindness that I almost forgot my previous misfortunes.

I noticed one thing that appeared to me very unusual. Everyone, including the king, rode on horseback without saddle, bridle, or stirrups. One day I took the liberty to ask His Majesty why such things were not used in his city. He replied that he had never heard of the articles of which I spoke.

I immediately went to a workman, and gave him a model from which to make the base of a saddle. When he had finished, I myself covered the saddle with leather, richly embroidered in gold, and stuffed it with hair. I then went to a locksmith who made me a bit and some stirrups according to the patterns I gave him.

These things I presented to the king, who was delighted with them. As a sign of his approval, he bestowed upon me, as a wife, a lady, beautiful, rich, and accomplished, with whom I lived happily for some time, although I often thought regretfully of my native city of Baghdad and longed to return there.

One day, the wife of one of my neighbors, with whom I was very friendly, fell sick and died. I· went to console the widower, and, finding him in the deepest grief, said to him, "May God preserve you, and grant you a long life."

"Alas!" he replied, "I have only one hour to live. This very day, according to the custom of the country, I shall be buried with my wife."

While I was still mute with horror at this barbarous custom, his relations and friends came to make arrangements for the funeral. They dressed the corpse of the woman as though for her wedding, and decorated her with jewels. Then they placed her on an open bier and the procession set out. The husband, dressed in mourning, went next, and the relations followed. They climbed a high mountain, on the summit of which was a deep pit covered with a large stone, into which the body was lowered. The husband, to whom was given a jug of water and seven small loaves of bread, then took leave of his friends and allowed himself to be lowered into the pit, and the stone was replaced.

I was very distressed by this and expressed my horror to the king. "What can I do, Sindbad?" he replied. "It is a law common to everyone. Even I must submit to it. I shall be interred alive with the queen, my consort, if she happens to die first."

"And must strangers submit to this cruel custom?" I asked.

"Certainly," said the king. "They are not exempt when they marry on the island."

After this you may imagine my distress when my wife died after a few days' illness. I almost regretted that I had not been eaten by the cannibals. And though the funeral procession was honored by the presence of the king and his whole court, I was not in the least consoled. I followed the body of my wife, deploring my miserable destiny. At the last moment I tried to save my life by pleading my position as a stranger. But in vain. I was lowered into the pit with

my seven loaves of bread and jug of water, and the stone was replaced on the opening.

In spite of the horrors of my situation, I lived for some days on my provisions. But one day, when they were finished, and I was preparing to die of starvation, I heard the sound of loud breathing and footsteps. I felt my way in that direction and saw a shadow which fled before me. I followed it until, at last, I saw a small peck of light resembling a star. I continued toward it until I arrived at an opening in the rock, through which I scrambled and found myself on the seashore. Then I discovered that the object I had followed was a small animal, which lived among the rocks.

I cannot describe my joy at this escape. After a time, I ventured to return to the cave and collect a great quantity of jewels and gold ornaments, which had been buried with the dead. These I tied about me and then returned to the shore just in time to see a large ship approaching.

I managed to attract attention by shouting and waving my turban, was taken on board, and at length arrived safely once more in Baghdad.

Sindbad here concluded the story of his fourth voyage. He repeated his present of a hundred gold coins to Hindbad, whom he requested, with the rest of the company, to return on the following day, when he began the account of his fifth voyage.

THE FIFTH VOYAGE

It was not long before the peaceful and pleasant life I led became dull. This time I built a vessel of my own, on which I took several other merchants as passengers. We set sail with a fair wind and a rich cargo. The first place at which we stopped was a desert island, where we found the egg of a roc, as large as the one I spoke of on a former occasion. It contained a small roc, almost hatched. Its beak had begun to pierce the shell. My companions, in spite of my advice, broke open the egg with hatchets, and roasted the young bird, bit by bit.

They had scarcely finished their meal when two immense clouds appeared in the air at a considerable distance. The captain realized that the parents of the young roc were coming, and warned us to reembark as quickly as possible, to escape the danger that threatened us. We took his advice and set sail immediately.

The two rocs approached, uttering the most terrible screams, which they redoubled on finding their egg broken and their young one destroyed. Then they flew away toward the mountains from where they had come. We hoped we had seen the last of them.

But they soon returned, each with an enormous piece of rock in its claws, which, when they were directly over our ship, they let

fall. Our ship was smashed. Everyone on board, with the exception of myself, was either crushed to death or drowned.

I was under water for some time, but, coming to the surface, was able to seize a piece of wreckage with the aid of which I reached an island.

When I had rested awhile, I proceeded farther inland and was charmed by the beauty of all I saw. I ate the ripe fruit which hung from the trees on every side and drank from the crystal streams.

When night came I lay down to rest on a mossy bank. When the sun rose I continued on my way until I came to a little rivulet, beside which I saw an aged man seated.

I saluted him and asked what he was doing there. Instead of answering, he made signs to me to take him on my shoulders and cross the brook, making me understand that he wanted to gather some fruit on the other side.

Accordingly, taking him on my back I waded through the stream. When I had reached the other side, I stooped for him to alight. Instead he clambered onto my shoulders, crossed his legs round my neck, and gripped me so tightly around the throat that I was nearly strangled and fell to the ground.

But he still stayed on my shoulders and kicked me so hard that I was forced to rise. He then made me walk under some trees, the fruit of which he gathered and ate. He didn't release his hold during the day. And at night he laid himself on the ground, still clinging to my neck.

From this time forward I was his beast of burden. All attempts to dislodge him were in vain. Finally, one day, I chanced to find on the ground several dried gourds that had fallen from the tree that bore them. I took a large one, and, after having cleared it out I squeezed into it the juice of several bunches of grapes, which the island produced in great abundance. This I left in a particular spot for some days, when, returning, I found the juice changed into wine.

I drank some of it and it had such an exhilarating effect that, in spite of my burden, I began to dance and sing. Noticing this, the old man indicated that he also wished to taste the liquor. He liked it so well that he emptied the gourd. The wine went almost immediately to his head, and he began to sway to and fro on my shoulders. Before long his grasp relaxed and I was able to throw him to the ground.

I was delighted to have got rid of this old man and I set out toward the seashore, where I met some people who belonged to a

vessel that had anchored there to get fresh water. They were much astonished at seeing me and hearing the account of my adventure.

"You had fallen," they said, "into the hands of the Old Man of the Sea, and you are the first of his captives whom he has not strangled sooner or later. Because of him the sailors and merchants who land here never dare approach except in a strong body."

They then took me to their ship and I sailed with them. In a few days we anchored in the harbor of a large city.

One of the merchants on the ship had become very friendly with me. When we landed he gave me a large sack, and then introduced me to some others who were also furnished with sacks. He said, "Follow these people, and do as they do."

We set off together and arrived at a large forest of coconut trees, the trunks of which were so smooth that it was impossible for any to climb, except the monkeys who lived among the branches.

My companions collected stones which they threw at the monkeys, who retaliated by hurling coconuts at us. In this way, we easily obtained enough to fill our sacks.

By selling these coconuts to merchants in the city, in the course of time I made a considerable sum.

I then obtained a passage in a ship that called for a cargo of coconuts. It was bound for the Island of Kamari, which was celebrated for its pearl fishery.

Here I hired divers and was fortunate to obtain a number of fine pearls, with which I again set sail. I landed in Basra, having still further increased my riches, a tenth part of which I bestowed in charity, as was now my custom on returning from a voyage.

At the end of this narrative Sindbad, as usual, gave a hundred pieces of gold to Hindbad, who left with all the other guests. The same party returned the next day. After their host had fed them in as sumptuous a manner as on the preceding days, he began the account of his sixth voyage.

THE SIXTH VOYAGE

About a year after my return from my fifth voyage, I again embarked on a ship, the captain of which intended to make a long voyage.

Long indeed it proved to be, for the captain and pilot lost their way and did not know how to navigate. When, at last, the captain discovered our whereabouts, he threw his turban on the deck, tore his beard, and beat his head like a man distraught.

On being asked the reason for this behavior, he replied, "We are in the greatest peril. A rapid current is pushing the ship, and we shall all perish in less than a quarter of an hour. Pray Allah to deliver us from this dreadful danger. Nothing can save us unless He takes pity on us."

He then gave orders to hoist more sail, but the ropes broke in the attempt. The ship became quite unmanageable and was dashed by the current against a rock, where it split into pieces. Nevertheless, we had time to remove our provisions, as well as the most valuable part of the cargo.

When we were assembled on the shore the captain said, "Allah's will be done. Here we may dig our graves for we are in a place so desolate that no one else cast on this shore has ever returned to his own home."

We were at the foot of a mountain, which formed part of an island. The coast was covered with wreckage and all kinds of valuable merchandise in bales and chests that had been thrown up by the sea. Indeed, if we could have lived on gold or jewels, all might have been well. As it was, starvation was bound to overcome us before very long.

There was, however, one strange thing about the place: a river of fresh water ran from the sea and disappeared into a cavern in the mountain.

We remained on the shore in a hopeless condition. The mountain was too steep to climb and so we were without any means of escape. The fate we feared gradually overcame us. Those who died first were buried by the others. I had the dismal job of burying my last companion, for I had eaten more sparingly of my share of the stock provisions which had been divided among us and so lived the longest. Nevertheless, when I buried the last of them I had so little food left that I imagined I must soon follow him.

But Allah had pity on me and inspired me with the thought of examining the river that lost itself in the recesses of the cave. Having done so, I decided to make a raft, trust myself to the current, and see where it would take me. If I perished, I would change only the manner of my death.

I set to work at once and made a strong framework of wood bound with rope, of which there was an abundance scattered about the shore. I then selected from among the wreckage the chests containing the most gold and valuable jewels. When I had carefully stowed these to balance the raft, I embarked on my vessel, guiding it with the little oar I had made.

The current carried me under the vault of the cavern and I soon found myself in darkness. I rowed, for what seemed to be days, without seeing a single ray of light.

During this time, I ate the last of my hoarded stock of provisions. I then either fell asleep or became unconscious. When I came to I

was astonished to find myself in open country, near a bank of the river, to which my raft was fastened, and surrounded by a number of black men.

I felt so overcome with joy that I could scarcely believe myself awake. At last, convinced that my deliverance was not a dream, I gave thanks aloud; and one of the men who understood Arabic, advanced and said, "Do not be alarmed at the sight of us. The river that issues from yonder mountain is that from which we get water for our fields. When we saw your raft being borne toward us, we swam to it, and guided it to shore. And now I beg you to tell us from where you came."

I replied, "I will do so, with pleasure, when I have eaten. I am at the point of starvation."

I satisfied my hunger and then proceeded to satisfy their curiosity. They then said they must take me to their king. So, having procured a horse for me, they pulled my raft ashore and followed me with it on their shoulders to the city of Serendib, where their king received me with great kindness.

To him I related all that had befallen me. He was so pleased with the story of my adventures that he ordered it to be written in letters of gold and preserved among the archives of his kingdom. The raft was then produced and, prostrating myself before him, I said: "If Your Majesty will honor me by accepting my cargo, it is all at your disposal."

But, although he smiled and appeared pleased, he refused my offer, and said that when I left his kingdom I should take with me proof of his regard.

After I had spent some days exploring the city and its surroundings, I begged to be allowed to return to my own country. The king not only gave me permission, together with a gift of great value, but also did me the high honor of entrusting me with a letter and gifts for the Caliph Haroun Alraschid. These gifts included a vase made of a single ruby, filled with pearls, and a female slave of marvelous beauty who wore jewels worth a king's ransom.

After a long but pleasant voyage, we landed at Basra, from where I returned to Baghdad. At once I presented the letter and the gifts of the King of Serendib to the caliph, who, after he had asked me a number of questions about the country from which I had returned, dismissed me with a handsome present.

Sindbad here finished his tale, and his visitors left, Hindbad, as usual, receiving his hundred gold pieces. The guests and the porter returned on the following day and Sindbad began to tell of his seventh and last voyage.

THE SEVENTH AND LAST VOYAGE

I now decided, since I was past the prime of life, to go to sea no more, but to enjoy a pleasant and restful existence at home.

But one day the caliph sent for me.

"Sindbad," he said, "I want you to do me a service. You must go once more to the King of Serendib with my answer and presents. It is only right that I should reply properly to him."

"Commander of the Faithful," I replied, "I humbly beg you to consider that I am exhausted by all I have undergone in my six voyages. I have even made a vow never again to leave Baghdad."

I then related the long tale of my adventures. When I had finished, the caliph said, "I confess that these are extraordinary adventures. Nevertheless, they must not prevent you from making the voyage I propose, which is only to the island of Serendib. You must agree that it would be wrong if I remained under obligation to the king of that island."

Since it was clear that the caliph was insisting that I go, I signified that I was ready to obey his commands. He then provided me with a thousand pieces of gold to cover the expenses of the voyage.

In a few days, having received the presents from the caliph, together with a letter written by his own hand, I set off for Basra,

where I embarked and, after a pleasant voyage, arrived at the island
of Serendib.

I soon obtained an audience with the king, who showed pleasure
at the sight of me. "Welcome, Sindbad," he said. "I assure you I
have often thought of you since your departure. Blessed be this day
in which I see you again."

After thanking the king for his kindness, I delivered the caliph's
letter and presents, which he received with great pleasure.

The caliph had sent the king a complete bolt of gold tissue, fifty
robes of a very rare material, a hundred more of the finest white
linen, a bolt of crimson velvet, and another of a different pattern
and color. In addition, he sent a vase of agate, carved in the most
wonderful manner.

Soon after this, I requested leave to depart, which the king
granted, at the same time giving me a handsome present. I then
reembarked. But three or four days after we set sail we were at-
tacked by pirates, who quickly made themselves masters of our
vessel. Those who tried to resist lost their lives. I and all those who
had the prudence to submit quietly were made slaves. After they
had stripped us and clothed us in rags instead of our own gar-
ments, the pirates bent their course toward a distant island, where
they sold us.

I was purchased by a rich merchant who took me home with
him. Some days later he asked me if I could shoot with a bow and
arrow.

I replied that I had practiced that sport in my youth and that I did
not think I had entirely lost my skill. He then gave me a bow and
some arrows and, making me mount behind him on an elephant,
took me to a vast forest some hours' journey from the city. We
went a great way into the forest, until the merchant came to a
particular spot, where he made me alight. Then he showed me a
large tree. "Climb that tree," he said, "and shoot at the elephants

that pass under it. There are many of these animals in this forest. If one should fall, come and let me know.''

He then left me some provisions and returned to the city.

During the first night no elephants came. But the next day, as soon as the sun had risen, a great number made their appearance. I shot many arrows at them and at last one fell. The others immediately ran away, and left me at liberty to go and inform my master of my success.

He praised me and, returning with me, we dug a pit and buried the elephant, so that the body might rot and the tusks be more easily secured.

I continued my new occupation for two months. Not a day passed on which I did not kill an elephant. But one day, instead of passing on as usual, the elephants herded together and came toward me, trumpeting loudly, and in such numbers that the ground trembled under their tread. They approached my tree and their eyes all fixed upon me. At this surprising spectacle I was so unnerved that my bow and arrows fell from my hands.

After the elephants had viewed me for some time, one of the largest twisted his trunk around the trunk of the tree, tore it up by the roots, and threw it on the ground. I fell with the tree. The animal lifted me up with his trunk and placed me on his shoulders, where I lay more dead than alive. The huge beast now put himself at the head of his companions and carried me to a little hill, where he set me down, and then went away with the rest.

After I had waited some time, seeing no other elephants, I rose, and saw that the hill was entirely covered with bones and tusks of elephants. Evidently this was their cemetery and they had brought me here to show it to me so that I would stop destroying them merely for the sake of possessing their tusks. I did not stay there long, but turned my steps toward the city. After walking for a day and a night, I arrived at my master's.

As soon as he saw me, he exclaimed, "Ah, my poor Sindbad! I have been wondering what could have become of you. I have been to the forest where I found a tree newly torn up by the roots and your bow and arrows on the ground. And so I despaired of ever seeing you again. Pray tell me by what fortunate chance you are still alive."

I satisfied his curiosity and the following day he accompanied me to the hill and, with great joy, convinced himself of the truth of my story. We loaded the elephant on which we had come with as many tusks as it could carry. When we returned my master said, "Brother, I give you your freedom. Up to now we have not been able to get ivory without risking the lives of our slaves. Now our whole city will be enriched because of you. I shall see that you are rewarded accordingly."

To this I replied, "The only reward I want is permission to return to my own country."

"Well," he replied, "you will have an opportunity shortly, for the monsoon will bring us vessels, which come to be filled with ivory. On one of these you may obtain passage."

The ships finally arrived. My master chose the one in which I was to embark, loaded it with ivory, signing more than half the cargo to me, which I ultimately sold for a large sum.

Arriving in Baghdad without any further adventures, I immediately presented myself to the caliph, who told me that my long absence had caused him some uneasiness, which made him the more delighted to see me return safely.

He bestowed more presents and honors upon me. After this I returned to my own home in this my native city of Baghdad, which I have not since left and where I hope to end my days.

Sindbad thus concluded the recital of his seventh and last voyage. Addressing himself to Hindbad, he added, "Well, my friend, have

103

you ever heard of anyone who has suffered more than I have, or has been in so many trying situations? Is it not right that after so many troubles I should enjoy an agreeable and quiet life?"

Hindbad kissed his hand and said, "I must confess that you have encountered frightful perils. You not only deserve a quiet life, but are worthy of all the riches you possess, since you make so good a use of them!"

Sindbad gave Hindbad another hundred pieces of gold. In addition he continued to show him so much kindness that Hindbad, who now had no need to continue as porter, for the remainder of his days had every reason to bless the name of Sindbad the Sailor.

FUTURE 1

English for Work, Life, and Academic Success

Second Edition

Series Consultants
Sarah Lynn
Ronna Magy
Federico Salas-Isnardi

Authors
Marjorie Fuchs
Lisa Johnson
Sarah Lynn
Irene Schoenberg

 Pearson

Future 1
English for Work, Life, and Academic Success
Copyright © 2021 by Pearson Education, Inc.
All rights reserved. No part of this publication may be reproduced, stored in a retrieval system, or transmitted in any form or by any means, electronic, mechanical, photocopying, recording, or otherwise, without the prior permission of the publisher.

Pearson Education, 221 River Street, Hoboken, NJ 07030 USA

Staff credits: The people who made up the **Future** team, representing content development, design, manufacturing, marketing, multimedia, project management, publishing, rights management, and testing, are Pietro Alongi, Jennifer Castro, Dave Dickey, Gina DiLillo, Warren Fischbach, Pamela Fishman, Gosia Jaros-White, Joanna Konieczna, Michael Mone, Mary Rich, Katarzyna Starzyńska-Kościuszko, Claire Van Poperin, Joseph Vella, Gabby Wu

Text composition: ElectraGraphics, Inc.
Cover Design: EMC Design Ltd
Illustration credits: See Credits page 282.
Photo credits: See Credits page 282.
Audio: CityVox

Library of Congress Cataloging-in-Publication Data
A catalog record for the print edition is available from the Library of Congress.

ISBN-13: 9780137359271 (Student Book with App and MyEnglishLab)
ISBN-10: 0137359276 (Student Book with App and MyEnglishLab)

ISBN-13: 9780137360321 (Student Book with App)
ISBN-10: 0137360320 (Student Book with App)
16 2022

pearsonenglish.com

CONTENTS

Welcome to *Future: English for Work, Life, and Academic Success*

Future is a six-level, standards-based English language course for adult and young adult students. *Future* provides students with the contextualized academic language, strategies, and critical thinking skills needed for success in workplace, life, and academic settings. *Future* is aligned with the requirements of the Workforce Innovation and Opportunity Act (WIOA), the English Language Proficiency (ELP) and College and Career Readiness (CCR) standards, and the National Reporting System (NRS) level descriptors. The 21st century curriculum in *Future*'s second edition helps students acquire the basic literacy, language, and employability skills needed to meet the requirements set by the standards.

Future develops students' academic and critical thinking skills, digital literacy and numeracy, workplace and civic skills, and prepares students for taking standardized tests. Competency and skills incorporating standards are in the curriculum at every level, providing a foundation for academic rigor, research-based teaching strategies, corpus-informed language, and the best of digital tools.

In revising the course, we listened to hundreds of *Future* teachers and learners and studied the standards for guidance. *Future* continues to be the most comprehensive English communication course for adults, with its signature scaffolded lessons and multiple practice activities throughout. *Future*'s second edition provides enhanced content, rigorous academic language practice, and cooperative learning through individual and collaborative practice. Every lesson teaches the interpretive, interactive, and productive skills highlighted in the standards.

Future's Instructional Design

Learner Centered and Outcome Oriented

The student is at the center of *Future*. Lessons start by connecting to student experience and knowledge, and then present targeted skills in meaningful contexts. Varied and dynamic skill practice progresses from controlled to independent in a meticulously scaffolded sequence.

Headers highlighting Depth of Knowledge (DOK) terms are used throughout *Future* to illuminate the skills being practiced. Every lesson culminates in an activity in which students apply their learning, demonstrate their knowledge, and express themselves orally or in writing. A DOK glossary for teachers includes specific suggestions on how to help students activate these cognitive skills.

Varied Practice

Cognitive science has proven what *Future* always knew: Students learn new skills through varied practice over time. Content-rich units that contextualize academic and employability skills naturally recycle concepts, language, and targeted skills. Individual and collaborative practice activities engage learners and lead to lasting outcomes. Lessons support both student collaboration and individual self-mastery. Students develop the interpretative, productive, and interactive skills identified in the NRS guidelines, while using the four language skills of reading, writing, listening, and speaking.

Goal Setting and Learning Assessment

For optimal learning to take place, students need to be involved in setting goals and in monitoring their own progress. *Future* addresses goal setting in numerous ways. In the Student Book, Unit Goals are identified on the unit opener page. Checkboxes at the end of lessons invite students to evaluate their mastery of the material, and suggest additional online practice.

High-quality assessment aligned to the standards checks student progress and helps students prepare to take standardized tests. The course-based assessment program is available in print and digital formats and includes a bank of customizable test items. Digital tests are assigned by the teacher and reported back in the LMS online gradebook. All levels include a midterm and final test. Test items are aligned with unit learning objectives and standards. The course Placement Test is available in print and digital formats. Test-prep materials are also provided for specific standardized tests.

One Integrated Program

Future provides everything adult English language learners need in one integrated program using the latest digital tools and time-tested print resources.

Integrated Skills Contextualized with Rich Content

Future contextualizes grammar, listening, speaking, pronunciation, reading, writing, and vocabulary in meaningful activities that simulate real workplace, educational, and community settings. A special lesson at the end of each unit highlights soft skills at work. While providing relevant content, *Future* helps build learner knowledge and equips adults for their many roles.

Meeting Work, Life, and Education Goals

Future recognizes that every adult learner brings a unique set of work, life, and academic experiences, as well as a distinct skill set. With its diverse array

WL 09.30.2022 1017

learners with multiple opportunities to practice with contextualized materials to build skill mastery. Specialized lessons for academic and workplace skill development are part of *Future*'s broad array of print and digital resources.

In addition to two units on employment in each level, every unit contains a Workplace, Life, and Community Skills lesson as well as a Soft Skills at Work lesson.

Workplace, Life, and Community Skills Lessons

In the second edition, the Life Skills lesson has been revised to focus on workplace, life, and community skills and to develop the real-life language and civic literacy skills required today. Lessons integrate and contextualize workplace content. In addition, every lesson includes practice with digital skills on a mobile device.

Soft Skills at Work Lessons

Future has further enhanced its development of workplace skills by adding a Soft Skills at Work lesson to each unit. Soft skills are the critical interpersonal communication skills needed to succeed in any workplace. Students begin each lesson by discussing a common challenge in the workplace. Then, while applying the lesson-focused soft skill, they work collaboratively to find socially appropriate solutions to the problem. The log at the back of the Student Book encourages students to track their own application of the soft skill, which they can use in job interviews.

Academic Rigor

Rigor and respect for the ability and experiences of the adult learner have always been central to *Future*. The standards provide the foundation for academic rigor. The reading, writing, listening, and speaking practice require learners to analyze, use context clues, interpret, cite evidence, build knowledge, support a claim, and summarize from a variety of

content-rich materials develop academic language and build knowledge. Interactive activities allow for collaboration and exchange of ideas in workplace and in academic contexts. *Future* emphasizes rigor by highlighting the critical thinking and problem solving skills required in each activity.

Writing Lessons

In addition to the increased focus on writing in Show What You Know activities, *Future* has added a cumulative writing lesson to every unit, a lesson that requires students to synthesize and apply their learning in a written outcome. Through a highly scaffolded approach, students begin by analyzing writing models before planning and finally producing written work of their own. Writing frameworks, Writing Skills, and a checklist help guide students through the writing process.

Reading lessons

All reading lessons have new, information-rich texts and a revised pedagogical approach in line with the CCR and ELP standards and the NRS descriptors. These informational texts are level appropriate, use high-frequency vocabulary, and focus on interpretation of graphic information. The readings build students' knowledge and develop their higher-order reading skills by teaching citation of evidence, summarizing, and interpretation of complex information from a variety of text formats.

Future Grows with Your Student

Future takes learners from absolute beginner level through low-advanced English proficiency, addressing students' abilities and learning priorities at each level. As the levels progress, the curricular content and unit structure change accordingly, with the upper levels incorporating more advanced academic language and skills in the text and in the readings.

Future Intro	Future Level 1	Future Level 2	Future Level 3	Future Level 4	Future Advanced
NRS Beginning ESL Literacy	NRS Low Beginning ESL	NRS High Beginning ESL	NRS Low Intermediate ESL	NRS High Intermediate ESL	NRS Advanced ESL
ELPS Level 1	**ELPS** Level 1	**ELPS** Level 2	**ELPS** Level 3	**ELPS** Level 4	**ELPS** Level 5
CCRS Level A	**CCRS** Level A	**CCRS** Level A	**CCRS** Level B	**CCRS** Level C	**CCRS** Level D
CASAS 180 and below	**CASAS** 181–190	**CASAS** 191–200	**CASAS** 201–210	**CASAS** 211–220	**CASAS** 221–235

English App provides easy mobile access to all of the audio files, plus Grammar Coach videos and activities and the new Pronunciation coach videos. Listen and study on the go—anywhere, any time!

Abundant Opportunities for Student Practice

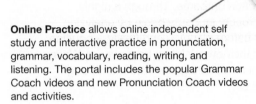

Student

a complete student resource, including lessons in grammar, listening and speaking, pronunciation, reading, writing, vocabulary, and Soft Skills at Work, taught and practiced in contextual and interactive activities in the eBook.

Workbook—with audio—provides additional practice for each lesson in the student book, with new readings and practice in writing, grammar, listening and speaking, plus activities for new Soft Skills at Work lessons.

Online Practice allows online independent self study and interactive practice in pronunciation, grammar, vocabulary, reading, writing, and listening. The portal includes the popular Grammar Coach videos and new Pronunciation Coach videos and activities.

Teacher's Edition includes culture notes, teaching tips, and numerous optional and extension activities, with lesson-by-lesson correlations to CCR and ELP standards. Rubrics are provided for evaluation of students' written and oral communication.

Outstanding Teacher Resources

Teacher

College and Career Readiness Plus Lessons supplement the student book with challenging reading and writing lessons for every level above Intro.

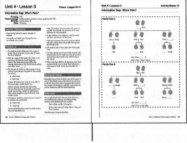

Presentation tool for front-of-classroom projection of the student book, includes audio at point of use and pop-up activities, including grammar examples, academic conversation stems, and reader's anticipation guide.

Assessment Program, accessed online with interactive and printable tests and rubrics, includes a Placement Test, multi-level unit, mid-term and final exams, and computer-based Test Generator with additional ready-to-use and customizable tests. In addition, sample high-stakes test practice is included with CASAS test prep for listening and reading.

Multilevel Communicative Activities provide an array of reproducible communication activities and games that engage students through different modalities. Teachers' notes provide multilevel options for pre-level and above-level students, as well as extension activities for additional speaking and writing practice.

Go to the Teacher's Portal for easy reference, correlations to federal and state standards, and course updates. pearsonenglish.com

Preview questions activate student background knowledge and help the teacher assess how much students know about the unit theme.

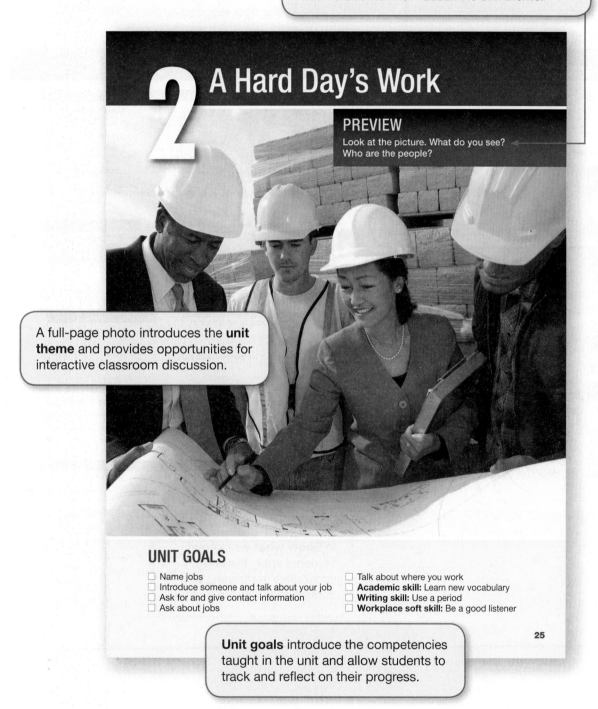

2 A Hard Day's Work

PREVIEW

Look at the picture. What do you see? Who are the people?

A full-page photo introduces the **unit theme** and provides opportunities for interactive classroom discussion.

UNIT GOALS

- ☐ Name jobs
- ☐ Introduce someone and talk about your job
- ☐ Ask for and give contact information
- ☐ Ask about jobs
- ☐ Talk about where you work
- ☐ **Academic skill:** Learn new vocabulary
- ☐ **Writing skill:** Use a period
- ☐ **Workplace soft skill:** Be a good listener

25

Unit goals introduce the competencies taught in the unit and allow students to track and reflect on their progress.

Key **vocabulary** is contextualized and practiced in connection to the unit theme.

Study tips introduce the learning skills and strategies students need to meet the rigor required by the CCRS.

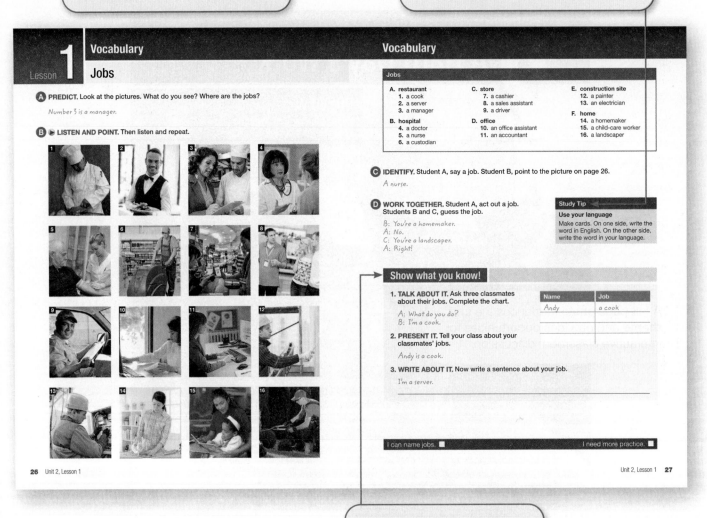

In **Show what you know!**, students apply the target vocabulary in meaningful conversations and in writing.

UNIT TOUR

Three **Listening and Speaking** lessons provide students opportunities for realistic conversations in work, community, and educational settings.

Pronunciation activities help students learn, practice, and internalize the patterns of spoken English and relate them to their own lives.

Lesson 2

Listening and Speaking

Introduce someone and talk about your job

1 BEFORE YOU LISTEN

TALK ABOUT IT. Look at the picture. Where are they?

Omar, this is Rosa. Rosa, this is Omar.

Hi, Omar. Nice to _____ you.

Hi, Rosa. _____ to meet you, _____.

2 LISTEN

A ▶ **LISTEN.** Complete the conversation in the picture.

B ▶ **LISTEN.** What is Rosa's question?

a. What do you do?　　b. Where are you from?

C ▶ **LISTEN FOR DETAILS.** Complete the sentences.

1. Omar is a landscaper and _____.
   a. a driver　　b. a student

2. Rosa is a student and _____.
   a. a sales assistant　　b. a nurse

D ▶ **EXPAND.** Listen to the whole conversation. What is Emilio's job?

a.

b.

Listening and Speaking

3 PRONUNCIATION

A ▶ **PRACTICE.** Listen. Then listen and repeat.

A: What do you do?
B: I'm a student.

A: What's your name?
B: I'm Peter.

Falling intonation in statements and *Wh-* questions

In *Wh-* questions and in statements, the voice goes down ↘ at the end.

B ▶ **APPLY.** Practice saying the sentences. Then listen and repeat.

Where are you from?
I'm from China.
What about you?

4 CONVERSATION

A ▶ **LISTEN AND READ.** Then listen and repeat.

A: So, what do you do?
B: I'm a landscaper. And I'm a student at Greenville Adult School.
A: Really? I'm a student there, too. And I'm a sales assistant.
B: Oh, that's interesting.

B **WORK TOGETHER.** Practice the conversation in Exercise A.

C **CREATE.** Make new conversations. Use the pictures.

A: What do you do?
B: I'm _____.
A: Really? I'm _____, too. And I'm _____.
B: Oh, that's interesting.

D **MAKE CONNECTIONS.** Make your own conversations.

Conversations carefully scaffold student learning and build language fluency.

I can introduce someone and talk about my job. ■　　I need more practice. ■

Multiple listening opportunities progress from listening for general understanding, to listening for details, to listening to an extended version of the conversation.

Checkpoints at the end of lessons provide students an opportunity to reflect on their progress and identify further resources for more practice.

Predict activities focus students on the social context of the conversation.

Each unit presents three **Grammar** lessons in a systematic grammar progression. Every Grammar lesson focuses on language introduced in the preceding Listening and Speaking lesson. Additional grammar practice is available in the Grammar Review and online.

Images provide scaffolding for meaningful grammar practice.

Lesson 3

Grammar

A/An; Singular and plural nouns

A/An

| He is | a | landscaper. | She is | an | accountant. |

Grammar Watch
- Use *a* before consonant sounds.
- Use *an* before vowel sounds.

A **IDENTIFY.** Cross out the incorrect words.

1. **A:** That's Fang. She's **a / an** office assistant.
   B: Oh, really? I'm **a / an** office assistant, too.

2. **A:** Paul is **a / an** teacher, right?
   B: No. He's not **a / an** teacher. He's **a / an** nurse.

3. **A:** I'm **a / an** landscaper. What about you?
   B: I'm **a / an** electrician.

4. **A:** This is Dr. and Mrs. Silver. He's **a / an** doctor, and she's **a / an** accountant.
   B: Nice to meet you. I'm Mary Green. I'm **a / an** child-care worker.

5. **A:** So, Ana, what do you do?
   B: I'm **a / an** homemaker.

B ▶ **SELF-ASSESS.** Listen and check your answers.

C **WORK TOGETHER.** Practice the conversations in Exercise A.

D **COMPLETE.** Use *a* or *an*. Then complete sentence 8.

1. Bob is ___*a*___ cashier.
2. Joe is _____ electrician.
3. Kevin is _____ driver.
4. John is _____ cook.
5. Sarah is _____ office assistant.
6. Hai is _____ accountant.
7. Faha is _____ student.
8. My classmate is _____.

Grammar

Singular and plural nouns

| John is | **a cook.** | John and Linda are | **cooks.** |

Grammar Watch
- Add *-s* to form most plurals.
- For irregular plural nouns, see page 259.

E **APPLY.** Look at the pictures. Complete the sentences.

1. Bob is ___*a nurse*___.
2. Rosa is _____.
3. Jill, Mei, and I are _____.
4. They're _____.

Show what you know!

1. **RANK.** These are the five most common jobs in the U.S. Which job is number 1? Number 2? 3? 4? 5? Guess. Write the numbers next to the jobs.

   ____ cashiers ____ sales assistants ____ food preparers and servers
   ____ office assistants ____ nurses

2. **TALK ABOUT IT.** What do you think? Talk about your answers in Exercise 1.

   A: I think cashiers are number 1.
   B: Me, too.
   C: No, I think . . .

3. ▶ **SELF-ASSESS.** Listen and check your answers.

4. **WRITE ABOUT IT.** What do you think about the most common jobs or other jobs you know? Write a sentence. Use words from the box.

   | friendly | good | great | helpful | smart |

   Most ___*sales assistants*___ are helpful.
   Most _____

I can use *a/an* and singular and plural nouns. ☐   I need more practice. ☐

Grammar activities progress from controlled to open practice, leading students from understanding to mastery of the target grammar.

Grammar charts present the target grammar point in a clear and simple format.

Every **Show what you know!** integrates an interactive exchange and a writing task so students demonstrate their mastery of the grammar point using a range of language skills.

UNIT TOUR

Workplace, Life, and Community skills lessons develop real-life language and civic literacy while encouraging community participation.

Interactive activities develop real-life communication and collaboration skills.

Workplace, Life, and Community Skills

Lesson 4 — Ask for and give contact information

1 IDENTIFY PHONE NUMBERS

A **MAKE CONNECTIONS.** Think about numbers in your life. When do you use numbers? Do you use numbers at work?

B ▶ **LISTEN AND POINT.** Then listen and repeat.

0 zero	1 one	2 two	3 three	4 four
5 five	6 six	7 seven	8 eight	9 nine

C ▶ **LISTEN.** Circle the phone numbers you hear.

1. a. 212-960-5334
   b. 412-960-5334
2. a. 619-464-2083
   b. 619-464-2093
3. a. 305-576-1169
   b. 395-576-1169

4. a. 323-865-4191
   b. 323-835-4191
5. a. 214-847-3726
   b. 214-847-3126
6. a. 773-395-2114
   b. 773-399-2114

Cumar Rahim
My number
(415) 555-7934

D ▶ **COMPLETE.** Listen to the voicemail messages. Write the missing numbers.

1.
Mr. Fernandez
Center Hospital
Landscaper job
(562) 555-_____

2.
Grace Simms
Grace's Office Supplies
Cashier Job
(_____) 555-_____

3.
Jin Wu
Greenville Store
Sales assistant job
(_____) 555-_____

4.
Ms. Rodriguez
Carla's Restaurant
Manager job
(_____) _____ - _____

Workplace, Life, and Community Skills

2 IDENTIFY EMAIL ADDRESSES

A ▶ **MAKE CONNECTIONS.** Think about email in your life. When do you use email? Do you use email at work?

B ▶ **LISTEN AND POINT.** Look at the email. Listen and point to the email addresses. Then listen and repeat.

From: amy.smith@mymail.com
To: rosa.medina@mymail.com
Subject: ESL class

C ▶ **LISTEN.** Circle the email addresses you hear.

1. a. dan.silver@ccmail.edu
   b. dans.ilver@ccmail.edu
2. a. gsimms@hmail.com
   b. g.simms@hmail.com

3. a. tlopez719@gomail.com
   b. tlopez715@gomail.com
4. a. jin.wu@newmail.edu
   b. jin.hu@newmail.edu

3 GET CONTACT INFORMATION

A ▶ **LISTEN AND READ.** Then listen and repeat.

A: What's your phone number?
B: 213-555-4963?
A: 213-555-4563?
B: No. It's 213-555-4963.
A: OK. And what's your email address?
B: asad.bilan@hmail.com.

B **WORK TOGETHER.** Ask two classmates for their phone number and email address. Complete the chart.

Name	Phone Number	Email address
Asad	(213) 555-4963	asad.bilan@hmail.com
1.		
2.		

C **GO ONLINE.** Add two new contacts in your phone.

| I can ask for and give contact information. ■ | I need more practice. ■ |

In **Go Online** activities, students use their devices to practice concrete online tasks, such as researching information or inputting data.

All new informational **Reading lessons** develop academic language and build content knowledge to meet the rigorous requirements of the CCRS.

Close-reading activities require that students return to the reading to find textual evidence of detail, to summarize for general understanding, and to make inferences.

Students develop **numeracy** skills by interpreting numeric information in charts and graphs.

Lesson 7

Reading
Read about healthcare jobs in the U.S.

1 BEFORE YOU READ

A CHOOSE. Complete the sentences with the vocabulary from the box.

| CNA | nursing home | orderly |

1. He's an _____. 2. She's a _____. 3. They live in a _____.

B TALK ABOUT IT. What kinds of jobs are there in a hospital?

2 READ

▶ Listen and read.

Academic Skill: Learn new vocabulary

The words in Exercise 1A will be important when you read *Healthcare Jobs in the U.S.* Write the words in your notebook. Underline the words when you see them in the article.

Healthcare Jobs in the U.S.

Many people in the U.S. work in healthcare. How many? More than 12 million.

The biggest number of jobs in healthcare is for nurses. They work in hospitals, doctors' offices, schools, and
5 nursing homes. You need a lot of training to be a nurse. Nurses go to school for many years.

That is not true for all jobs in healthcare. For some jobs, a high school diploma is enough. For example, you can be an orderly or a CNA. (CNA means "certified
10 nursing assistant.") Most orderlies get training on the job. CNAs take a training course and an exam.

The U.S. has more than 1.5 million CNAs and orderlies. They work in hospitals and nursing homes. They need to be strong because sometimes they lift
15 patients out of bed. They also help people eat, wash, or get dressed.

Hospitals and nursing homes need other kinds of workers, too. They need cooks, housekeepers, custodians, and electricians. They need clerks to do
20 office work.

Healthcare in the U.S. is growing. It will need more workers in the future.

Top Jobs in the U.S.

	What's the job?	How many people do it?	How much money do they make in a year?
1.	Sales assistant	4.5 million	about $25,000
2.	Cashier	3.3 million	about $20,000
3.	Food preparer and server	3.0 million	about $19,000
4.	Office assistant	2.8 million	about $30,000
5.	Registered nurse	2.7 million	about $69,000

Source: U.S. Bureau of Labor Statistics

Reading

3 CLOSE READING

A CITE EVIDENCE. Complete the sentences. Where is the information? Write the line number.

Lines

1. More than _____ million people work in healthcare in the U.S.
   a. 12   b. 15   c. 21   _____
2. You need many years of school to be _____.
   a. a CNA   b. an orderly   c. a nurse   _____
3. _____ do office work in hospitals.
   a. Clerks   b. Housekeepers   c. Electricians   _____
4. There will be _____ jobs in healthcare in the future.
   a. more   b. the same number of   c. not so many   _____

B INTERPRET. Complete the sentences about the chart.

1. The chart shows _____ in the U.S.
   a. the jobs with the most workers   b. who makes the most money   c. the best jobs
2. There are _____ nurses in the U.S.
   a. 2.7 million   b. 7 million   c. 12 million
3. There are more nurses in the U.S. than _____.
   a. cashiers   b. office assistants   c. doctors
4. Most nurses make about _____ a year.
   a. $39,000   b. $69,000   c. $89,000

4 SUMMARIZE

Complete the summary with the words in the box.

| CNA | healthcare | nurses | training |

More than 12 million people in the U.S. work in (1) _____. The biggest number of jobs are for (2) _____. They need a lot of (3) _____, but you can be a (4) _____ or an orderly after you finish high school. There are many other jobs in healthcare, too.

Show what you know!

1. **THINK ABOUT IT.** Do you know people who work in healthcare? What are their jobs? Where do they work?
2. **WRITE ABOUT IT.** Now write about someone you know who works in healthcare.

   _____ works in healthcare. (He/She) is a _____. (He/She) works at _____.

I can learn new vocabulary. ☐   I need more practice. ☐

To read more, go to MyEnglishLab.

Graphs and charts introduce students to information in a variety of formats, developing their visual literacy.

Academic tasks, such as summarizing, are introduced from the beginning and scaffolded to support low-level learners.

Informational readings containing level-appropriate complex text introduce academic language and build content knowledge.

Writing lessons follow a robust and scaffolded writing-process approach, engaging students in analyzing writing models, planning, and producing a final product.

A **Writing Skill** explains and models appropriate writing. Later in the lesson, students apply the skill to their own writing.

New **Soft Skills at Work** lessons engage students in real-life situations that develop the personal, social, and cultural skills critical for career success, and help students meet the WIOA requirements.

A brief scenario introduces a common workplace problem that can be solved using **critical thinking** and **soft skills**.

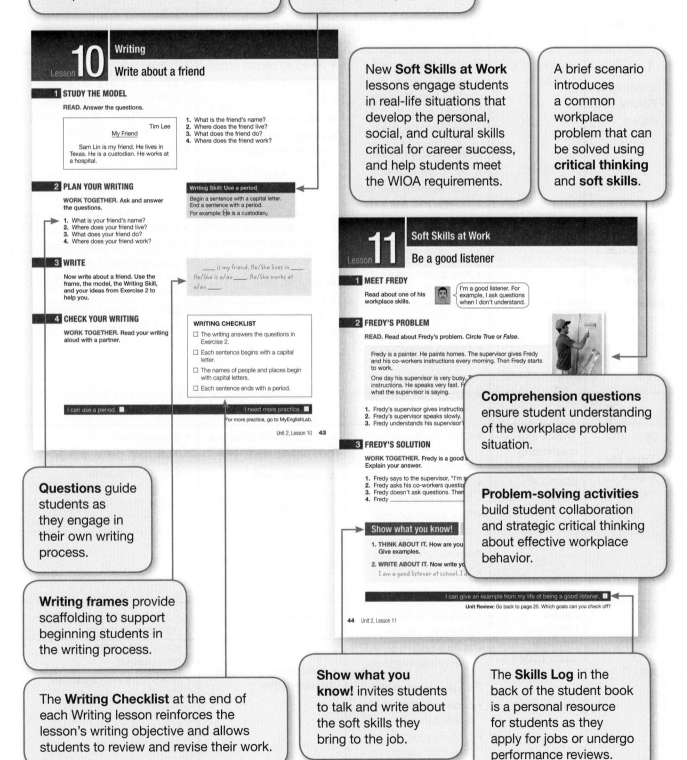

Questions guide students as they engage in their own writing process.

Writing frames provide scaffolding to support beginning students in the writing process.

Comprehension questions ensure student understanding of the workplace problem situation.

Problem-solving activities build student collaboration and strategic critical thinking about effective workplace behavior.

The **Writing Checklist** at the end of each Writing lesson reinforces the lesson's writing objective and allows students to review and revise their work.

Show what you know! invites students to talk and write about the soft skills they bring to the job.

The **Skills Log** in the back of the student book is a personal resource for students as they apply for jobs or undergo performance reviews.

SCOPE AND SEQUENCE

Unit	Vocabulary	Listening and Speaking	Reading	Grammar
Pre-Unit **Welcome to Class** *page 2*	Classroom instructions; Ask for help	• Follow classroom instructions • Ask for help	• Locate the U.S. map in your book	• Introduction to imperatives
1 **Getting to Know You** *page 5*	Regions and countries	• Introduce yourself • Identify people and ask where they are from • Talk about school **Pronunciation skills:** • Sentence stress • The different sounds in *he's* and *she's*	• Read an article about immigrants in the U.S. **Academic skill:** • Analyze text structure—Use the title	• Subject pronouns • Simple present of *be*: Affirmative and negative statements • Contractions with *be* • Negative contractions with *be*
2 **A Hard Day's Work** *page 25*	Jobs; Workplaces	• Introduce someone and talk about your job • Ask about jobs • Talk about where you work **Pronunciation skills:** • Falling intonation in statements and *Wh-* questions • Rising intonation in *yes/no* questions	• Read an article about healthcare jobs in the U.S. **Academic skill:** • Learn new vocabulary related to healthcare	• *A/an* • Singular and plural nouns • Simple present of *be*: Yes/no questions and short answers • Simple present affirmative: *work* and *live*
3 **Time for Class** *page 45*	Things in a classroom; People and places at school	• Give and follow classroom instructions • Talk about things in the classroom • Talk about people and places at school **Pronunciation skills:** • Voiced *th* sound • Word stress	• Read an article about helpful study habits **Academic skill:** • Analyze text structure—Use the headings	• Imperatives • *This, that, these, those* • Object pronouns
4 **Family Ties** *page 65*	Family members; Physical descriptions	• Talk about family • Describe people • Give a child's age and grade in school **Pronunciation skills:** • Pronunciation of possessive *'s* • Linking words together: consonant to vowel	• Read an article about blended families **Academic skill:** • Read closely—Make connections	• Possessive adjectives and possessive nouns • *Have* and *be* for descriptions • Questions with *How old*

Writing	Document Literacy Numeracy	Workplace, Life, and Community Skills	Soft Skills At Work
• Write about yourself **Writing skill:** • Use a capital letter for people and places	• Interpret a bar graph	• Say and spell first and last names • Use appropriate titles **Digital skill:** • Go online and find common American last names	• Be friendly
• Write about a friend **Writing skill:** • Begin a sentence with a capital letter • End a sentence with a period	• Learn cardinal numbers 0–9 • Interpret a chart	• Identify phone numbers • Identify email addresses • Ask for and give contact information **Digital skill:** • Go online and add new contacts in your phone	• Be a good listener
• Write about your study habits **Writing skill:** • Recognize and use a verb in a sentence	• Count classroom items	• Identify places at school • Give locations of places at school **Digital skill:** • Go online and find a school in your neighborhood	• Be flexible
• Write about a family member **Writing skill:** • Use a capital letter for months	• Interpret a calendar • Learn ordinal numbers 1st–31st • Interpret a pie chart • Understand percentages • Calculate age based on date of birth	• Talk about months • Talk about and write dates **Digital skill:** • Go online and find the date of the next holiday on your calendar	• Separate work and home life

Text in purple refers to workplace and employability topics.

Unit	Vocabulary	Listening and Speaking	Reading	Grammar
5 **Shop, Shop, Shop** *page 85*	Colors and clothes	• Talk about things you need or want • Ask for sizes and colors • Return something to a store **Pronunciation skill:** • Sentence stress	• Read an article about credit cards and debit cards **Academic skill:** • Read closely—Make inferences	• Simple present affirmative • Simple present: *Yes/no* questions and short answers • Simple present negative
6 **Home, Sweet Home** *page 105*	Rooms of a house; Furniture and appliances	• Talk about a house for rent • Ask about an apartment for rent • Give directions **Pronunciation skill:** • Stress in compound nouns	• Read an article about smoke alarms and fire safety at home **Academic skill:** • Read closely—Read multiple times to get all the details	• *There is/There are* • *Is there/Are there* • Prepositions of direction and location
7 **Day After Day** *page 125*	Daily routines and leisure activities; Clock times	• Make plans with someone • Talk about weekend activities • Talk about ways to relax **Pronunciation skills:** • The weak pronunciation of *do you* in questions • Extra syllable in *-es* endings	• Read an article about how Americans spend their free time **Academic skill:** • Read closely—Make predictions	• Simple present: *When* and *What time* • Prepositions of time • Adverbs of frequency • Questions with *How often* • Expressions of frequency
8 **From Soup to Nuts** *page 145*	Common foods	• Talk about foods you like and don't like • Order a meal in a restaurant • Plan a healthy meal **Pronunciation skill:** • Intonation of choice questions with *or*	• Read an article about food safety **Academic skill:** • Analyze text structure—Read captions before reading an article	• Count and non-count nouns • Choice questions with *or* • Questions and short answers with *How many* and *How much*

Writing	Document Literacy Numeracy	Workplace, Life, and Community Skills	Soft Skills At Work
• Write about the clothes you wear **Writing skill:** • Use commas between words in a list	• Count U.S. money • Calculate the total on a receipt • Make a bar graph about where classmates shop • Interpret a pie chart	• Identify U.S. money • Talk about prices • Read receipts **Digital skill:** • Go online and find the tax rate in your city	• Be professional
• Write about your favorite room at home **Writing skill:** • Use details in your writing	• Talk about numbers of rooms in a home • Compare rents of two homes	• Say and write addresses • Read housing ads **Digital skill:** • Go online and find the address of a home for rent in or near your neighborhood	• Find information
• Write about your favorite day of the week **Writing skill:** • Use a capital letter for days of the week	• Tell time • Count hours worked in a day or week • Interpret a pie chart	• Talk about work schedules • Read and complete a time sheet **Digital skill:** • Go online and find the next event on your calendar	• Be a team player
• Write about the foods you usually eat **Writing skill:** • Choose the correct verb to use with food and drinks	• Understand U.S. measurements of weight • Read store flyers and compare prices • Understand nutritional information on food labels	• Compare food prices • Read food labels • Talk about healthy food **Digital skill:** • Go online and look up the number of calories in your favorite food	• Take action

Text in purple refers to workplace and employability topics.

SCOPE AND SEQUENCE

Unit	Vocabulary	Listening and Speaking	Reading	Grammar
9 **Rain or Shine** *page 165*	Weather, seasons, and temperature	• Talk about what you are doing now • Ask what someone is doing now • Understand a weather report	• Read an article about hurricanes **Academic skill:** • Read closely—Focus on details	• Present continuous: Statements • Present continuous: *Yes/no* questions and short answers • Adverbs of degree
10 **Around Town** *page 185*	Places in the community; Kinds of transportation	• Give locations of places in the community • Ask about bus routes and costs • Talk about weekend plans **Pronunciation skills:** • Stressed syllable in a two-syllable word • Unstressed words (*do, the, to, at*)	• Read an article about resources available at the public library **Academic skill:** • Read closely—Give your own examples	• Prepositions of place • Simple present questions with *How, How much,* and *Where* • Present continuous for future plans
11 **Health Matters** *page 205*	Parts of the body; Symptoms and illnesses	• Call to explain an absence • Talk about health problems • Give advice **Pronunciation skill:** • Pronunciation of *was/were* and *wasn't/weren't*	• Read an article about the health benefits of walking **Academic skill:** • Read closely—Apply what you read	• Review: Simple present • Past of *be*: Statements • Statements with *should*
12 **Help Wanted** *page 225*	Job duties	• Respond to a help-wanted sign • Talk about hours you can work • Talk about work experience **Pronunciation skills:** • Sentence stress: *Can* and *can't* in statements • Sentence stress: *Can* and *can't* in short answers	• Read an article about making a good first impression in a job interview **Academic skill:** • Read closely—Mark up a text when reading	• *Can*: Statements • *Can*: *Yes/no* questions and short answers • Past of *be*: Questions and answers

Writing	Document Literacy Numeracy	Workplace, Life, and Community Skills	Soft Skills At Work
• Write about the weather in your native country **Writing skill:** • Use *because* to give a reason	• Read a thermometer in degrees Fahrenheit	• Talk about bad weather and emergencies • Plan for an emergency **Digital skill:** • Go online and add emergency numbers to your phone	• Be ready to learn new skills
• Write about your street **Writing skill:** • Use the correct preposition in a sentence	• Understand traffic signs • Understand bus schedules	• Talk about kinds of transportation • Read traffic signs • Read bus signs and schedules **Digital skill:** • Go online and use a transportation website or app to find public transportation to a supermarket	• Be reliable
• Write about your healthy habits **Writing skill:** • Start each paragraph with a topic sentence	• Read medicine labels and understand correct dosages	• Make a doctor's appointment • Follow a doctor's instructions • Read medicine labels **Digital skill:** • Go online and find the phone number for a clinic in or near your neighborhood	• Make good decisions
• Write about a job you want and your job skills **Writing skill:** • Recognize and use a subject in a sentence	• Calculate weekly earnings based on hourly wages	• Read job postings • Identify different ways to find a job **Digital skill:** • Go online and find a job listing for a job you want	• Respond well to feedback

Text in purple refers to workplace and employability topics.

CORRELATIONS

Unit	CASAS Reading Standards (correlated to CASAS Reading Standards 2016)	CASAS Listening Standards (correlated to CASAS Listening Basic Skills Content Standards)	
1	**L1:** RDG 1.1, 1.4, 1.5, 1.7, 2.1, 1.8, 3.2, 2.9, 3.4, 3.5; **L2:** RDG 1.1, 1.5, 1.7, 2.9; **L3:** RDG 1.1, 1.5, 1.7, 2.2, 2.9, 3.3, 3.10; **L4:** RDG 1.1, 1.5, 1.7, 2.2, 2.9; **L5:** RDG 1.1, 1.5, 1.7, 2.10, 2.9; **L6:** RDG 1.1, 1.5, 1.7, 1.8, 3.2, 3.4, 3.5, 3.8, 4.2; **L7:** RDG 1.1, 1.5, 1.7, 2.9; **L8:** RDG 1.1, 1.5, 1.7, 2.10, 2.9; **L10:** RDG 1.1, 1.5, 1.7, 1.8, 3.2, 3.14; **L11:** RDG 1.1, 1.5, 1.7, 1.8, 3.2	**L1:** 2.1, 2.3, 2.9; **L2:** 1.3, 1.4, 2.1, 2.3, 4.1, 4.2; **L3:** 1.3, 2.1, 2.2, 2.3, 4.1, 4.2; **L4:** 1.2, 2.1, 2.3, 4.1, 4.2; **L5:** 2.1, 2.3, 3.1, 3.3, 3.5, 4.1, 4.2; **L6:** 2.1, 2.3, 4.1, 4.2; **L7:** 2.1, 2.3, 4.1, 4.2, 4.3; **L8:** 2.1, 2.3, 3.1, 3.3, 3.5, 4.1, 4.2; **L9:** 2.1, 2.3, 3.1, 3.3, 3.5; **L10:** 2.1, 2.3; **L11:** 2.1, 2.3, 4.1, 4.2;	
2	**L1:** RDG 2.3; **L2:** RDG 1.1, 1.5, 1.7, 2.9; **L3:** RDG 2.6, 1.8, 3.2, 2.9, 3.6, 1.4; **L4:** RDG 1.1, 1.5, 1.7, 2.9, 1.4; **L5:** RDG 1.1, 1.7, 2.9; **L6:** RDG 1.7, 3.6, 2.9; **L7:** RDG 1.1, 1.5, 1.7, 1.8, 3.2, 1.4, 3.4, 3.10, 4.2; **L8:** RDG 1.1, 1.7, 2.9; **L10:** RDG 1.1, 1.5, 1.7, 1.8, 3.2, 3.14; **L11:** RDG 1.1, 1.5, 1.7, 1.8, 3.2	**L1:** 2.1, 2.4, 2.9, 4.2; **L2:** 1.3, 1.4, 2.1, 2.3, 2.4, 3.6, 4.1, 4.2; **L3:** 1.2, 2.3, 2.4, 3.7, 4.2; **L4:** 1.3, 2.1, 2.3, 4.1, 4.2; **L5:** 1.3, 1.4, 2.1, 2.3, 2.4, 3.6, 4.1, 4.2; **L6:** 1.3, 1.4, 2.1, 2.3, 2.4, 3.3, 3.6, 4.1, 4.2; **L7:** 2.4, 2.9, 4.2; **L8:** 1.3, 2.1, 2.3, 2.4, 4.1, 4.2; **L9:** 2.1, 2.3, 3.1; **L10:** 2.1, 2.3, 3.6; **L11:** 2.1, 2.3	
3	**L1:** RDG 2.3; **L2:** RDG 1.1, 1.5, 1.7, 2.9, 2.8, 3.6; **L3:** RDG 2.10, 3.6, 2.9; **L4:** RDG 1.1, 1.5, 1.7, 1.8, 3.2, 3.10, 4.2; **L5:** RDG 1.1, 1.5, 1.7, 2.9, 3.6; **L7:** RDG 1.1, 1.5, 1.7, 2.9, 3.6, 3.4, 3.5; **L8:** RDG 1.1, 1.5, 1.7, 2.9; **L10:** RDG 1.1, 1.5, 1.7, 1.8, 3.2, 3.14; **L11:** RDG 1.1, 1.5, 1.7, 1.8, 3.2	**L1:** 2.1, 2.4, 2.9, 4.2; **L2:** 1.3, 2.1, 2.3, 4.2, 5.4; **L3:** 1.3, 2.1, 2.3, 2.4, 3.3, 3.4, 4.1, 4.2; **L4:** 2.4, 2.9, 4.2; **L5:** 1.3, 2.1, 2.3, 2.9, 4.2; **L6:** 2.1, 2.3, 3.2, 3.6; **L7:** 1.3, 2.1, 2.3, 2.9, 4.2; **L8:** 1.3, 1.4, 2.1, 2.3, 2.9, 4.2; **L9:** 2.1, 2.3, 3.1, 3.2; **L10:** 2.1, 2.3, 3.6; **L11:** 2.1, 2.3	
4	**L1:** RDG 2.3; **L2:** RDG 1.1, 1.5, 1.7, 2.9; **L3:** RDG 2.10, 2.6, 2.9; **L4:** RDG 1.1, 1.5, 1.7, 1.8, 3.2, 3.4, 3.5, 4.2; **L5:** RDG 1.1, 1.5, 1.7, 2.9; **L6:** RDG 1.1, 1.5, 1.7, 2.9; **L7:** RDG 1.1, 1.5, 1.7, 2.2, 1.4; **L8:** RDG 1.1, 1.5, 1.7, 2.9; **L10:** RDG 1.1, 1.5, 1.7, 1.8, 3.2, 3.14; **L11:** RDG 1.1, 1.5, 1.7, 1.8, 3.2	**L1:** 2.1, 2.9, 4.2; **L2:** 1.3, 2.1, 2.3, 4.2; **L3:** 1.2, 2.1, 2.3, 3.2, 3.3, 3.8; **L4:** 2.3, 2.9, 4.2; **L5:** 1.3, 2.1, 2.3, 4.2; **L6:** 2.1, 2.3, 3.1, 4.2; **L7:** 1.3, 2.1, 2.3, 4.2; **L8:** 1.1, 1.3, 1.4, 2.1, 2.3, 4.2; **L9:** 2.1, 2.3, 3.6; **L10:** 2.1, 2.3, 3.5; **L11:** 2.1, 2.3	
5	**L1:** RDG 2.3, 2.11; **L2:** 1.1, 1.5, 1.7, 2.9; **L3:** 2.9; **L4:** 1.1, 1.5, 1.7, 2.9, 1.4; **L5:** 1.1, 1.5, 1.7, 2.9, 3.7, 3.10; **L6:** 2.9; **L7:** 1.1, 1.5, 1.7, 1.8, 3.2, 3.4, 3.5, 4.2, 4.3; **L8:** 1.1, 1.5, 1.7, 2.2, 2.9; **L10:** 1.1, 1.5, 1.7, 1.8, 3.2, 3.14; **L11:** 1.1, 1.5, 1.7, 1.8, 3.2	**L1:** 2.1, 2.9, 4.2; **L2:** 1.3, 2.1, 2.3, 2.4, 4.1, 4.2; **L3:** 1.2, 2.1, 2.3, 3.1, 4.2; **L4:** 1.3, 2.1, 2.3, 2.4, 4.2; **L5:** 1.3, 1.4, 2.1, 2.3, 2.4, 4.2; **L6:** 2.1, 2.3, 3.1, 3.3, 3.6, 4.2; **L7:** 2.3, 2.9, 4.2; **L8:** 1.3, 2.1, 2.3, 2.4, 4.2; **L9:** 2.1, 2.3, 3.1, 3.3, 3.5; **L10:** 2.1, 2.3, 3.6; **L11:** 2.1, 2.3	
6	**L1:** RDG 2.3; **L2:** RDG 1.1, 1.5, 1.7, 2.9; **L3:** RDG 1.1, 1.5, 1.7 2.10, 2.9, 1.4; **L4:** RDG 1.1, 1.5, 1.7, 1.8, 3.2, 3.4, 3.5, 3.7, 3.10, 4.2; **L5:** RDG 1.1, 1.5, 1.7, 2.9; **L6:** RDG 2.10; **L7:** RDG 1.1, 1.5, 1.3, 1.7, 2.2, 1.8, 3.2, 1.4; **L8:** RDG 1.1, 1.5, 1.7, 1.8, 3.2, 1.4, 3.4, 3.5; **L10:** RDG 1.1, 1.5, 1.7, 1.8, 3.2, 3.14; **L11:** RDG 1.1, 1.5, 1.7, 3.2	**L1:** 2.1, 2.4, 2.9, 4.2; **L2:** 1.3, 2.1, 2.3, 2.4, 4.2; **L3:** 2.1, 2.3, 3.1, 3.3, 4.2; **L4:** 2.3, 2.9, 4.2; **L5:** 1.3, 1.7, 2.1, 2.3, 2.4, 2.9, 4.2; **L6:** 2.1, 2.3, 3.1, 3.3, 4.2; **L7:** 2.3, 2.4, 2.9, 4.2; **L8:** 2.3, 2.3, 2.9, 4.2, 5.4; **L9:** 2.1, 2.3, 3.9,; **L10:** 2.1, 2.3, 3.6; **L11:** 2.1, 2.3, 2.4	
7	**L1:** RDG 1.4, 2.3; **L2:** RDG 1.1, 1.5, 1.7, 1.8, 3.2, 1.4; **L3:** RDG 2.9, 3.4; **L4:** RDG 2.9, 1.4, 3.4; **L5:** RDG 1.1, 1.5, 1.7, 1.8, 3.2, 3.6; **L6:** RDG 2.9, 1.4, 3.4; **L7:** RDG 1.1, 1.5, 1.7, 1.8, 3.2, 3.4, 3.5, 3.7, 3.10, 3.8, 4.2; **L8:** RDG 1.1, 1.5, 1.7, 1.8, 3.2; **L10:** RDG 1.1, 1.5, 1.7, 1.8, 3.2, 3.14; **L11:** RDG 1.1, 1.5, 1.7, 1.8, 3.2	**L1:** 2.1, 2.4, 2.9, 4.2; **L2:** 1.4, 1.5, 2.3, 2.4, 4.2, 4.4; **L3:** 2.1, 2.3, 2.4, 3.1, 3.6, 4.2; **L4:** 2.3, 2.4, 4.2; **L5:** 1.4, 2.3, 2.4, 4.2; **L6:** 2.1, 2.3, 2.4, 3.9, 4.2; **L7:** 2.3, 2.9, 4.2; **L8:** 1.2, 2.3, 2.4, 2.9, 4.2; **L9:** 2.1, 2.3, 3.1, 3.9; **L10:** 2.1, 2.3, 3.6; **L11:** 2.1, 2.3, 2.4	
8	**L1:** RDG 2.3, 3.4, 3.5; **L2:** RDG 1.1, 1.5, 1.7, 1.8, 3.2; **L3:** RDG 2.9; **L4:** RDG 1.1, 1.5, 1.7, 1.8, 3.2, 4.2, 3.10; **L5:** RDG 1.1, 1.5, 1.7, 1.8, 3.2, 3.6; **L7:** RDG 2.2, 1.4, 3.16; **L8:** RDG 1.1, 1.5, 1.7, 1.8, 3.2; **L9:** RDG 2.9; **L10:** RDG 1.1, 1.5, 1.7, 1.8, 3.2, 3.14; **L11:** RDG 1.1, 1.5, 1.7, 1.8, 3.2	**L1:** 2.1, 2.9, 4.2; **L2:** 2.3, 2.4, 2.9, 4.2; **L3:** 2.1, 2.3, 2.4, 3.7, 4.2; **L4:** 2.3, 2.4, 4.2; **L5:** 1.4, 2.3, 2.4, 4.2; **L6:** 2.1, 2.3, 2.4, 3.6, 4.2, 4.4; **L7:** 2.3, 2.4, 2.9, 4.2; **L8:** 2.3, 2.4, 2.9, 4.2; **L9:** 2.3, 3.6, 3.7; **L10:** 2.1, 2.3, 3.6; **L11:** 2.1, 2.3, 2.4	
9	**L1:** RDG 1.3, 2.3; **L2:** RDG 1.1, 1.5, 1.7, 1.8, 3.2, 3.4, 3.5; **L3:** RDG 2.9; **L4:** RDG 1.1, 1.5, 1.7, 2.3, 1.8, 3.2, 1.4; **L5:** RDG 1.1, 1.5, 1.7, 1.8, 3.2, 2.3; **L6:** RDG 2.10, 2.9; **L7:** RDG 1.1, 1.5, 1.3, 1.7, 2.3, 1.8, 3.2, 3.4, 3.5, 3.7, 3.10, 4.2; **L8:** RDG 1.1, 1.5, 1.3, 1.7, 2.3, 1.8, 3.2, 3.4, 3.5; **L9:** RDG 1.1, 1.5, 1.7, 2.9; **L10:** RDG 1.1, 1.5, 1.7, 1.8, 3.2, 3.14; **L11:** RDG 1.1, 1.5, 1.7, 1.8, 3.2	**L1:** 2.1, 4.2; **L2:** 2.3, 2.4, 2.9, 4.2; **L3:** 2.1, 2.3, 3.3, 3.9, 4.2; **L4:** 2.3, 2.4, 4.2; **L5:** 2.3, 2.4, 4.2; **L6:** 2.1, 2.3, 2.4, 3.6, 4.2; **L7:** 2.1, 2.3, 2.4, 2.9, 4.2; **L8:** 2.3, 2.4, 2.9, 4.2; **L9:** 2.1, 2.3, 3.9; **L10:** 2.1, 2.3, 3.6; **L11:** 2.1, 2.3, 2.4	
10	**L1:** RDG 2.3; **L2:** RDG 1.1, 1.5, 1.7, 1.8, 3.2, 3.4, 3.5; **L3:** RDG 2.9, 3.4, 3.5; **L4:** RDG 1.3, 2.2, 2.3, 1.4, 3.4; **L5:** RDG 1.1, 1.5, 1.7, 1.8, 3.2, 1.4, 2.3; **L6:** RDG 2.9; **L7:** RDG 1.1, 1.5, 1.7, 2.3, 1.8, 3.2, 3.7, 3.10, 4.2; **L8:** RDG 1.1, 1.5, 1.7, 2.3, 1.8, 3.2; **L9:** RDG 1.1, 1.5, 1.7, 2.9; **L10:** RDG 1.1, 1.5, 1.7, 1.8, 3.2, 3.14; **L11:** RDG 1.1, 1.5, 1.7, 1.8, 3.2	**L1:** 2.1, 2.3, 2.4, 4.2; **L2:** 1.4, 2.3, 2.4, 2.9, 4.2; **L3:** 2.3, 3.9, 4.2; **L4:** 2.3, 2.4, 4.2; **L5:** 1.4, 2.3, 2.4, 4.2; **L6:** 2.1, 2.3, 2.4, 3.6, 4.2; **L7:** 2.1, 2.3, 2.4, 2.9, 4.2; **L8:** 2.3, 2.4, 2.9, 4.2; **L9:** 2.1, 2.3, 3.9; **L10:** 2.1, 2.3, 3.6; **L11:** 2.3, 2.4	
11	**L1:** RDG 2.3; **L2:** RDG 1.1, 1.5, 1.7, 1.8, 3.2; **L3:** RDG 2.9; **L4:** RDG 2.2, 2.3, 1.8, 3.2; **L5:** RDG 1.1, 1.5, 1.7, 1.8, 3.2, 1.4, 2.3; **L6:** RDG 2.10, 2.9, 3.4; **L7:** RDG 1.1, 1.5, 1.7, 2.3, 1.8, 3.2, 3.7, 3.10, 4.2; **L8:** RDG 1.1, 1.5, 1.7, 1.8, 3.2, 3.4; **L9:** RDG 1.1, 1.5, 1.7, 2.2, 2.10; **L10:** RDG 1.1, 1.5, 1.7, 1.8, 3.2, 3.14; **L11:** RDG 1.1, 1.5, 1.7, 1.8, 1.4	**L1:** 2.1, 2.2, 4.2; **L2:** 2.3, 2.4, 2.9, 4.2; **L3:** 3.1, 3.6, 4.2; **L4:** 2.3, 2.4, 4.2; **L5:** 1.4, 2.3, 2.4, 4.2; **L6:** 2.1, 2.3, 2.4, 3.9, 4.2; **L7:** 2.1, 2.3, 2.4, 2.9, 4.2; **L8:** 2.3, 2.4, 2.9, 4.2; **L9:** 2.1, 2.3, 3.3, 3.9; **L10:** 2.1, 2.3, 3.6; **L11:** 2.3, 2.4	
12	**L1:** RDG 2.3; **L2:** RDG 1.1, 1.5, 1.7, 2.10, 1.8, 3.2; **L3:** RDG 2.10, 2.9, 3.4; **L4:** RDG 1.1, 1.5, 1.7, 2.2, 2.3, 1.8, 3.2, 1.4; **L5:** RDG 1.1, 1.5, 1.7, 2.10, 1.8, 3.2, 2.3, 1.4; **L6:** RDG ; **L7:** RDG 1.1, 1.5, 1.7, 2.3, 1.8, 3.2, 3.7, 3.10, 4.2; **L8:** RDG 1.1, 1.5, 1.7, 1.8, 3.2; **L9:** RDG 2.10; **L10:** RDG 1.1, 1.5, 1.7, 1.8, 3.2, 3.14; **L11:** RDG 1.1, 1.5, 1.7, 1.8, 3.2	**L1:** 2.1, 2.4, 4.2; **L2:** 1.4, 2.4, 2.9, 3.3, 4.2; **L3:** 2.1, 2.4, 3.1, 3.3, 3.5, 4.2; **L4:** 2.3, 2.4, 4.2; **L5:** 1.4, 2.3, 2.4, 4.2; **L6:** 2.1, 2.4, 3.6, 4.2; **L7:** 2.3, 2.4, 2.9, 4.2; **L8:** 2.3, 2.4, 2.9, 4.2; **L9:** 2.1, 2.4, 3.3, 3.9; **L10:** 2.1, 2.3, 2.4, 3.6; **L11:** 2.3, 2.4	

CASAS: Comprehensive Adult Student Assessment System
CCRS: College and Career Readiness Standards (R=Reading; W=Writing; SL=Speaking/Listening; L=Language)
ELPS: English Language Proficiency Standards

CASAS Competencies (correlated to CASAS Competencies: Essential Life and Work skills for Youth and Adults)	CCRS Correlations, Level A	ELPS Correlations, Level 1
L1: 0.1.2, 0.1.5, 0.2.1, 7.4.1; **L2:** 0.1.2, 0.1.4, 0.1.5, 0.2.1; **L3:** 0.1.2, 0.1.4, 0.1.5, 0.1.6, 0.2.1, 0.2.2, 7.7.3; **L4:** 0.1.2, 0.1.4, 0.1.5, 0.1.6, 0.2.1; **L5:** 0.1.2, 0.1.4, 0.1.5, 0.1.6, 0.2.1, 7.4.1; **L6:** 0.1.2, 0.1.4, 0.1.5, 0.2.1, 6.7.2, 6.8.1; **L7:** 0.1.2, 0.1.4, 0.1.5, 0.1.6, 0.2.1; **L8:** 0.1.2, 0.1.4, 0.1.5, 0.1.6, 0.2.1; **L9:** 0.1.2; **L10:** 0.1.2, 0.1.5, 0.1.6, 0.2.1; **L11:** 0.1.2, 0.1.5;	**L1:** RI.1.4, SL.1.1, SL.K.6, L1. 4, L.1.5a, L.1.5b, L.1.5c, L1.6; **L2:** SL.K.3, SL.1.4; **L3:** W.1.7, W.1.8; **L4:** SL.K.3; SL.1.4; **L5:** L.1.1e, L.1.1f; **L6:** L1.6, RI.1.2, RI.1.3, RI.1.4, RI.1.7, W.1.7, W.1.8, SL.K.2; **L7:** SL.K.3, SL.1.4; **L8:** L.1.1e, L.1.1f, L.1.1g; **L9:** L.1.1e, L.1.1g; **L10:** W.1.3, W.1.5, W.1.7, W.1.8, SL.1.1a, SL.1.1b, SL.1.1c, SL.K.6, L.1.1l, L.1.2b; **L11:** RI.1.8	ELPS 1–3, 5–10
L1: 0.1.2, 0.1.5, 0.2.1, 7.4.1; **L2:** 0.1.2, 0.1.5, 0.2.1; **L3:** 0.1.2, 0.1.5, 0.1.6, 4.1.3, 4.1.8, 7.4.1, 7.4.2; **L4:** 0.1.2, 0.1.5, 0.2.1, 2.1.7, 7.7.3, 7.7.4; **L5:** 0.1.2, 0.1.5, 0.2.1, 4.1.8; **L6:** 0.1.2, 0.1.5, 0.1.6, 0.2.1, 4.1.8; **L7:** 0.1.2, 0.1.5, 0.2.1, 4.4.3, 7.4.1, 7.4.2; **L8:** 0.1.2, 0.1.5, 0.2.1, 4.1.8; **L9:** 0.1.2, 0.1.5, 0.2.1, 4.1.8; **L10:** 0.1.2, 0.1.5, 0.1.6, 0.2.1; **L11:** 0.1.2	**L1:** RI.1.4, L.1. 4, L.1.6, W.1.7, W.1.8, L.1.5a, L.1.5b, L.1.5c; **L2:** SL.K.3, SL.1.4; **L3:** L.1.1b, L.1.1c, L.1.1g, L.1.1i; **L4:** W.1.7, W.1.8, SL.1.1a, SL.1.1b, SL.1.1c, SL.K.6; **L5:** SL.K.3, SL.1.4, SL.1.1, SL.K.6; **L6:** L.1.1g, L.1.1k; **L7:** RI.1.4, RI.1.7, L.1.6; **L8:** SL.K.3, SL.1.4; **L9:** L.1.1c, L.1.1e, L.1.1g; **L10:** W.1.3, W.1.5, W.1.7, W.1.8, L.1.1i, L.1.2a, L.1.2b, L.1.2c, L.1.2d; **L11:** RI.1.8	ELPS 1–3, 5–10
L1: 0.1.2, 0.1.5, 7.4.1, 7.4.2, 7.4.3; **L2:** 0.1.2, 0.1.5, 0.1.7, 0.2.1; **L3:** 0.1.2, 0.1.5, 0.1.7; **L4:** 0.1.2, 0.1.5, 0.2.1, 7.4.1, 7.4.9; **L5:** 0.1.2, 0.1.5; **L6:** 0.1.2, 0.1.5; **L7:** 0.1.2, 0.1.5, 2.2.1; **L8:** 0.1.2, 0.1.4, 0.1.5, 4.1.8; **L9:** 0.1.2, 0.1.5, 0.1.7, 0.2.1, 2.2.1; **L10:** 0.1.2, 0.1.5, 0.2.1, 7.4.1; **L11:** 0.1.2, 0.1.5	**L1:** RI.1.4, L.1. 4a, L.1.6, L.1.5a, L.1.5b, L.1.5c; **L2:** SL.K.3, SL.1.4, SL.1.1a, SL.1.1b, SL.1.1c, SL.K.6; **L3:** L.1.1e, L.1.1g; **L4:** RI.1.4, RI.1.5, L.1.6, RI/RL.1.1, RI.1.2, RI.1.3, SL.K.2; **L5:** SL.K.3, SL.1.4; **L6:** ; **L7:** W.1.7, W.1.8; **L8:** SL.K.3, SL.1.4; **L9:** L.1.1d; **L10:** W.1.2, W.1.5, W.1.7, W.1.8, L.1.1l, L.1.2a, L.1.2c, L.1.2d; **L11:** RI.1.8, SL.1.1a, SL.1.1b, SL.1.1c, SL.K.6	ELPS 1–3, 5–10
L1: 0.1.2, 0.1.5, 7.4.1, 7.4.2; **L2:** 0.1.2, 0.1.4, 0.1.5, 0.2.1; **L3:** 0.1.2, 0.1.5; **L4:** 0.1.2, 0.1.5, 0.2.1, 7.4.1; **L5:** 0.1.2, 0.1.5, 0.2.1; **L6:** 0.1.2, 0.1.5, 0.2.1; **L7:** 0.1.2, 0.1.5, 0.2.1; **L8:** 0.1.2, 0.1.4, 0.1.5, 0.2.1; **L9:** 0.1.2, 0.1.5; **L10:** 0.1.2, 0.1.5, 0.2.1; **L11:** 0.1.2, 0.1.5	**L1:** RI.1.4, L.1. 4a, L.1.6, L.1.5a, L.1.5b, L.1.5c, L1.6; **L2:** SL.K.3, SL.1.4, SL.1.1a, SL.1.1b, SL.1.1c, SL.K.6; **L3:** L.1.1b, SL.1.1a, SL.1.1b, SL.1.1c, SL.K.6; **L4:** RI.1.4, RI.1.7, L.1.6, RI/RL.1.1, RI.1.2, RI.1.3, SL.K.2; **L5:** SL.K.3, SL.1.4; **L6:** L.1.1c, L.1.1e, L.1.1f, L.1.1g, W.1.7, W.1.8; **L7:** W.1.7, W.1.8; **L8:** SL.K.3, SL.1.4; **L9:** L.1.1k; **L10:** W.1.2, W.1.5, W.1.7, W.1.8, L.1.1l, L.1.2a, L.1.2c, L.1.2d; **L11:** RI.1.8	ELPS 1–3, 5–10
L1: 0.1.2, 0.1.5, 0.2.1, 7.4.1; **L2:** 0.1.2, 0.1.5, 0.2.1; **L3:** 0.1.2, 0.1.5, 0.2.1; **L4:** 0.1.2, 0.1.5, 0.2.1, 1.1.6, 1.6.4, 5.4.2, 7.7.3; **L5:** 0.1.2, 0.1.4, 0.1.5, 1.2.9; **L6:** 0.1.2, 0.1.5, 0.2.1; **L7:** 0.1.2, 0.1.5, 0.2.1, 1.3.1, 7.4.1; **L8:** 0.1.2, 0.1.4, 0.1.5, 1.3.3; **L9:** 0.1.2, 0.1.5; **L10:** 0.1.2, 0.1.5, 0.2.1; **L11:** 0.1.2, 0.1.5	**L1:** RI.1.4, L.1.4, L.1.6, W.1.7, W.1.8, L.1.5a, L.1.5b, L.1.5c; **L2:** SL.K.3, SL.1.4; **L3:** L.1.1c, L.1.1e, L.1.1g; **L4:** W.1.7, W.1.8; **L5:** SL.K.3, SL.1.4, SL.1.1a, SL.1.1b, SL.1.1c, SL.K.6; **L6:** L.1.1c, L.1.1e, L.1.1g, L.1.1k; **L7:** RI.1.4, RI.1.7, L.1.6, RI/RL.1.1, RI.1.2, RI.1.3, SL.K.2; **L8:** SL.K.3, SL.1.4; **L9:** L.1.1e, L.1.1g; **L10:** W.1.2, W.1.5, W.1.2, SL.1.1, SL.K.6, L.1.1l, L.1.2a, L.1.2c, L.1.2d, L.1.2e, L.1.2g, L.1.2h, L.1.2i; **L11:** RI.1.8	ELPS 1–10
L1: 0.1.2, 0.1.5, 7.4.1, 7.4.2; **L2:** 0.1.2, 0.1.5, 1.4.1; **L3:** 0.1.2, 0.1.5, 1.4.1, 1.4.2; **L4:** 0.1.2, 0.1.5, 0.2.1, 1.4.1, 7.4.1; **L5:** 0.1.2, 0.1.5, 1.4.1; **L6:** 0.1.2, 0.1.5, 1.4.1; **L7:** 0.1.2, 0.1.5, 0.2.1, 1.4.1, 1.4.2; **L8:** 0.1.2, 0.1.5, 0.2.1, 2.2.1; **L9:** 0.1.2, 0.1.5, 2.2.1; **L10:** 0.1.2, 0.1.5, 0.2.1, 1.4.1; **L11:** 0.1.2, 0.1.4, 0.1.5	**L1:** RI.1.4, L.1. 4a, L.1.6, L.1.5a, L.1.5b, L.1.5c; **L2:** SL.K.3, SL.1.4; **L3:** L.1.1g; **L4:** RI.1.4, RI.1.7, L.1.6, RI/RL.1.1, RI.1.2, RI.1.3, SL.K.2; **L5:** SL.K.3, SL.1.4; **L6:** L.1.1g; **L7:** W.1.7, W.1.8, SL.1.1a, SL.1.1b, SL.1.1c, SL.K.6; **L8:** SL.K.3, SL.1.4, SL.1.1a, SL.1.1b, SL.1.1c, SL.K.6; **L9:** L.1.1j; **L10:** W.1.2, W.1.5, W.1.7, W.1.8, L.1.1l; **L11:** RI.1.8	ELPS 1–3, 5–10
L1: 0.1.2, 0.1.5, 0.2.1, 0.2.4, 7.4.1, 7.4.3; **L2:** 0.1.2, 0.1.4, 0.1.5, 0.2.1, 0.2.4; **L3:** 0.1.2, 0.1.5, 0.2.1, 0.2.4, 7.1.2; **L4:** 0.1.2, 0.1.5, 0.2.1, 2.8.3, 4.2.1, 7.4.4, 7.7.3; **L5:** 0.1.2, 0.1.4, 0.1.5, 0.2.1, 0.2.4; **L6:** 0.1.2, 0.1.5, 0.2.1, 0.2.4; **L7:** 0.1.2, 0.1.5, 0.2.1, 7.4.1; **L8:** 0.1.2, 0.1.5, 0.2.1, 0.2.4, 2.2.1; **L9:** 0.1.2, 0.1.5, 2.8.3; **L10:** 0.1.2, 0.1.5, 0.2.1, 0.2.4; **L11:** 0.1.2, 0.1.4, 0.1.5	**L1:** RI.1.4, L.1. 4, L.1.6, L.1.5a, L.1.5b, L.1.5c; **L2:** SL.K.3, SL.1.4; **L3:** L.1.1e, L.1.1g, L.1.1j, RI.1.7, W.1.7, W.1.8; **L4:** SL.1.1a, SL.1.1b, SL.1.1c, SL.K.6, W.1.7, W.1.8; **L5:** SL.1.1a, SL.1.1b, SL.1.1c, SL.K.3, SL.1.4, SL.K.6; **L6:** RI.1.4, L.1.6; **L7:** RI/RL.1.1, RI.1.2, RI.1.3, RI.1.7, SL.K.2; **L8:** SL.K.3, SL.1.4; **L9:** L.1.1k; **L10:** W.1.2, W.1.5, W.1.7, W.1.8, L.1.1l, L.1.2; **L11:** RI.1.8	ELPS 1–3, 5–10
L1: 0.1.2, 0.1.5, 0.2.4, 1.2.8, 7.4.1, 7.4.3; **L2:** 0.1.2, 0.1.5, 0.2.1, 0.2.4, 1.2.8; **L3:** 0.1.2, 0.1.5, 1.2.8; **L4:** 0.1.2, 0.1.5, 0.2.1, 1.6.1, 1.2.8, 3.5.3; **L5:** 0.1.2, 0.1.4, 0.1.5, 0.2.1, 0.2.4, 1.2.8, 2.6.4; **L6:** 0.1.2, 0.1.5, 0.2.1, 0.2.4, 1.2.8; **L7:** 0.1.2, 0.1.5, 0.2.1, 1.2.1, 1.2.2, 1.2.8, 3.5.1, 3.5.2; **L8:** 0.1.2, 0.1.5, 0.2.1, 0.2.4, 1.2.8, 3.5.2, 3.5.3; **L9:** 0.1.2, 0.1.5, 1.2.8; **L10:** 0.1.2, 0.1.5, 0.2.1, 0.2.4, 1.2.8; **L11:** 0.1.2, 0.1.4, 0.1.5, 1.2.8, 4.6.4, 7.3.1, 7.3.2	**L1:** RI.1.4, L.1. 4a, L.1.6; **L2:** SL.K.3, SL.1.4; **L3:** L.1.1b, L.1.1c, L.1.1g; **L4:** RI.1.4, RI.1.5, L.1.6, RI/RL.1.1, RI.1.2, RI.1.3, SL.K.2; **L5:** SL.K.3, SL.1.4; **L6:** L.1.1h, L.1.1k; **L7:** L.1.5a, L.1.5b, L.1.5c, W.1.7, W.1.8; **L8:** SL.1.1a, SL.1.1b, SL.1.1c, SL.K.3, SL.1.4, SL.K.6; **L9:** SL.1.1a, SL.1.1b, SL.1.1c, SL.K.6, L.1.1k; **L10:** W.1.2, W.1.5, W.1.7, L.1.1l; **L11:** RI.1.8	ELPS 1–3, 5–10
L1: 0.1.2, 0.1.5, 2.3.3, 7.4.1; **L2:** 0.1.2, 0.1.4, 0.1.5, 0.2.1, 0.2.4, 2.3.3; **L3:** 0.1.2, 0.1.5, 2.3.3; **L4:** 0.1.2, 0.1.5, 0.2.1, 2.3.1, 2.3.3, 7.7.3; **L5:** 0.1.2, 0.1.5, 0.2.1; **L6:** 0.1.2, 0.1.5, 0.2.1; **L7:** 0.1.2, 0.1.5, 0.2.1, 2.3.3; **L8:** 0.1.2, 0.1.5, 0.2.1, 2.3.3; **L9:** 0.1.2, 0.1.5, 0.2.1, 2.3.3; **L10:** 0.1.2, 0.1.5, 0.2.1, 2.3.3; **L11:** 0.1.2, 0.1.4, 0.1.5, 7.3.2, 7.5.7	**L1:** RI.1.4, L.1. 4a, L.1.6, W.1.7, W.1.8; **L2:** SL.K.3, SL.1.4, L.1.5a, L.1.5b, L.1.5c, SL.1.1a, SL.1.1b, SL.1.1c, SL.K.6; **L3:** L.1.1e, L.1.1g, L.1.2g, L.1.2h, L.1.2i; **L4:** W.1.7, W.1.8; **L5:** SL.K.3, SL.1.4; **L6:** L.1.1e, L.1.1g, L.1.1k; **L7:** RI/RL.1.1, RI.1.2, RI.1.3, RI.1.4, RI.1.7, L.1.6; **L8:** SL.K.3, SL.1.4; **L9:** L.1.1f, L.1.1j; **L10:** W.1.2, W.1.5, W.1.7, W.1.8, SL.1.1a, SL.1.1b, SL.1.1c, SL.K.6, L.1.1l; **L11:** RI.1.8	ELPS 1–10
L1: 0.1.2, 0.1.5, 2.2.1, 7.4.1; **L2:** 0.1.2, 0.1.4, 0.1.5, 0.1.7, 2.2.1; **L3:** 0.1.2, 0.1.5, 2.2.1; **L4:** 0.1.2, 0.1.5, 0.2.1, 2.2.4, 2.3.1, 7.4.4, 7.7.3; **L5:** 0.1.2, 0.1.3, 0.1.4, 0.1.5; **L6:** 0.1.2, 0.1.5, 0.2.1; **L7:** 0.1.2, 0.1.5, 2.5.6, 7.4.1; **L8:** 0.1.2, 0.1.5, 0.2.1, 0.2.4; **L9:** 0.1.2, 0.1.5, 0.2.1; **L10:** 0.1.2, 0.1.5, 0.2.1; **L11:** 0.1.2, 0.1.4, 0.1.5, 7.3.2, 7.5.7	**L1:** L.1.4a, L.1.5a, L.1.5b, L.1.5c, L.1.6; **L2:** SL.K.3, SL.1.4; **L3:** L.1.1j; **L4:** W.1.7, W.1.8; **L5:** SL.1.1a, SL.1.1b, SL.1.1c, SL.K.3, SL.1.4, SL.K.6; **L6:** SL.1.1a, SL.1.1b, SL.1.1c, SL.K.6, L.1.1e, L.1.1g, L.1.1k; **L7:** RI/RL.1.1, RI.1.2, RI.1.3, RI.1.4, RI.1.7, SL.K.2, L.1.6; **L8:** SL.K.3, SL.1.4; **L9:** L.1.1e; **L10:** W.1.2, W.1.5, W.1.7, W.1.8, L.1.1j, L.1.1l; **L11:** RI.1.8	ELPS 1–3, 5–10
L1: 0.1.2, 0.1.5, 3.6.1, 7.4.1, 7.4.3; **L2:** 0.1.2, 0.1.4, 0.1.5, 2.8.6, 3.6.1; **L3:** 0.1.2, 0.1.5, 0.1.8; **L4:** 0.1.2, 0.1.5, 3.3.1, 3.3.2, 3.3.4, 7.7.3; **L5:** 0.1.2, 0.1.3, 0.1.4, 0.1.5; **L6:** 0.1.2, 0.1.5; **L7:** 0.1.2, 0.1.5, 3.5.9, 7.4.1; **L8:** 0.1.2, 0.1.3, 0.1.5, 3.6.3, 3.6.4; **L9:** 0.1.2, 0.1.3, 0.1.5, 3.4.1; **L10:** 0.1.2, 0.1.3, 0.1.5, 0.2.1, 3.5.9; **L11:** 0.1.2, 0.1.5, 3.5.9, 7.3.2, 7.5.7	**L1:** RI.1.4, L.1.4a, L.1.5a, L.1.5b, L.1.5c, L1.6; **L2:** SL.K.3, SL.1.4; **L3:** L.1.1e, L.1.1g; **L4:** W.1.7, W.1.8, SL.1.1a, SL.1.1b, SL.1.1c, SL.K.6; **L5:** SL.K.3, SL.1.4; **L6:** L.1.1e, L.1.1g; **L7:** RI/RL.1.1, RI.1.2, RI.1.3, RI.1.4, RI.1.7, SL.K.2, L.1.6; **L8:** SL.K.3, SL.1.4; **L9:** L.1.1g; **L10:** W.1.2, W.1.5, W.1.7, W.1.8, L.1.1l; **L11:** RI.1.8, SL.1.1a, SL.1.1b, SL.1.1c, SL.K.6	ELPS 1–3, 5–10
L1: 0.1.2, 0.1.5, 4.1.8, 7.4.1, 7.4.2, 7.4.3; **L2:** 0.1.2, 0.1.4, 0.1.5, 4.1.3, 4.1.8; **L3:** 0.1.2, 0.1.5, 4.1.8; **L4:** 0.1.2, 0.1.5, 4.1.3, 4.1.8, 7.4.4, 7.7.3; **L5:** 0.1.2, 0.1.4, 0.1.5; **L6:** 0.1.2, 0.1.5, 4.1.8; **L7:** 0.1.1, 0.1.2, 0.1.5, 4.1.5, 4.1.7; **L8:** 0.1.2, 0.1.4, 0.1.5, 0.2.1; **L9:** 0.1.2, 0.1.5, 4.1.5; **L10:** 0.1.2, 0.1.5, 0.2.1, 4.1.8; **L11:** 0.1.2, 0.1.3, 0.1.5, 4.6.1, 7.3.2, 7.5.3, 7.5.7	**L1:** RI.1.4, W.1.7, L.1.4a, L.1.5a, L.1.5b, L.1.5c, L1.6; **L2:** SL.K.3, SL.1.4; **L3:** ; **L4:** W.1.7, W.1.8; **L5:** SL.K.3, SL.1.4; **L6:** L.1.1k; **L7:** RI/RL.1.1, RI.1.2, RI.1.3, RI.1.4, RI.1.7, SL.1.1a, SL.1.1b, SL.1.1c, SL.K.2, L.1.6; **L8:** SL.1.1a, SL.1.1b, SL.1.1c, SL.K.3, SL.1.4, SL.K.6; **L9:** L.1.1e, L.1.1g, L.1.1k; **L10:** W.1.2, W.1.5, W.1.7, W.1.8, L.1.1l; **L11:** RI.1.8	ELPS 1–3, 5–10

All units of *Future* meet most of the **EFF Content Standards**. For details, as well as for correlations to other state standards, go to www.pearsoneltusa.com/future 2e.

ABOUT THE SERIES CONSULTANTS AND AUTHORS

AUTHOR, SERIES CONSULTANT, AND LEARNING EXPERT

Sarah Lynn is an ESOL teacher trainer, author, and curriculum design specialist. She has taught adult learners in the U.S. and abroad for decades, most recently at Harvard University's Center for Workforce Development. As a teacher-trainer and frequent conference presenter throughout the United States and Latin America, Ms. Lynn has led sessions and workshops on topics such as: fostering student agency and resilience, brain-based teaching techniques, literacy and learning, and teaching in a multilevel classroom. Collaborating with program leaders, teachers, and students, she has developed numerous curricula for college and career readiness, reading and writing skill development, and contextualized content for adult English language learners. Ms. Lynn has co-authored several Pearson ELT publications, including *Business Across Cultures, Future, Future U.S. Citizens,* and *Project Success.* She holds a master's degree in TESOL from Teachers College, Columbia University.

SERIES CONSULTANTS

Ronna Magy has worked as an ESOL classroom teacher, author, teacher-trainer, and curriculum development specialist. She served as the ESL Teacher Adviser in charge of professional development for the Division of Adult and Career Education of the Los Angeles Unified School District. She is a frequent conference presenter on the College and Career Readiness Standards (CCRS), the English Language Proficiency Standards (ELPS), and on the language, literacy, and soft skills needed for academic and workplace success. Ms. Magy has authored/co-authored and trained teachers on modules for CALPRO, the California Adult Literacy Professional Development Project, including modules on integrating and contextualizing workforce skills in the ESOL classroom and evidence-based writing instruction. She is the author of adult ESL publications on English for the workplace, reading and writing, citizenship, and life skills and test preparation. Ms. Magy holds a master's degree in social welfare from the University of California at Berkeley.

Federico Salas-Isnardi has worked in adult education as a teacher, administrator, professional developer, materials writer, and consultant. He contributed to a number of state projects in Texas including the adoption of adult education content standards and the design of statewide professional development and accountability systems.

Over nearly 30 years he has conducted professional development seminars for thousands of teachers, law enforcement officers, social workers, and business people in the United States and abroad. His areas of concentration have been educational leadership, communicative competence, literacy, intercultural communication, citizenship, and diversity education. He has taught customized workplace ESOL and Spanish programs as well as high-school equivalence classes, citizenship and civics, labor market information seminars, and middle-school mathematics. Mr. Salas-Isnardi has been a contributing writer or series consultant for a number of ESL publications, and he has co-authored curriculum for site-based workforce ESL and Spanish classes.

Mr. Salas-Isnardi is a certified diversity trainer. He has a Masters Degree in Applied Linguistics and doctoral level coursework in adult education.

AUTHORS

Marjorie Fuchs has taught ESL at New York City Technical College and LaGuardia Community College of the City University of New York and EFL at Sprach Studio Lingua Nova in Munich, Germany. She has a master's degree in applied English linguistics and a certificate in TESOL from the University of Wisconsin–Madison. She has authored or co-authored many widely used books and multimedia materials, notably *Focus on Grammar: An Integrated Skills Approach* (levels 3 and 4), *Longman English Interactive 3 and 4, Grammar Express (Basic and Intermediate), OPD Workplace Skills Builder,* and workbooks for the *Oxford Picture Dictionary* (*High Beginning and Low Intermediate*), *Grammar Express Basic,* and *Focus on Grammar* (levels 3 and 4).

Lisa Johnson has taught ESL in the United States and abroad and is currently an instructor and curriculum specialist at City College of San Francisco, where she has taught for the past two decades. Ms. Johnson holds a master's degree in TESOL from the University of Northern Iowa. She co-authored *Apply Yourself: English for Job Search Success,* co-authored or edited the Communication Companions for the Pearson English Interactive course, and contributed to *Talking Business Intermediate: Mastering the Language of Business.* She has also developed curricula for numerous ESL and VESL projects.

Irene Schoenberg has taught ESL for more than two decades at Hunter College's International English Language Institute and at Columbia University's American Language Program. Ms. Schoenberg holds a master's degree in TESOL from Teachers College, Columbia University. She has trained teachers at Hunter College, Columbia University, and the New School University, and she has given workshops and academic presentations at ESL programs and conferences throughout the world. Ms. Schoenberg is the author or co-author of numerous publications, including *True Colors; Speaking of Values 1; Topics from A to Z,* Books 1 and 2; and *Focus on Grammar: An Integrated Skills Approach* (levels 1 and 2).

ACKNOWLEDGMENTS

The Publisher would like to acknowledge the teachers, students, and survey and focus-group participants for their valuable input. Thank you to the following reviewers and consultants who made suggestions, contributed to this *Future* revision, and helped make *Future: English for Work, Life, and Academic Success* even better in this second edition. There are many more who also shared their comments and experiences using *Future*—a big thank you to all.

Fuad Al-Daraweesh The University of Toledo, Toledo, OH

Denise Alexander Bucks County Community College, Newtown, PA

Isabel Alonso Bergen Community College, Hackensack, NJ

Veronica Avitia LeBarron Park, El Paso, TX

Maria Bazan-Myrick Houston Community College, Houston, TX

Sara M. Bulnes Miami Dade College, Miami, FL

Alexander Chakshiri Santa Maria High School, Santa Maria, CA

Scott C. Cohen, M.A.Ed. Bergen Community College, Paramus, NJ

Judit Criado Fiuza Mercy Center, Bronx, NY

Megan Ernst Glendale Community College, Glendale, OH

Rebecca Feit-Klein Essex County College Adult Learning Center, West Caldwell, NJ

Caitlin Floyd Nationalities Service Center, Philadelphia, PA

Becky Gould International Community High School, Bronx, NY

Ingrid Greenberg San Diego Continuing Education, San Diego Community College District, San Diego, CA

Steve Gwynne San Diego Continuing Education, San Diego, CA

Robin Hatfield, M.Ed. Learning Institute of Texas, Houston,TX

Coral Horton Miami Dade College, Kendall Campus, Miami, FL

Roxana Hurtado Miami-Dade County Public Schools, Miami, FL

Lisa Johnson City College of San Francisco, San Francisco, CA

Kristine R. Kelly ATLAS @ Hamline University, St. Paul, MN

Jennifer King Austin Community College, Austin, TX

Lia Lerner, Ed.D. Burbank Adult School, Burbank, CA

Ting Li The University of Toledo, Ottawa Hills, OH

Nichole M. Lucas University of Dayton, Dayton, OH

Ruth Luman Modesto Junior College, Modesto, CA

Josephine Majul El Monte-Rosemead adult School, El Monte, CA

Dr. June Ohrnberger Suffolk County Community College, Selden, NY

Sue Park The Learning Institute of Texas, Houston, TX

Dr. Sergei Paromchik Adult Education Department, Hillsborough County Public Schools, Tampa, FL

Patricia Patton Uniontown ESL, Uniontown, PA

Matthew Piech Amarillo College, Amarillo, TX

Guillermo Rocha Essex County College, NJ

Audrene Rowe Essex County School, Newark, NJ

Naomi Sato Glendale Community College, Glendale, CA

Alejandra Solis Lone Star College, Houston, TX

Geneva Tesh Houston Community College, Houston, TX

Karyna Tytar Lake Washington Institute of Technology, Kirkland, WA

Miguel Veloso Miami Springs Adult, Miami, FL

Minah Woo Howard Community College, Columbia, MD

1 MEET YOUR TEACHER

▶ Look at the picture. Listen. Then listen and repeat.

2 FOLLOW CLASSROOM INSTRUCTIONS

Look at the pictures. Listen to your teacher. Repeat the sentences.

Take out your book.

Point to the picture.

Read the information.

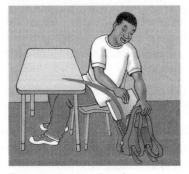

Put away your book.

Look at the board.

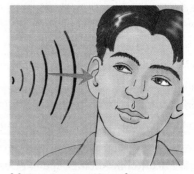

Listen to your teacher.

Open your notebook.

Write sentences.

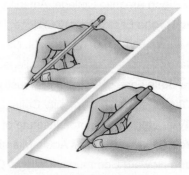

Use a pencil./Use a pen.

3 ASK FOR HELP

A Look at the pictures. Complete the conversations.

~~Can you speak more slowly?~~	Can you repeat that?
How do you pronounce this?	How do you spell that?
What does this word mean?	What's this called in English?

1.

Where are you from?

I'm sorry. *Can you speak more slowly?*

Oh, sorry. Where are you from?

I'm from Korea.

2.

_____

It's a pencil sharpener.

Thank you.

3.

Excuse me.
_____

Registration.

New Student Registration ____

Registration?

Yes. That's right.

4.

Can you help me?

Sure.

_____
_____

Occupation? It means a job or career.

5.

Please turn to page 45.

I'm sorry. ____
_____

Sure. Please turn to page 45.

6.

My name is Chiao.

Chiao? _____

C-H-I-A-O.

Thanks.

B **WORK TOGETHER.** Practice the conversations in Exercise A.

Welcome to Class

4 LEARN ABOUT *FUTURE*

A Turn to page iii. Answer the questions.

1. How many units are in this book? _____
2. Which unit is about families? _____
3. Which unit is about health? _____
4. Which units are about work? _____
5. Which unit is about shopping? _____
6. Which unit is about education/school? _____

B Look in the back of your book. Find each section. Write the page numbers.

Map of the World _____

Grammar Reference _____

Map of the U.S. and Canada _____

Grammar Review _____

Alphabet _____

Numbers _____

Word List _____

Audio Script _____

C Look at Unit 1. Write the page numbers.

Lesson 1: Vocabulary _____

Lesson 2: Listening and Speaking _____

Lesson 3: Workplace, Life, and
    Community Skills _____

Lesson 5: Grammar _____

Lesson 6: Reading _____

Lesson 10: Writing _____

Lesson 11: Soft Skills at Work _____

D Look inside the front cover. How will you get the Pearson Practice English app with audio?

_____

5 THINK ABOUT YOUR ENGLISH

A **THINK ABOUT IT.** What is most important for you? Put number 1 next to it. Then number 2-6.

_____ Listening

_____ Speaking

_____ Writing

_____ Grammar

_____ Vocabulary

_____ Reading

B **TALK ABOUT IT.** Tell the class what is most important for you.

1 Getting to Know You

PREVIEW

Look at the picture. What do you see?
Where are the people?

UNIT GOALS

- [ ] Identify regions and countries
- [ ] Introduce yourself
- [ ] Say and spell names
- [ ] Use titles
- [ ] Identify people and ask where they are from
- [ ] Talk about school

- [ ] **Academic skill:** Use the title to help understand a reading
- [ ] **Writing skill:** Use a capital letter for names and places
- [ ] **Workplace soft skill:** Be friendly

Regions and countries

A **PREDICT.** Look at the map. What are the regions and countries?

Letter A is North America. Number 2 is the United States.

B ▶ **LISTEN AND POINT.** Then listen and repeat.

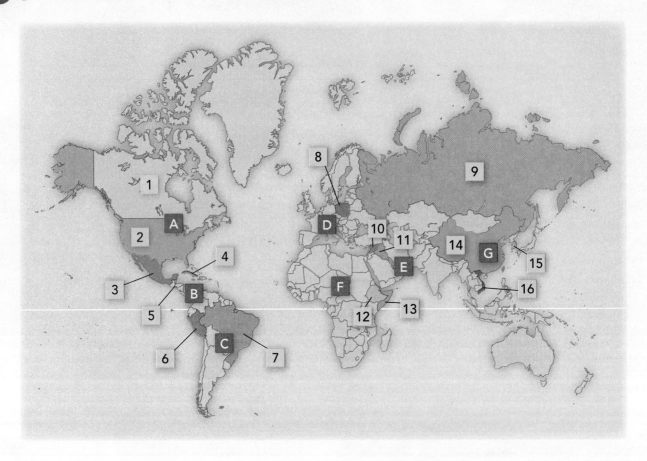

Vocabulary

Regions and countries

A. North America
1. Canada
2. the United States

B. Central America
3. Mexico
4. Cuba
5. El Salvador

C. South America
6. Peru
7. Brazil

D. Europe
8. Poland
9. Russia

E. The Middle East
10. Syria
11. Iraq

F. Africa
12. Ethiopia
13. Somalia

G. Asia
14. China
15. South Korea
16. Vietnam

C **IDENTIFY.** Student A, look at the map. Say a country. Student B, point to the country.

Vietnam.

D **NAME.** Student A, look at the word box. Say the region and the first letter of a country. Student B, say the country.

A: It is in Europe. The first letter is P.
B: Poland?
A: Yes!

Study Tip

Test yourself
Cover the word box. Say the words you remember.

Show what you know!

1. TALK ABOUT IT. What country are you from? Point to the map. Tell your group.

A: I'm from China. What about you?
B: I'm from Mexico. What about you?
C: I'm from Somalia.

2. PRESENT IT. Tell your class about one classmate from your group.

Ana is from Mexico.

3. WRITE ABOUT IT. Now write a sentence about where you are from.

I'm from the United States.

I can identify regions and countries. ☐   I need more practice. ☐

For more practice, go to MyEnglishLab.

1 BEFORE YOU LISTEN

A **LABEL.** Write the words under the pictures.

| bow | hug | shake hands |

1. _____ 2. _____ 3. _____

B **MAKE CONNECTIONS.** In the United States and Canada, people shake hands when they meet for the first time. What about in your native country?

2 LISTEN

A **PREDICT.** Look at the picture of Carla and Boris. Where are they?

Boris

Carla

B ▶ **LISTEN.** Choose the correct picture for the conversation.

a.  b.

C ▶ **LISTEN FOR DETAILS.** What does Carla say?

a. Nice to meet you, too.   **b.** Nice to meet you.

D ▶ **EXPAND.** Listen to the whole conversation. Complete the sentences.

1. Boris is from ____.   **a.** Russia   **b.** Poland
2. Carla is from ____.   **a.** Mexico   **b.** Peru

Listening and Speaking

3 PRONUNCIATION

A ▶ **PRACTICE. Listen. Then listen and repeat.**

Nice to **meet** you.   **Nice** to meet **you, too**.

B ▶ **APPLY. Listen. Then listen again and put a dot (•) on the stressed words.**

Where are you from?   I'm from China.   What about you?

> **Sentence stress**
>
> In English, important words in a sentence are stressed. Stressed words sound long and strong.

---

4 CONVERSATION

A ▶ **LISTEN AND READ. Then listen and repeat.**

B **WORK TOGETHER. Practice the conversation. Use your own names and countries.**

A: Hi, I'm _____.

B: Hi, I'm _____.

A: Nice to meet you.

B: Nice to meet you, too.

A: Where are you from?

B: I'm from _____. What about you?

A: I'm from _____.

C **MAKE CONNECTIONS. Walk around the room. Meet other classmates.**

I can introduce myself. ■   I need more practice. ■

For more practice, go to MyEnglishLab.

Lesson 3

Spell names and use titles

1 SAY AND SPELL YOUR NAME

A ▶ **LISTEN AND READ.** Then listen and repeat.

A: What's your first name?
B: My first name is Andre.
A: How do you spell that?
B: A-N-D-R-E.
A: A-N-D-R-E?
B: Right.
A: And what's your last name?
B: Mirov.
A: OK. Thanks.

B **MAKE CONNECTIONS.** Practice the conversation. Talk to five classmates. Write their names.

First Name	Last Name
Andre	Mirov

C GO ONLINE. Find common American last names.

_____   _____
_____   _____
_____   _____
_____   _____
_____   _____

I can say and spell my first and last name. ■   I need more practice. ■

For more practice, go to MyEnglishLab.

Workplace, Life, and Community Skills

2 USE TITLES

A ▶ **LISTEN AND POINT.** Then listen and repeat.

Mr. Johnson

Miss Chan / Ms. Chan

Mrs. Brown / Ms. Brown

B **MAKE CONNECTIONS.** Read the information. Which title do you use?

> **Using Titles**
>
> Use *Mr.* for both single and married men.
> Use *Ms.* for both single and married women.
> Use *Miss* for single women.
> Use *Mrs.* for married women.
> Use titles with last names, not first names.
> *John Smith = Mr. Smith, not* ~~Mr. John~~

C **IDENTIFY.** Look at the pictures. Check (✓) the correct title.

1.
☐ Mr. Rivas
☐ Mrs. Rivas

2.
☐ Miss Parker
☐ Mrs. Parker

3.
☐ Ms. Lee
☐ Mr. Lee

D ▶ **APPLY.** Listen. Complete the form.

1.
Student Registration

Title
● Mr. ○ Miss ○ Mrs. ○ Ms.

Name

	Chen
First	Last

2.
Student Registration

Title
○ Mr. ○ Miss ○ Mrs. ○ Ms.

Name

Vera	
First	Last

3.
Student Registration

Title
○ Mr. ○ Miss ○ Mrs. ○ Ms.

Name

Ana	
First	Last

I can use titles. ■   I need more practice. ■

For more practice, go to MyEnglishLab.

Listening and Speaking

Identify people and ask where they are from

1 BEFORE YOU LISTEN

A **READ.** Look at the pictures and read.

B **IDENTIFY.** Look at your classmates. Answer the question.

Who is absent?

_____

2 LISTEN

A **PREDICT.** Look at the picture. Carla and Sen are classmates. Where are they?

a. in their classroom
b. outside their classroom

B ▶ **LISTEN.** Circle the questions Carla asks.

a. Who's that?
b. Where is he?
c. Where's he from?

C ▶ **LISTEN FOR DETAILS.** Complete the sentences.

1. The man in the picture is _____.
   a. Max   **b.** Boris

2. Max is from _____.
   a. Mexico   **b.** Russia

D ▶ **EXPAND.** Listen to the whole conversation. Choose the correct picture of Boris.

a.

b.

Listening and Speaking

3 PRONUNCIATION

A ▶ **PRACTICE.** Listen. Notice the different sounds in *he's* and *she's*. Then listen and repeat.

He's from Mexico.   She's absent.

he =    she = 

he's = he is   she's = she is

B ▶ **CHOOSE.** Listen. Circle the words you hear.

1. a. He's **b.** She's
2. a. He's **b.** She's
3. a. He's **b.** She's
4. a. He's **b.** She's
5. a. He's **b.** She's
6. a. He's **b.** She's

4 CONVERSATION

A ▶ **LISTEN AND READ.** Then listen and repeat.

A: Who's that?
B: That's Boris.
A: No, that's not Boris.
B: Oh, you're right. That's Max.
A: Max? Where's he from?
B: He's from Mexico.

B **WORK TOGETHER.** Practice the conversation in Exercise A.

C **CREATE.** Make new conversations. Use the information in the boxes.

A: Who's that?
B: That's the teacher.
A: No, that's not the teacher.
B: Oh, you're right. That's ________.
A: ________? Where's ________ from?
B: ________'s from ________.

 Jin Su	he	South Korea
 Laura	she	Mexico
 Sagal	she	Somalia

D **MAKE CONNECTIONS.** Make your own conversations. Ask about your classmates.

I can identify people and ask where they are from. ☐   I need more practice. ☐

For more practice, go to MyEnglishLab.

Affirmative of *be* with *I, he,* and *she*		
I	**am**	
He		from Russia.
She	**is**	
Boris		

Grammar Watch

We usually use contractions in conversation.

Contractions
I am = **I'm**
he is = **he's**
she is = **she's**

A **REWRITE.** Write contractions for the underlined words.

1. My name is Carla Cruz. ~~I am~~ *I'm* in level 1. I am from Peru.

2. That's Victor. He is in my class.

3. Ms. Reed is the teacher. She is from Canada.

4. Pedro is a new student. He is from Mexico.

5. Frida is from Mexico, too. She is in Level 3.

B ▶ **SELF-ASSESS.** Listen and check your answers.

C **COMPLETE.** Look at the pictures. Complete the sentences. Use contractions.

1. ___*I'm*___ from Mexico.
2. ___*She's*___ from Vietnam.
3. _____ from El Salvador.

4. _____ from Peru.
5. _____ from South Korea.
6. _____ from China.

Grammar

Negative of *be* with *I*, *he*, and *she*				
I	am			
He				
She	is	not	in Level 3.	
Carla				

Grammar Watch

Contractions
I am not = ***I'm not***
he is not = ***he's not***
she is not = ***she's not***

D **IDENTIFY. Look at the identification cards. Cross out the incorrect words.**

Greenville Adult School

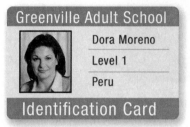

Dora Moreno
_____
Level 1
_____
Peru

Identification Card

Greenville Adult School

Kofi Solomon
_____
Level 1
_____
Ethiopia

Identification Card

1. **She's / ~~She's not~~** from Peru.
2. **She's / She's not** from Ethiopia.

3. **He's / He's not** in Level 3.
4. **He's / He's not** in Level 1.

E **WORK TOGETHER. Look at the chart. Student A, make sentences about a person. Student B, guess the person.**

A: *She's from Peru. She's absent.*
B: *Carla?*
A: *No! Dora.*

Level 1 Attendance		Monday		
Name	Country	Here	Absent	Late
Mr. Carlos Delgado	Mexico			✓
Ms. Carla Cruz	Peru	✓		
Ms. Ting Wong	China	✓		
Ms. Mi Young Lim	South Korea		✓	
Ms. Dora Moreno	Peru		✓	
Mr. Kofi Solomon	Ethiopia	✓		

Show what you know!

1. **TALK ABOUT IT. Say a sentence about yourself.**

A: *I'm Carmen Garcia.*
B: *I'm not from Peru.*
C: *I'm a student.*

2. **WRITE ABOUT IT. Now write two sentences about a classmate.**

Mi Young is not from Peru.
_____

_____

I can use affirmative and negative *be* with *I*, *he*, and *she*. ☐   I need more practice. ☐

For more practice, go to MyEnglishLab.

Read about immigrants to the U.S.

1 BEFORE YOU READ

A CHOOSE. Complete the sentences with the vocabulary in the box.

easy	hard	safe

1. They are _____.

2. This is _____.

3. This is not easy. It is _____.

B TALK ABOUT IT. Talk about living in the U.S. What's hard? What's easy?

2 READ

▶ Listen and read.

Academic Skill: Use the title

Before you read an article, look at the title. It can help you understand the article.

IMMIGRANTS IN THE U.S.

Every year, many immigrants come to the U.S. They come from different places and for different reasons.

Why do immigrants come to the U.S.?
Some people come for work. They get jobs in the U.S. Some people come to be safe. There are problems in their countries. Some people come to be with their family.
5 For example, the parents come first. The children come later to be with their parents.

Where are immigrants from?
Many immigrants come from Central or South America. They come from countries
10 like Mexico and Brazil. Many immigrants come from countries in Asia. For example, they come from China or India. Some immigrants are from Europe or Africa. Some are from other places.

15 *Are immigrants happy to be here in the U.S.?*
It is not easy to leave your home. It is hard to start a new life in a new country. But more than 70% of immigrants in the U.S. say they are happy to be here.

Source: www.publicagenda.org

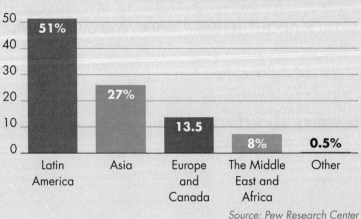

Immigrants Living in the U.S. by Region of Birth

- Latin America: 51%
- Asia: 27%
- Europe and Canada: 13.5
- The Middle East and Africa: 8%
- Other: 0.5%

Source: Pew Research Center

Reading

3 CLOSE READING

A **CITE EVIDENCE.** Complete the sentences. Where is the information? Write the line number.

Lines

1. People come to live in the U.S. for different _____.
   a. families   b. reasons   c. immigrants   _____

2. Some immigrants come to _____ in the U.S.
   a. get jobs   b. live an easy life   c. make new friends   _____

3. More than _____ percent (%) of immigrants in the U.S. say they are happy here.
   a. 50   b. 70   c. 90   _____

B **INTERPRET.** Complete the sentences about the bar graph.

1. More than 50% of immigrants living in the U.S. are from _____.
   a. Europe   b. Latin America   c. Africa

2. About _____ of immigrants living in the U.S. are from Asia.
   a. 17%   b. 24%   c. 27%

3. About 8% of immigrants living in the U.S. are from _____.
   a. Africa and the Middle East   b. Europe and Canada   c. North America

4 SUMMARIZE

Complete the summary with the words in the box.

family	happy	immigrants	safe

Many (1) _____ come to the U.S. They come for different reasons. Some come to work, some come to be (2) _____, and some come to be with their (3) _____. Most immigrants say they are (4) _____ living in the U.S.

Show what you know!

1. **TALK ABOUT IT.** Complete the chart with information about the other people in your group. Ask, "What's your name? Where are you from?"

Name	Country	Region

2. **WRITE ABOUT IT.** Now write about 3 people from your group. Tell where they are from.

_____ is from _____. It's in _____.

I can use the title to help understand a reading. ☐   I need more practice. ☐

To read more, go to MyEnglishLab.

7 Listening and Speaking

Talk about school

1 BEFORE YOU LISTEN

A **LABEL.** Write the words under the pictures.

| boring | easy | ~~good~~ |
| great | hard | interesting |

B **COMPARE.** Look at your answers. Compare with a partner.

1. _____good_____   2. _____   3. _____

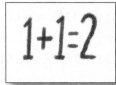 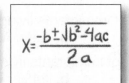 

4. _____   5. _____   6. _____

2 LISTEN

A ▶ **LISTEN.** Look at the picture. Listen to the conversation. What are they talking about?

a. a test   b. a class   c. a book

B ▶ **LISTEN FOR DETAILS.** Complete the sentences.

1. Boris and Mimi are in _____.
   a. Level 1   b. Level 2

2. The students are _____.
   a. interesting   b. great

C ▶ **EXPAND.** Listen to the whole conversation. Complete the sentence.

Boris says, "English! It's _____."

Min Jung   Boris   Mimi

3 CONVERSATION

A ▶ **LISTEN AND READ.** Then listen and repeat.

A: Hi. So, what class are you in?
B: We're in Level 1.
A: Oh. How is it?
C: It's good. The teacher is great.
A: How are the students?
B: They're great, too.

B **WORK TOGETHER.** Practice the conversation in Exercise A.

C **CREATE.** Make new conversations. Use the words in the boxes.

A: Hi. What class are you in?

B: We're in Level 1.

A: Oh. How is it?

C: It's _____. The teacher is _____.

A: How are the students?

B: They're _____, too.

easy	great	interesting

helpful	smart	friendly

D **MAKE CONNECTIONS.** Make your own conversations.
Talk about your English class.

I can talk about school. ■   I need more practice. ■

Grammar

Be with *we*, *you*, *they*, and *it*

Affirmative of *be* with *we*, *you*, *they*, and *it*					
We Carla and I					
You	are	in Level 1.	It The book	is	interesting.
They Sen and Boris					

Grammar Watch

Contractions
we are = ***we're***
you are = ***you're***
they are = ***they're***
it is = ***it's***

you
(singular)

you
(plural)

A **APPLY.** Complete the sentences. Use contractions.

1. **Mr. Salas:** You_'re_____ in Level 1.

   Student A: Thanks.

2. **Mr. Salas:** Here. You_____ in Level 2.

   Student B: Thank you.

3. **Student A:** So, you and Tom are in Level 2.

   Student B: Yes. We_____ in Level 2.

   Student A: How is your class?

   Student B: It_____ interesting.

   Student A: And how are the students?

   Student B: They_____ great.

B **WORK TOGETHER.** Practice the conversations in Exercise A.

Grammar

Negative of *be* with *we*, *you*, *they*, and *it*								
We **Carla and I**								
You	**are**	**not**	late.	**It** **The book**	**is**	**not**	easy.
They **Sen and Boris**								

Grammar Watch

Contractions
*we are not = **we're not***
*you are not = **you're not***
*they are not = **they're not***
*it is not = **it's not***

C **IDENTIFY.** Read the conversations. Cross out the incorrect words.

1. **Students:** Oh, no. **We're / ~~We're not~~** late.
   Teacher: It's OK. You're on time. **You're / You're not** late.

2. **Teacher:** Where are the students? **They're / They're not** here.
   Students: Oh. **We're / We're not** here. Sorry we're late.

3. **Student A:** My class is good. **It's / It's not** interesting. How is your class?
   Student B: My class **is / is not** interesting, too.

4. **Student A:** How are the students?
   Student B: They're great. **They're / They're not** friendly.

D **WORK TOGETHER.** Practice the conversations.

Show what you know!

1. **TALK ABOUT IT.** Talk about your class. Use words from the box.

boring	easy	friendly	good	great	hard	helpful	interesting	smart

   A: How is your class?
   B: It's not good . . .

2. **WRITE ABOUT IT.** Now write an affirmative and a negative sentence about your class.

   My class is good. It's not boring.

   _____

   _____

I can use affirmative and negative of *be* with *we*, *you*, *they*, and *it*. ☐   I need more practice. ☐

For more practice, go to MyEnglishLab.

Other negative contractions with *be*		
He		
She	**isn't**	
Carla		
You		late.
We	**aren't**	
They		

Grammar Watch

Contractions
isn't = is not
aren't = are not

A **COMPLETE. Write *isn't* or *aren't*.**

1. My teacher _____isn't_____ from Canada.
2. My classmates _____ from the United States.
3. Ana _____ absent.
4. Our books _____ boring.
5. It _____ easy.
6. Her last name _____ Brown. It's Wilson.

B **COMPLETE. Write *is*, *isn't*, *are*, or *aren't*.**

1. Carlos _____isn't_____ in Peru. He's in the United States.
2. Ana _____ absent. She's here.
3. My book _____ hard. It isn't easy.
4. My classmates _____ here. They're absent.
5. Lila and Rob _____ in Level 2. They aren't in Level 1.
6. They _____ from Canada. They're from the United States.

C ▶ **LISTEN. Complete the sentences.**

1. _____ in Level 3.
   a. He's   (b.) He's not

2. Level 3 _____ easy.
   a. is   b. isn't

3. _____ late.
   a. We're   b. We're not

4. _____ in my class.
   a. They're   b. They're not

5. _____ absent.
   a. They're   b. They aren't

6. The teachers _____ helpful.
   a. are   b. aren't

I can use other negative contractions with *be*. ■   I need more practice. ■

For more practice, go to MyEnglishLab.

Write about yourself

1 STUDY THE MODEL

READ. Answer the questions.

Marta Banas

My Class

    I'm Marta Banas. My first name is Marta. My last name is Banas. I'm from Warsaw, Poland. Now I'm in Chicago, Illinois. I'm an English student. My class is helpful. The students are friendly.

1. What are the writer's first and last names?
2. Where is she from?
3. Where is she now?
4. How is her class?

2 PLAN YOUR WRITING

WORK TOGETHER. Ask and answer the questions.

1. What are your first and last names?
2. Where are you from?
3. Where are you now?
4. How is your class?

Writing Skill: Use capital letters

Names of people and places begin with a capital letter. For example:

Marta Banas, Warsaw

3 WRITE

Now write about yourself. Use the frame, the model, the Writing Skill, and your ideas from Exercise 2 to help you.

I'm _____. My first name is _____. My last name is _____. I'm from _____, _____. Now I'm in _____, _____. I'm a/an _____ student. My class is _____. The students are _____.

4 CHECK YOUR WRITING

WORK TOGETHER. Read your writing aloud with a partner.

WRITING CHECKLIST

☐ The writing answers the questions in Exercise 2.

☐ The names of people and places begin with a capital letter.

I can use a capital letter for names and places. ■   I need more practice. ■

For more practice, go to MyEnglishLab.

Be friendly

1 MEET AKI

Read about one of her workplace skills.

> I'm friendly. For example, I smile and say hi to my co-workers. I call my co-workers by their first name.

2 AKI'S PROBLEM

READ. Circle *True* or *False*.

Aki works at a store. She is a sales assistant. She works with people from different countries. She learns their names. She asks her co-workers questions to get to know them.

One day, Aki sees a new co-worker. The co-worker says, "Hi, Aki." Aki wants to talk to her, but she doesn't know her name.

1. Aki works with people from her native country.	True	False
2. Aki asks her co-workers questions.	True	False
3. Aki knows the new co-worker's name.	True	False

3 AKI'S SOLUTION

A **WORK TOGETHER.** Aki is friendly. What is the friendly thing to do? Explain your answer.

1. Aki says "Hi" and leaves.
2. Aki says, "Hi. I'm sorry. I don't know your name."
3. Aki says nothing.
4. Aki says, "_____"

B **ROLE-PLAY.** Look at your answers to 3A. Role-play Aki's conversation.

Show what you know!

1. **THINK ABOUT IT.** How are you friendly at school? At work? Give examples.

2. **WRITE ABOUT IT.** Now write your example in your Skills Log.

   I smile and say "hi" to my classmates.

I can give an example of how I am friendly. ■

Unit Review: Go back to page 5. Which goals can you check off?

2 A Hard Day's Work

PREVIEW

Look at the picture. What do you see?
Who are the people?

UNIT GOALS

- [ ] Name jobs
- [ ] Introduce someone and talk about your job
- [ ] Ask for and give contact information
- [ ] Ask about jobs
- [ ] Talk about where you work
- [ ] **Academic skill:** Learn new vocabulary
- [ ] **Writing skill:** Use a period
- [ ] **Workplace soft skill:** Be a good listener

25

Vocabulary

Jobs

A **PREDICT.** Look at the pictures. What do you see? Where are the jobs?

Number 3 is a manager.

B ▶ **LISTEN AND POINT.** Then listen and repeat.

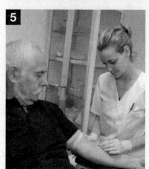

Vocabulary

Jobs

A. restaurant
1. a cook
2. a server
3. a manager

B. hospital
4. a doctor
5. a nurse
6. a custodian

C. store
7. a cashier
8. a sales assistant
9. a driver

D. office
10. an office assistant
11. an accountant

E. construction site
12. a painter
13. an electrician

F. home
14. a homemaker
15. a child-care worker
16. a landscaper

C IDENTIFY. Student A, say a job. Student B, point to the picture on page 26.

A nurse.

D WORK TOGETHER. Student A, act out a job. Students B and C, guess the job.

B: You're a homemaker.
A: No.
C: You're a landscaper.
A: Right!

Study Tip

Use your language
Make cards. On one side, write the word in English. On the other side, write the word in your language.

Show what you know!

1. **TALK ABOUT IT.** Ask three classmates about their jobs. Complete the chart.

   A: What do you do?
   B: I'm a cook.

Name	Job
Andy	a cook

2. **PRESENT IT.** Tell your class about your classmates' jobs.

   Andy is a cook.

3. **WRITE ABOUT IT.** Now write a sentence about your job.

   I'm a server.

I can name jobs. ■   I need more practice. ■

For more practice, go to MyEnglishLab.

1 BEFORE YOU LISTEN

TALK ABOUT IT. Look at the picture. Where are they?

Omar, this is Rosa. Rosa, this is Omar.

Hi, Omar. Nice to _____ you.

Hi, Rosa. _____ to meet you, _____.

2 LISTEN

A ▶ **LISTEN. Complete the conversation in the picture.**

B ▶ **LISTEN. What is Rosa's question?**

  a. What do you do?   **b.** Where are you from?

C ▶ **LISTEN FOR DETAILS. Complete the sentences.**

  1. Omar is a landscaper and _____.
    a. a driver   **b.** a student

  2. Rosa is a student and _____.
    a. a sales assistant   **b.** a nurse

D ▶ **EXPAND. Listen to the whole conversation. What is Emilio's job?**

a.

b.

Listening and Speaking

3 PRONUNCIATION

A ▶ **PRACTICE. Listen. Then listen and repeat.**

A: What do you do?
B: I'm a student.

A: What's your name?
B: I'm Peter.

> **Falling intonation in statements and *Wh-* questions**
>
> In *Wh-* questions and in statements, the voice goes down ↘ at the end.

B ▶ **APPLY. Practice saying the sentences. Then listen and repeat.**

Where are you from?
I'm from China.
What about you?

4 CONVERSATION

A ▶ **LISTEN AND READ. Then listen and repeat.**

A: So, what do you do?
B: I'm a landscaper. And I'm a student at Greenville Adult School.
A: Really? I'm a student there, too. And I'm a sales assistant.
B: Oh, that's interesting.

B **WORK TOGETHER. Practice the conversation in Exercise A.**

C **CREATE. Make new conversations. Use the pictures.**

A: What do you do?
B: I'm   .
A: Really? I'm   , too. And I'm   .
B: Oh, that's interesting.

D **MAKE CONNECTIONS. Make your own conversations.**

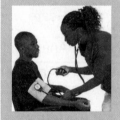

I can introduce someone and talk about my job. ■   I need more practice. ■

For more practice, go to MyEnglishLab.

Lesson 3

A/An; Singular and plural nouns

A/An					
He is	**a**	landscaper.	She is	**an**	accountant.

Grammar Watch

- Use **a** before consonant sounds.
- Use **an** before vowel sounds.

A IDENTIFY. Cross out the incorrect words.

1. **A:** That's Fang. She's **a / an** office assistant.
   B: Oh, really? I'm **a / an** office assistant, too.

2. **A:** Paul is **a / an** teacher, right?
   B: No. He's not **a / an** teacher. He's **a / an** nurse.

3. **A:** I'm **a / an** landscaper. What about you?
   B: I'm **a / an** electrician.

4. **A:** This is Dr. and Mrs. Silver. He's **a / an** doctor, and she's **a / an** accountant.
   B: Nice to meet you. I'm Mary Green. I'm **a / an** child-care worker.

5. **A:** So, Ana, what do you do?
   B: I'm **a / an** homemaker.

B ▶ SELF-ASSESS. Listen and check your answers.

C WORK TOGETHER. Practice the conversations in Exercise A.

D COMPLETE. Use a or an. Then complete sentence 8.

1. Bob is ____a____ cashier.
2. Joe is _____ electrician.
3. Kevin is _____ driver.
4. John is _____ cook.

5. Sarah is _____ office assistant.
6. Hai is _____ accountant.
7. Faha is _____ student.
8. My classmate is _____.

Grammar

Singular and plural nouns

| John is | **a cook**. | John and Linda are | **cooks**. |

Grammar Watch

- Add **-s** to form most plurals.
- For irregular plural nouns, see page 259.

E **APPLY. Look at the pictures. Complete the sentences.**

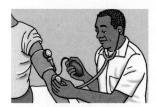

1. Bob is ___*a nurse*___.

2. Rosa is _____.

3. Jill, Mei, and I are _____.

4. They're _____.

Show what you know!

1. **RANK.** These are the five most common jobs in the U.S. Which job is number 1? Number 2? 3? 4? 5? Guess. Write the numbers next to the jobs.

   ____ cashiers   ____ sales assistants   ____ food preparers and servers

   ____ office assistants   ____ nurses

2. **TALK ABOUT IT. What do you think? Talk about your answers in Exercise 1.**

   A: I think cashiers are number 1.
   B: Me, too.
   C: No, I think . . .

3. ▶ **SELF-ASSESS. Listen and check your answers.**

4. **WRITE ABOUT IT. What do you think about the most common jobs or other jobs you know? Write a sentence. Use words from the box.**

   | friendly | good | great | helpful | smart |

   Most ___*sales assistants*___ are helpful.

   Most _____.

I can use *a/an* and singular and plural nouns. ☐   I need more practice. ☐

For more practice, go to MyEnglishLab.

Lesson 4

Ask for and give contact information

1 IDENTIFY PHONE NUMBERS

A MAKE CONNECTIONS. Think about numbers in your life. When do you use numbers? Do you use numbers at work?

B ▶ LISTEN AND POINT. Then listen and repeat.

0 zero	1 one	2 two	3 three	4 four
5 five	6 six	7 seven	8 eight	9 nine

Cumar Rahim

My number
(415) 555-7934

C ▶ LISTEN. Circle the phone numbers you hear.

1. a. 212-960-5334
   b. 412-960-5334

2. a. 619-464-2083
   b. 619-464-2093

3. a. 305-576-1169
   b. 395-576-1169

4. a. 323-865-4191
   b. 323-835-4191

5. a. 214-847-3726
   b. 214-847-3126

6. a. 773-395-2114
   b. 773-399-2114

D ▶ COMPLETE. Listen to the voicemail messages. Write the missing numbers.

1.
Mr. Fernandez
Center Hospital
Landscaper job
(562) 555-_____

2.
Grace Simms
Grace's Office Supplies
Cashier Job
(_____) 555-_____

3.
Jin Wu
Greenville Store
Sales assistant job
(_____) 555-_____

4.
Ms. Rodriguez
Carla's Restaurant
Manager job
(_____) _____ - _____

Workplace, Life, and Community Skills

2 IDENTIFY EMAIL ADDRESSES

A **MAKE CONNECTIONS.** Think about email in your life. When do you use email? Do you use email at work?

B ▶ **LISTEN AND POINT.** Look at the email. Listen and point to the email addresses. Then listen and repeat.

● ● ●

From: amy.smith@mymail.com
To: rosa.medina@mymail.com
Subject: ESL class

C ▶ **LISTEN.** Circle the email addresses you hear.

1. **a.** dan.silver@ccmail.edu
   b. dans.ilver@ccmail.edu

2. **a.** gsimms@hmail.com
   b. g.simms@hmail.com

3. **a.** tlopez719@gomail.com
   b. tlopez715@gomail.com

4. **a.** jin.wu@newmail.edu
   b. jin.hu@newmail.edu

3 GET CONTACT INFORMATION

A ▶ **LISTEN AND READ.** Then listen and repeat.

A: What's your phone number?
B: 213-555-4963.
A: 213-555-4563?
B: No. It's 213-555-4963.
A: OK. And what's your email address?
B: asad.bilan@hmail.com.

B **WORK TOGETHER.** Ask two classmates for their phone number and email address. Complete the chart.

Name	Phone Number	Email address
Asad	(213) 555-4963	asad.bilan@hmail.com
1.		
2.		

C GO ONLINE. Add two new contacts in your phone.

I can ask for and give contact information. ☐   I need more practice. ☐

For more practice, go to MyEnglishLab.

Lesson 5 — Ask about jobs

1 BEFORE YOU LISTEN

LABEL. Write the jobs under the pictures.

| cashier | cook | homemaker | ~~server~~ |

1. _____server_____   2. _____   3. _____   4. _____

2 LISTEN

A **PREDICT.** Look at the picture. Where are they?

B ▶ **LISTEN.** Complete the sentence.

Sara is a _____.
a. student   **b.** teacher

Boris   Marta   Sara

C ▶ **LISTEN FOR DETAILS.** Complete the sentences.

1. Sara is a _____, too.
   a. cashier   **b.** nurse

2. Boris is a _____.
   a. server   **b.** cook

D ▶ **EXPAND.** Listen to the whole conversation. Complete the sentences.

1. Marta says, "I'm _____." (Choose all the correct answers.)
   a. an electrician   **c.** a cook   **e.** a server
   b. a child-care worker   **d.** a cashier   **f.** a doctor

2. Marta is _____. (Choose one answer.)
   a. a homemaker   **b.** a landscaper   **c.** a painter

Listening and Speaking

3 PRONUNCIATION

A ▶ **PRACTICE. Listen. Then listen and repeat.**

Are you a student?   Is he a cook?

> **Rising intonation in *yes/no* questions**
>
> In *yes/no* questions, the voice goes up (↗) at the end.

B ▶ **CHOOSE. Listen to the sentences. Does the voice go up (↗) or down (↘) at the end?**

	1.	2.	3.	4.	5.	6.	7.	8.
Up	☑	☐	☐	☐	☐	☐	☐	☐
Down	☐	☐	☐	☐	☐	☐	☐	☐

4 CONVERSATION

A ▶ **LISTEN AND READ. Then listen and repeat.**

A: Who's that? Is she a teacher?
B: No, she's not. She's a student. And she's a cashier at Al's Restaurant.
A: Oh, that's interesting. And what do you do?
B: I'm a cook.

B **WORK TOGETHER. Practice the conversation in Exercise A.**

C **CREATE. Make new conversations. Use the words in the boxes.**

A: Who's that? Is _____ a teacher?
B: No, _____'s not. _____'s a student. And _____'s _____.
A: Oh, that's interesting. And what do you do?
B: I'm _____.

she	a cashier	a sales assistant

he	an electrician	a painter

she	a nurse	an accountant

D **MAKE CONNECTIONS. Make your own conversations. Ask about people and their jobs.**

I can ask about jobs. ◻   I need more practice. ◻

For more practice, go to MyEnglishLab.

Be: Yes/no questions and short answers

Yes/no questions		
Are	you	
Is	he she	a teacher?
Are	you they	teachers?

Short answers			
Yes,	I **am**.	**No,**	I'm **not**.
	he **is**. she **is**.		he's **not** / he **isn't**. she's **not** / she **isn't**.
	we **are**. they **are**.		we're **not** / we **aren't**. they're **not** / they **aren't**.

A **APPLY.** Now write *yes/no* questions.

1. John / a / landscaper / Is   <u>Is John a landscaper?</u>
2. cook / she / a / Is   _____
3. they / Are / sales assistants   _____
4. a / Are / server / you   _____
5. Is / painter / he / a   _____
6. managers / you / Are   _____

Is she a cook?

B **COMPLETE.** Use capital letters when necessary.

1. **A:** _____<u>Are</u>_____ they servers?
   B: No, ___<u>they're not</u>___. (OR ___<u>they aren't</u>___.)

2. **A:** _____ she a cook?
   B: Yes, _____.

3. **A:** _____ Marta and Kim office assistants?
   B: Yes, _____.

4. **A:** _____ you an electrician?
   B: No, _____.

5. **A:** _____ he an accountant?
   B: No, _____.

6. **A:** _____ Mr. Garcia a painter?
   B: Yes, _____.

Grammar

C **APPLY.** Look at the pictures. Complete the conversations. Add *a* or *an* when necessary.

1. A: <u>Is she an</u> accountant?

   B: <u>Yes, she is.</u>

2. A: _____ drivers?

   B: _____

3. A: _____ electrician?

   B: _____

4. A: _____ nurse?

   B: _____

5. A: _____ landscapers?

   B: _____

6. A: _____ server?

   B: _____

Show what you know!

1. **ACT IT OUT.** Student A, choose a job. Act it out. Students B and C, guess the job.

   B: Are you a painter?
   A: No, I'm not.
   C: Are you a cook?
   A: Yes, I am.

2. **WRITE ABOUT IT.** Now write two *yes/no* questions and short answers about your classmates' jobs.

   Is Tom a driver? Yes, he is.

   _____

   _____

I can ask *yes/no* questions and give short answers with *be*. ■   I need more practice. ■

For more practice, go to MyEnglishLab.

Read about healthcare jobs in the U.S.

1 BEFORE YOU READ

A CHOOSE. Complete the sentences with the vocabulary from the box.

CNA	nursing home	orderly

1. He's an _____.   **2.** She's a _____.   **3.** They live in a _____.

B TALK ABOUT IT. What kinds of jobs are there in a hospital?

2 READ

▶ Listen and read.

> **Academic Skill: Learn new vocabulary**
>
> The words in Exercise 1A will be important when you read *Healthcare Jobs in the U.S.* Write the words in your notebook. Underline the words when you see them in the article.

Healthcare Jobs in the U.S.

Many people in the U.S. work in healthcare. How many? More than 12 million.

The biggest number of jobs in healthcare is for nurses. They work in hospitals, doctors' offices, schools, and 5 nursing homes. You need a lot of training to be a nurse. Nurses go to school for many years.

That is not true for all jobs in healthcare. For some jobs, a high school diploma is enough. For example, you can be an orderly or a CNA. (CNA means "certified 10 nursing assistant.") Most orderlies get training on the job. CNAs take a training course and an exam.

The U.S. has more than 1.5 million CNAs and orderlies. They work in hospitals and nursing homes. They need to be strong because sometimes they lift 15 patients out of bed. They also help people eat, wash, or get dressed.

Hospitals and nursing homes need other kinds of workers, too. They need cooks, housekeepers, custodians, and electricians. They need clerks to do 20 office work.

Healthcare in the U.S. is growing. It will need more workers in the future.

Top Jobs in the U.S.		
What's the job?	**How many people do it?**	**How much money do they make in a year?**
1. Sales assistant	4.5 million	about $25,000
2. Cashier	3.3 million	about $20,000
3. Food preparer and server	3.0 million	about $19,000
4. Office assistant	2.8 million	about $30,000
5. Registered nurse	2.7 million	about $69,000

Source: U.S. Bureau of Labor Statistics

Reading

3 CLOSE READING

A **CITE EVIDENCE. Complete the sentences. Where is the information? Write the line number.**

Lines

1. More than _____ million people work in healthcare in the U.S.
   a. 12   **b.** 15   **c.** 21   _____
2. You need many years of school to be _____.
   a. a CNA   **b.** an orderly   **c.** a nurse   _____
3. _____ do office work in hospitals.
   a. Clerks   **b.** Housekeepers   **c.** Electricians   _____
4. There will be _____ jobs in healthcare in the future.
   a. more   **b.** the same number of   **c.** not so many   _____

B **INTERPRET. Complete the sentences about the chart.**

1. The chart shows _____ in the U.S.
   a. the jobs with the most workers   **b.** who makes the most money   **c.** the best jobs
2. There are _____ nurses in the U.S.
   a. 2.7 million   **b.** 7 million   **c.** 12 million
3. There are more nurses in the U.S. than _____.
   a. cashiers   **b.** office assistants   **c.** doctors
4. Most nurses make about _____ a year.
   a. $39,000   **b.** $69,000   **c.** $89,000

4 SUMMARIZE

Complete the summary with the words in the box.

CNA	healthcare	nurses	training

More than 12 million people in the U.S. work in (1) _____. The biggest number of jobs are for (2) _____. They need a lot of (3) _____, but you can be a (4) _____ or an orderly after you finish high school. There are many other jobs in healthcare, too.

Show what you know!

1. **THINK ABOUT IT. Do you know people who work in healthcare? What are their jobs? Where do they work?**

2. **WRITE ABOUT IT. Now write about someone you know who works in healthcare.**

   _____ works in healthcare. (He/She) is a _____. (He/She)
   works at _____.

I can learn new vocabulary. ■   I need more practice. ■

To read more, go to MyEnglishLab.

Lesson 8

Talk about where you work

1 BEFORE YOU LISTEN

**TALK ABOUT IT. Look at the picture.
What do they do? Where do they work?**

2 LISTEN

A ▶ **LISTEN. Dora, Omar, and Sali are at
a party. What is Sali talking about?**

a. her school   **b.** her job

B ▶ **LISTEN FOR DETAILS. Where does
Sali work?**

a.

b.

C ▶ **EXPAND. Listen to the whole conversation. Complete the sentences.**

1. Omar is a _____.
   a. nurse   **b.** teacher   **c.** student

2. Omar says, "It's _____."
   a. an interesting job   **b.** a hard job   **c.** a great job

D **DISCUSS.**

Sali says, "That's not a job." Omar says, "Yes, it is." Who is right, Sali or Omar?

3 CONVERSATION

A ▶ **LISTEN AND READ. Then listen and repeat.**

A: So, what do you do?
B: I'm a nurse.
A: Really? Where do you work?
B: I work at a school on Main Street. I'm a school nurse.
A: Oh. That's nice.

B **WORK TOGETHER. Practice the conversation in Exercise A.**

C **CREATE. Make new conversations.**
Use the information in the boxes.

A: What do you do?
B: I'm _____.
A: Really? Where do you work?
B: I work at _____ on Main
Street.
A: Oh. That's nice.

a carpenter

a construction site

a caregiver

a nursing home

D **MAKE CONNECTIONS. Make your own
conversations. Ask where your partner
works.**

A: Where do you work?
B: Oh, I'm a server at Alice's Restaurant.
   What about you?
A: I'm a server, too. I work at . . .

an assembly line
worker

a factory

a stock clerk

a supermarket

E **NETWORK. Find classmates with the
same job as you. Form a group. Ask the
people in your group, *Where do you work?***

I can talk about where I work. ■   I need more practice. ■

Simple present affirmative: *work* and *live*

Simple present affirmative: *work* and *live*		
I		
You	**live**	
We	**work**	
They		in Miami.
He		
She	**lives**	
Kate	**works**	

Grammar Watch

For spelling rules for the simple present, see page 259.

A IDENTIFY. Cross out the incorrect words.

1. That's my friend George. He ~~work~~ / **works** at a store.
2. George **live** / **lives** in New York. My wife and I **live** / **lives** in New York, too.
3. I **work** / **works** at a store, too! I'm a cashier.
4. This is Gloria. She **live** / **lives** in Florida. She **work** / **works** at a hospital.
5. Olga and Marcos **work** / **works** at a hospital, too. They're clerks.

B COMPLETE. Look at the ID cards. Complete the sentences. Use the verbs in parentheses and write the jobs.

1. Helen Lam (be) _____*is*_____ a _____. She (live) _____ in Los Angeles. She (work) _____ at General Hospital.

2. Luis Mendoza and Nadif Fall (be) _____ _____. They (live) _____ in Tampa. They (work) _____ for Andrews Accounting.

General Hospital — HELEN LAM — Nurse

Luis Mendoza — Accountant — ANDREWS ACCOUNTING

Nadif Fall — Accountant — ANDREWS ACCOUNTING

C WORK TOGETHER. Talk about what you do and where you work.

A: I'm a cook. I work at a restaurant.
B: Paul is a cook. He works at a restaurant. I'm a sales assistant. I work at a store.
C: Paul is a cook. He works at a restaurant. Sara is a sales assistant. She . . .

I can use the simple present affirmative with *work* and *live*. ■   I need more practice. ■

For more practice, go to MyEnglishLab.

1 STUDY THE MODEL

READ. Answer the questions.

> Tim Lee
>
> <u>My Friend</u>
>
> Sam Lin is my friend. He lives in Texas. He is a custodian. He works at a hospital.

1. What is the friend's name?
2. Where does the friend live?
3. What does the friend do?
4. Where does the friend work?

2 PLAN YOUR WRITING

WORK TOGETHER. Ask and answer the questions.

1. What is your friend's name?
2. Where does your friend live?
3. What does your friend do?
4. Where does your friend work?

Writing Skill: Use a period

Begin a sentence with a capital letter.
End a sentence with a period.
For example: He is a custodian.

3 WRITE

Now write about a friend. Use the frame, the model, the Writing Skill, and your ideas from Exercise 2 to help you.

_____ is my friend. He/She lives in _____. He/She is a/an _____. He/She works at a/an _____.

4 CHECK YOUR WRITING

WORK TOGETHER. Read your writing aloud with a partner.

WRITING CHECKLIST

☐ The writing answers the questions in Exercise 2.

☐ Each sentence begins with a capital letter.

☐ The names of people and places begin with capital letters.

☐ Each sentence ends with a period.

I can use a period. ■   I need more practice. ■

For more practice, go to MyEnglishLab.

1 MEET FREDY

Read about one of his workplace skills.

 I'm a good listener. For example, I ask questions when I don't understand.

2 FREDY'S PROBLEM

READ. Read about Fredy's problem. Circle *True* or *False*.

Fredy is a painter. He paints homes. The supervisor gives Fredy and his co-workers instructions every morning. Then Fredy starts to work.

One day his supervisor is very busy. The supervisor gives many instructions. He speaks very fast. Fredy doesn't understand what the supervisor is saying.

1. Fredy's supervisor gives instructions every morning.	True	False
2. Fredy's supervisor speaks slowly.	True	False
3. Fredy understands his supervisor's instructions.	True	False

3 FREDY'S SOLUTION

WORK TOGETHER. Fredy is a good listener. What is the right thing to do? Explain your answer.

1. Fredy says to the supervisor, "I'm sorry. Could you please repeat that?"
2. Fredy asks his co-workers questions when the supervisor leaves.
3. Fredy doesn't ask questions. Then he starts to work.
4. Fredy _____.

Show what you know!

1. **THINK ABOUT IT.** How are you a good listener at school? At work? At home? Give examples.

2. **WRITE ABOUT IT.** Now write your example in your Skills Log.

   I am a good listener at school. I don't talk when another student talks.

I can give an example from my life of being a good listener. ☐

Unit Review: Go back to page 25. Which goals can you check off?

3 Time for Class

PREVIEW

Look at the picture. What do you see?
Where are the people?

UNIT GOALS

- ☐ Identify things in the classroom
- ☐ Give and follow classroom instructions
- ☐ Talk about things in the classroom
- ☐ Talk about places at school
- ☐ Talk about people and places at school

- ☐ **Academic skill:** Use headings to help understand a reading
- ☐ **Writing skill:** Recognize and use a verb in a sentence
- ☐ **Workplace soft skill:** Be flexible

A **PREDICT.** Look at the pictures. What do you see? What are the things?

Number 3 is a tablet.

B ▶ **LISTEN AND POINT.** Then listen and repeat.

Vocabulary

Things in the classroom

1. a desk
2. a laptop
3. a tablet
4. a phone

5. a projector
6. a board
7. a marker
8. a book

9. a dictionary
10. a piece of paper
11. a sticky note
12. a notebook

13. an eraser
14. a three-ring binder
15. a folder
16. a backpack

C **IDENTIFY.** Student A, say a thing. Student B, point to the picture on page 46.

A dictionary.

D **CATEGORIZE.** Write the things in the chart.
Then compare answers.

Digital devices	Things you can read	Things you can write on
a laptop		

Study Tip

Draw pictures

Make cards. On one side, write the word in English. On the other side, draw a picture.

Show what you know!

1. **TALK ABOUT IT.** Talk about the things you have in your classroom. How many do you see?

   A: *We have one projector.*
   B: *We have twenty-five desks.*

2. **MAKE CONNECTIONS.** Talk about the things you have.

   I have a phone, a folder, and a book.

3. **WRITE ABOUT IT.** Now write a sentence about the things you have.

   I have _____.

I can identify things in the classroom. ■   I need more practice. ■

Lesson 2

Give and follow classroom instructions

1 BEFORE YOU LISTEN

MATCH. Look at the pictures. Complete the sentences with the words in the box.

| borrow | put away | take out | ~~turn off~~ |

1. Please _turn off_ your phone.

2. Please _____ your books.

3. Please _____ your notebook.

4. Can I _____ your pen?

2 LISTEN

A ▶ **LISTEN.** Look at the picture. Listen to the conversation. Complete the sentence.

The teacher is giving _____ to the students.
a. books
b. instructions
c. pencils

B ▶ **LISTEN FOR DETAILS.** Check (✓) the teacher's instructions.

☐ Take out your books.

☐ Put away your books.

☐ Borrow a pencil.

☐ Take out a piece of paper.

C ▶ **EXPAND.** Listen to the whole conversation. A phone is ringing. Complete the sentence.

It's _____ phone.
a. a student's
b. the teacher's

Listening and Speaking

3 CONVERSATION

A ▶ **LISTEN AND READ.** Then listen and repeat.

Teacher:	OK, everyone. Please put away your books. Take out a piece of paper.
Student A:	Can I borrow a pencil?
Student B:	Sure. Here you go.

B **WORK TOGETHER.** Practice the conversation in Exercise A.

C **CREATE.** Make new conversations. Use the pictures.

Teacher:	Please put away your _____. Take out _____.
Student A:	Can I borrow _____?
Student B:	Sure. Here you go.

D **ROLE-PLAY.** Make your own conversations. Student A, you're a teacher. Give instructions. Student B, you're a student. Follow the instructions.

A: Please take out your notebook.
B: OK.

I can give and follow classroom instructions. ■   I need more practice. ■

For more practice, go to MyEnglishLab.

Grammar

Imperatives

Imperatives			
Affirmative		**Negative**	
Use	a pencil.	**Don't use**	a pen.

A **MATCH.** Write the letters to match the pictures and the sentences.

_d_ **1.** Turn off your laptop.

____ **2.** Don't use your dictionary.

____ **3.** Write in your book.

____ **4.** Don't take out your notebook.

____ **5.** Don't turn off your laptop.

____ **6.** Use your dictionary.

____ **7.** Take out your notebook.

____ **8.** Don't write in your book.

a.

b.

c.

d.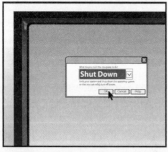

e.

f.

g.

h.

Grammar

B IDENTIFY. Look at the pictures. Cross out the incorrect words.

1.

Use / Don't use a Number 2 pencil.

2.
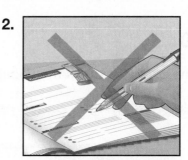
Use / Don't use a pen.

3.
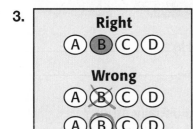
Fill in / Don't fill in the circles.

4.

Look / Don't look at your classmate's test.

C APPLY. Complete the sentences about classroom rules. Use the words in the box.
Add *Don't* when necessary.

answer	~~bring~~	come	~~eat~~	follow	listen

1. ___Bring___ a notebook and pencil.

2. ___Don't eat___ in class.

3. _____ to class on time.

4. _____ to your classmates.

5. _____ your teacher's instructions.

6. _____ your phone in class.

Show what you know!

1. TALK ABOUT IT. What are some *Dos* and *Don'ts* in your classroom?

A: Speak English in class.
B: Don't come late.

2. WRITE ABOUT IT. Now write one *Do* and one *Don't* for your class.

_____   _____

I can use imperatives. ☐   I need more practice. ☐

For more practice, go to MyEnglishLab.

Reading

Lesson 4

Read about good study habits

1 BEFORE YOU READ

A **CHOOSE. Complete the sentences with the vocabulary in the box.**

looking at study goals	studying for a short period	throwing out papers

1. He's _____

_____.

2. He's _____

_____.

3. He's _____

_____.

B **MAKE CONNECTIONS. What are your study habits? Where do you usually study? When do you usually study?**

2 READ

▶ Listen and read.

Academic Skill: Use headings

Headings are titles for each part of a reading. They are often in **bold**, so they are easy to see.

HELPFUL STUDY HABITS

Sam and Tim are in the same class. Sam plans to study vocabulary every Sunday night for 60 minutes. Tim plans to study vocabulary for 10 minutes 5 nights a week. Whose plan is better?

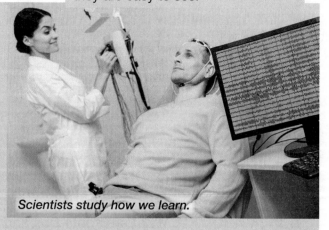

Scientists study how we learn.

5 Scientists study how people learn. They study how the brain remembers new information. What can scientists tell students?

Set study goals. Keep your goals small and write them in your notebook. For example, write "Listening: Watch TV
10 in English for ten minutes. Do it five days a week." Look at your goals every day. When you reach a goal, make a check mark ✓ next to it.

Be organized. Keep all your things for school in a bag or backpack. Keep important papers in a binder. Throw
15 out papers you don't need.

Do one thing at a time. You cannot learn when you are thinking about other things. Don't watch TV. Don't listen to music. Don't text friends when you study. Turn off your phone.

20 **Get enough sleep.** Most adults need about 7.5 hours of sleep. Sleep helps your brain work better.

Study for a short period every day. That's better than studying for a long time on one day. You will remember more. (Tim has the right idea!)

Reading

3 CLOSE READING

CITE EVIDENCE. Complete the sentences. Where is the information? Write the line number.

Lines

1. The information about study habits comes from _____.
   a. students   **b.** parents   **c.** scientists   _____

2. It is a good idea to write your _____ in your notebook.
   a. study goals   **b.** sleep habits   **c.** phone number   _____

3. Keep all your school things in a bag or backpack. It will help you _____.
   a. remember new words   **b.** be organized   **c.** read faster   _____

4. _____ papers you don't need.
   a. Throw out   **b.** Put away   **c.** Organize   _____

5. You cannot learn when you are _____.
   a. using your brain   **b.** studying for short periods   **c.** doing two things at the same time   _____

6. Most adults need about _____ hours of sleep.
   a. 6.5   **b.** 7.5   **c.** 8   _____

4 SUMMARIZE

Complete the summary with the words in the box.

goals	learn	organized	period

Good study habits help you (1) _____ better. For example, set study (2) _____. Be (3) _____ and keep all your school things in a bag or backpack. Do one thing at a time. Get the sleep your brain needs. Study for a short (4) _____ every day.

Show what you know!

1. **THINK ABOUT IT.** Think about your study habits and the ideas in the article. What can you do better? Make a plan.

2. **TALK ABOUT IT.** Talk about your study habits. Ask, *What can you do better? What is your plan?*

3. **WRITE ABOUT IT.** Now write about ways to have good study habits.

   Don't _____. Try to _____.

I can use headings to help understand a reading. ■   I need more practice. ■

To read more, go to MyEnglishLab.

Listening and Speaking

Talk about things in the classroom

1 BEFORE YOU LISTEN

LABEL. Look at the pictures. Write the words from the box on the lines.

keyboard
mouse
printer
screen

_____

_____

_____

_____

2 LISTEN

Ⓐ PREDICT. Look at the picture. Where are Carlos and Mimi? What are they looking at?

a. their books
b. their notebooks
c. their phones

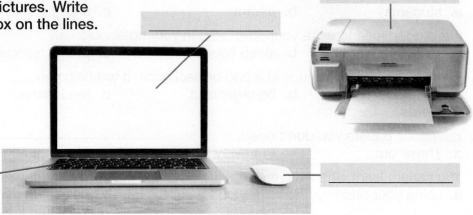

Carlos   Mimi

Ⓑ ▶ LISTEN. Carlos asks, "What's this called in _____?"

a. English   **b.** Spanish

Ⓒ ▶ LISTEN FOR DETAILS. What is Carlos asking about? Check (✓) all the correct answers.

☐ a mouse   ☐ a keyboard
☐ printers   ☐ screens

Ⓓ ▶ EXPAND. Listen to the whole conversation. Complete the sentence.

Carlos says, "This is a _____ of a _____, and that's a

_____ of _____."

Listening and Speaking

3 PRONUNCIATION

A ▶ **PRACTICE. Listen. Then listen and repeat.**

This	**Th**is is a laptop.
These	**Th**ese are printers.
That's	**Th**at's a keyboard.

B ▶ **CHOOSE. Listen. Then listen again and check (✓) the correct words.**

1. ☐ ten ☐ then
2. ☐ day ☐ they
3. ☐ Ds ☐ these

Voiced *th* sound

To say the *th* sound in *this*, *these*, and *that's*, put your tongue between your teeth.

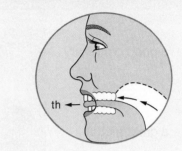

4 CONVERSATION

A ▶ **LISTEN AND READ. Then listen and repeat.**

A: What's this called in English?
B: It's a mouse.
A: And these? What are these called?
B: They're printers.

B **WORK TOGETHER. Practice the conversation in Exercise A.**

C **CREATE. Make new conversations. Use the pictures.**

A: What's this called in English?
B: It's _____.
A: And these? What are these called?
B: They're _____.

D **MAKE CONNECTIONS. Make your own conversations. Ask about things in your classroom.**

I can talk about things in the classroom. ■   I need more practice. ■

For more practice, go to MyEnglishLab.

Grammar

This, that, these, those

This, that, these, those: Statements

Singular		Plural	
This is	a good dictionary.	**These are**	good dictionaries.
That's	a great picture.	**Those are**	great pictures.

A **IDENTIFY.** Cross out the incorrect words.

1. **This is / These are** a good book.
2. **That's / Those are** my classmates.
3. **This is / These are** my markers.
4. **That's / Those are** my folders.
5. **That's / Those are** called a screen.

Grammar Watch

- Use **this** and **these** for people or things near you.
- Use **that** or **those** for people or things <u>not</u> near you.

Contraction
that is = **that's**

B **COMPLETE.** Look at the pictures. Complete the sentences with *This is, That's, These are,* and *Those are*.

1. *These are* our books.
2. _____ our teacher.
3. _____ nice binders.
4. _____ my backpack.

C **WRITE.** Write two sentences about things in your classroom. Use *this, that, these,* or *those*.

This is my book.

_____

_____

Grammar

This, that, these, those: Questions and answers

Is	this that	your book?	Yes, **it** is.	What is	this? that?	It's a pen.
Are	these those	your books?	Yes, **they** are.	What are	these? those?	**They**'re pens.

D **WORK TOGETHER. Look at the picture. Complete the conversations.**

Partners
Practice *this,*
that, these, those

What's _this_ called
1.
in English?

What _____ ?
2.

What _____ ?
3.

_____
4.

_____ a
5.
good book?

_____,
_____.
6.

_____
7.
markers?

_____,
_____.
8.

Show what you know!

1. **TALK ABOUT IT. Student A, you have ten seconds. Draw a picture of one or two things in your classroom. Student B, guess the object or objects.**

   A: *What are these?*
   B: *Are they folders?*
   A: *No. They're notebooks.*

2. **WRITE ABOUT IT. Now write a question and an answer about something in your classroom.**

   A: _____

   B: _____

I can use *this, that, these, those.* ☐

I need more practice. ☐

For more practice, go to MyEnglishLab.

Lesson 7

Workplace, Life, and Community Skills

Talk about places at school

1 IDENTIFY PLACES AT SCHOOL

A **LABEL.** Look at the floor plan. How many places around school do you know? Write the words from the box on the lines.

cafeteria	computer lab	elevator	hall
library	office	~~restroom~~	stairs

1. restroom
2. ______
3. ______
4. ______
5. ______
6. ______
7. ______
8. ______

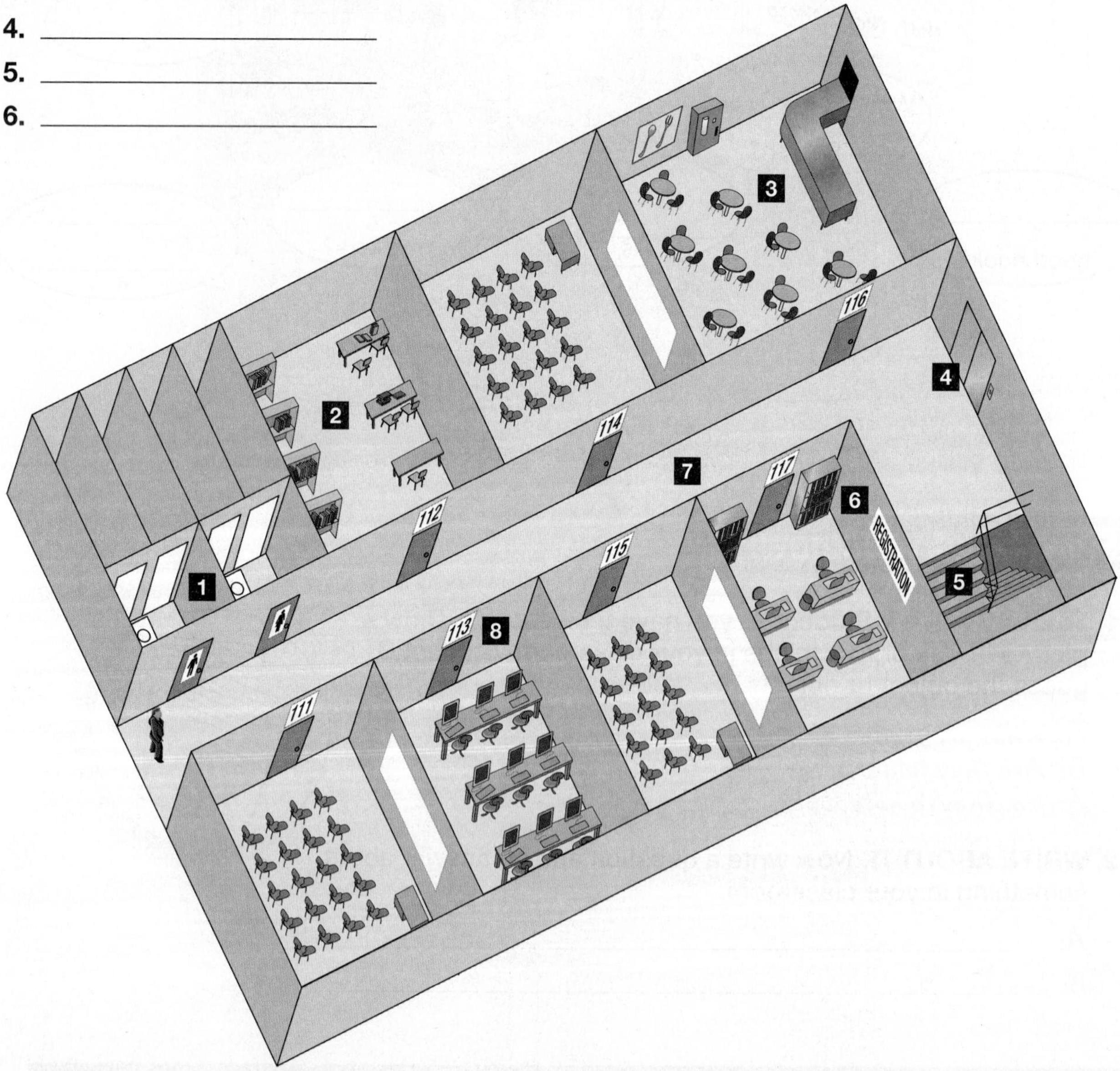

B **SELF-ASSESS.** Listen and check your answers. Then listen and repeat.

2 GIVE LOCATIONS OF PLACES AT SCHOOL

A **INTERPRET.** Look at the diagram. Then look at the floor plan on page 58. Circle *True* or *False*.

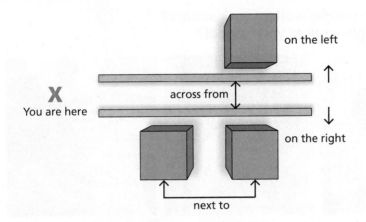

on the left

across from

X
You are here

on the right

next to

1. The library is on the right.	True	False
2. Room 115 is next to the computer lab.	True	False
3. Room 111 is across from the office.	True	False
4. The stairs are on the left.	True	False
5. The cafeteria is next to the restrooms.	True	False

B **REWRITE.** Correct the sentences in Exercise 2A.

C ▶ **LISTEN AND READ.** Then listen and repeat.

A: Where is Room 114?
B: It's on the left, next to the library.
A: Where is the computer lab?
B: It's on the right, across from the library.

D **ROLE-PLAY.** Make new conversations about other rooms on the floor plan on page 58.

E GO ONLINE. Find a school in your neighborhood.

I can talk about places at school. ■   I need more practice. ☐

For more practice, go to MyEnglishLab.

Talk about people and places at school

1 BEFORE YOU LISTEN

IDENTIFY. Look at the pictures. Which people work at your school? Check (✓) the people. What other people work at your school?

☐ custodian

☐ director

☐ librarian

☐ computer lab assistant

2 LISTEN

A **PREDICT. Look at the picture. What do you see?**

B ▶ **LISTEN. Ken is asking a question. Complete the sentence.**

Ken's first words are _____.
a. Help me.
b. Excuse me.
c. Look at me.

C ▶ **LISTEN FOR DETAILS. Answer the questions.**

1. What is Ken's question?
   a. Where is the computer lab?
   b. Is the computer lab open?
   c. Is the computer lab upstairs?

2. Who is the man in the room with Ken and Berta?
   a. a teacher
   b. an office assistant
   c. the computer lab assistant

Listening and Speaking

3 PRONUNCIATION

A ▶ **PRACTICE. Listen. Then listen and repeat.**

of fice   ex **cuse**   **li** brar y   li **brar** i an   caf e **te** ri a

> **Word stress**
>
> A syllable is part of a word. One syllable in each word has the most stress.

B ▶ **APPLY. Listen to the words. Mark (•) the syllable with the most stress.**

1. **o** pen   **2.** com pu ter   **3.** as sist ant   **4.** di rec tor   **5.** cus to di an

4 CONVERSATION

A ▶ **LISTEN AND READ. Then listen and repeat.**

A: Excuse me. Is the computer lab open?
B: Sorry. I don't know. Ask him.
A: Oh, OK. But . . . Who is he?
B: He's the computer lab assistant.

B **WORK TOGETHER. Practice the conversation in Exercise A.**

C **CREATE. Make new conversations. Use the words in the boxes.**

A: Excuse me. Is the ▭ open?
B: Sorry. I don't know. Ask ▭.
A: Oh, OK. But . . . Who is ▭?
B: ▭ 's the ▭.

Ask him.   Ask her.

cafeteria	him	he	custodian
office	her	she	office assistant
library	him	he	librarian
director's office	her	she	director

D **ROLE-PLAY. Make your own conversations. Talk about places at your school.**

I can talk about people and places at school. ▢	I need more practice. ▢

For more practice, go to MyEnglishLab.

Subject pronouns			Object pronouns	
I	am			**me**.
He	is			**him**.
She		new here.	Please help	**her**.
We	are			**us**.
They				**them**.

Grammar Watch

Subject Pronoun	Object Pronoun	
you	**you**	Are you the librarian? Can I ask **you** a question?
it	**it**	It's interesting. Read **it**.

A **IDENTIFY. Cross out the incorrect words.**

1. **A:** Where's the cafeteria?
   B: Sorry. I don't know. Ask ~~he~~ / **him**.

2. **A:** Are these the answers?
   B: Yes, but don't look at **they / them**.

3. **A:** Please show **us / we** your new pictures.
   B: Sure. Here they are.

4. **A:** What's the word for this in English?
   B: Sorry. I don't know. Ask **her / she**.

Where's the cafeteria?

Ask him.

B **APPLY. Change the underlined words. Use** *him*, *her*, *it*, *us*, **or** *them*.

1. Take out your book. Open ~~the book~~ to page 10. *it*

2. Please close your notebooks. Thanks.

3. Please don't use your phone in class. Use your phone in the cafeteria.

4. Ask Ms. Adams about the computer lab hours. She's the computer lab assistant.

5. Mr. and Mrs. Lin are new here. Please show Mr. and Mrs. Lin the library.

6. Mr. Tran doesn't understand. Please help Mr. Tran.

7. Ask Mr. Benson and me. We're both Level 1 teachers.

I can use object pronouns. ■	I need more practice. ■

For more practice, go to MyEnglishLab.

Write about study habits

1 STUDY THE MODEL

READ. Answer the questions.

> Marc Booker
> <u>My Study Habits</u>
>
> I study English four nights a week.
> I sit at my kitchen table. I read my
> class notes. I do my homework. I
> write new words in my notebook.

1. How many nights a week does Marc study?
2. Where does he study?
3. What does he read?
4. What does he write?

2 PLAN YOUR WRITING

WORK TOGETHER. Ask and answer the questions.

1. How many times a week do you study?
2. Where do you study?
3. What do you read?
4. What do you write?

> **Writing Skill: Recognize and use verbs**
>
> Every sentence has a verb. For example:
> I (study) English four nights a week.

3 WRITE

Now write about your study habits. Use the frame, the model, the Writing Skill, and your ideas from Exercise 2 to help you.

> I study _____ times a week. I sit _____. I read _____. I write _____.

4 CHECK YOUR WRITING

WORK TOGETHER. Read your writing aloud with a partner.

> **WRITING CHECKLIST**
>
> ☐ The writing answers the questions in Exercise 2.
>
> ☐ Each sentence begins with a capital letter.
>
> ☐ Each sentence has a verb.
>
> ☐ Each sentence ends with a period.

I can recognize and use a verb in a sentence. ■   I need more practice. ■

For more practice, go to MyEnglishLab.

11 | Soft Skills at Work

Be flexible

1 MEET YING

Read about one of her workplace skills.

> I'm flexible. For example, sometimes the work I do changes. I can make changes in my life.

2 YING'S PROBLEM

READ. Circle *True* or *False*.

Ying works in a restaurant. She is a server. She works every day from 9:00 to 5:00. She takes an English class in the evening. She really likes the class. The teacher is great, and the students are friendly.

One day the manager says to Ying, "You need to work in the evening." Ying wants to continue learning English, but she needs the job. She finds an online class. This is her first online class. It's not so friendly.

1. Ying works in a restaurant every day.	True	False
2. Ying doesn't like her English class.	True	False
3. Ying likes online classes.	True	False

3 YING'S SOLUTION

WORK TOGETHER. Ying is flexible. What is the flexible thing to do? Explain your answer.

1. Ying doesn't take the online class. She wants to wait until she works during the day again.
2. Ying takes the online class. Learning English is very important to her.
3. Ying quits her job so she can go to her class in the evening.
4. Ying _____.

Show what you know!

1. **THINK ABOUT IT.** How are you flexible at school? At work? At home? Give examples.

2. **WRITE ABOUT IT.** Now write your example in your Skills Log.

   Sometimes my schedule changes at school. That's OK for me.

3. **PRESENT IT.** Give a short presentation to show how you are flexible.

I can give an example from my life of being flexible. ☐

Unit Review: Go back to page 45. Which goals can you check off?

4 Family Ties

PREVIEW

Look at the picture. Who are the people?
Where are they?

UNIT GOALS

- [ ] Identify family members
- [ ] Talk about family
- [ ] Describe people
- [ ] Say and write dates
- [ ] Give a child's age and grade in school
- [ ] **Academic skill:** Make connections
- [ ] **Writing skill:** Use a capital letter for months
- [ ] **Workplace soft skill:** Separate work and home life

Vocabulary

Family members

A **PREDICT.** Look at the pictures of Sue's family. What are the family words?

Sue

Number 3 is Sue's mother.

B ▶ **LISTEN AND POINT.** Then listen and repeat.

Vocabulary

Family members

1. sister	**4.** father	**7.** wife	**10.** children
2. brother	**5.** parents	**8.** daughter	**11.** grandmother
3. mother	**6.** husband	**9.** son	**12.** grandfather

C **IDENTIFY.** Student A, point to a person in a picture on page 66. Talk about the person.

A: Who's this?
B: Sue's mother.

D **MATCH.** Student A, say a family member. Student B, say the matching male or female word.

A: Brother.
B: Sister.

E **LABEL.** Look at Sue's family tree. Write family words in the correct places.

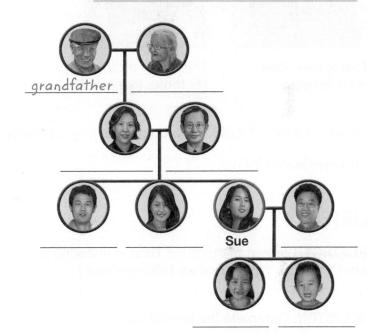

grandfather

Sue

Show what you know!

1. DRAW A PICTURE. Draw your family tree. Use names.

2. TALK ABOUT IT. Talk about your family.

Ben is my brother.

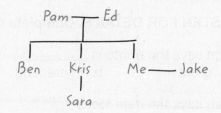

3. WRITE ABOUT IT. Now write a sentence about your family.

_____ is my _____.

I can identify family members. ■   I need more practice. ■

For more practice, go to MyEnglishLab.

Talk about family

1 BEFORE YOU LISTEN

A READ.

This is Dev Patel.
He is an actor.

This is my brother.
He **looks like** Dev Patel.

B MAKE CONNECTIONS. Who do people in your family look like?

My sister looks like me.

2 LISTEN

Gina   Kim

A PREDICT. Look at the picture. Gina is showing a photo to Kim. What are they talking about?

B ▶ LISTEN. Complete the sentence.

The man in the photo is _____.
a. Gina's father   b. Gina's grandfather

C ▶ LISTEN FOR DETAILS. Complete the sentences.

1. Kim says the photo is _____.
   a. great   b. interesting   c. nice

2. Kim says the man looks _____.
   a. great   b. interesting   c. nice

D ▶ EXPAND. Listen to the whole conversation. Read the sentences. Circle *True* or *False*.

1. Kim thinks Gina looks like the woman in the photo.   True   False
2. The woman is Gina's sister.   True   False

3 CONVERSATION

A ▶ **LISTEN AND READ. Then listen and repeat.**

A: That's a great photo. Who's that?
B: My father.
A: Oh, he looks nice.
B: Thanks.

B **WORK TOGETHER.** Practice the conversation in Exercise A.

C **CREATE.** Make new conversations.
Use the family tree.

A: That's a great photo. Who's that?

B: My _____.
           (family member)

A: Oh, _____ looks nice.
           (he / she)

B: Thanks.

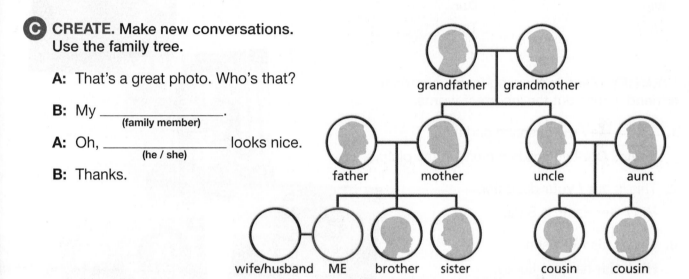

D **MAKE CONNECTIONS.** Make your own
conversations. Use a photo of a person
in your family. Talk about that person.

I can talk about family. ■   I need more practice. ■

For more practice, go to MyEnglishLab.

Possessive adjectives

Subject pronouns			Possessive adjectives	
I	am		**My**	
You	are		**Your**	
He	is	in the U.S.	**His**	family is in Peru.
She			**Her**	
We	are		**Our**	
They			**Their**	

A **IDENTIFY.** Maria is showing family photos to a friend. Cross out the incorrect words.

1. This is ~~his~~ / **my** husband and me.

   Their / Our two children aren't in the picture.

2. This is **our / your** daughter.

   His / Her name is Sara.

3. This is **his / our** son.

   His / Her name is Lucas.

4. These are **my / our** parents.

   Her / Their names are Frida and Luis.

B **COMPLETE.** Maria is showing more photos to her friend. Complete their conversation with *my, your, his, her,* and *their*.

Maria: This is _____*my*_____ daughter with _____ friend from school.

This is _____ son with _____ cousin. And here are

the children with _____ classmates.

Friend: Nice. _____ son looks like you.

Maria: I know. And _____ daughter looks like my husband.

C ▶ **SELF-ASSESS.** Listen and check your answers.

Grammar

Possessive nouns

Dora	is in the U.S.	Dora's	
Luis		Luis's	family is in Peru.
		Dora and Luis's	

Grammar Watch

Add **'s** to names to show possession.

Pronunciation of possessive 's

The **'s** adds an extra syllable after the sounds *s*, *z*, *sh*, and *ch* (*Luis's, Alex's, Liz's, Josh's,* and *Mitch's*).

D INTERPRET. Look at the family tree. Complete the sentences.

1. Ryan is _____*Eva's*_____ husband.

2. Meg is _____ wife.

3. Eva is Ross and _____ daughter.

4. Tess is _____ grandmother.

5. Ed is _____ husband.

6. Pat is Mary and _____ granddaughter.

Family tree:
Ross — Mary
Ryan — Eva
Tess — Ed
Pat
Alex — Meg
Jake

E ▶ SELF-ASSESS. Listen and check your answers. Then listen and repeat.

Show what you know!

1. TALK ABOUT IT. Say the names of two people in the family tree. Your partner says their relationship.

A: Ross and Alex.
B: Ross is Alex's grandfather.

2. WRITE ABOUT IT. Now write about a person in your family. Describe your relationship in two ways.

Rosa is my sister. I'm Rosa's brother.

_____ _____

I can use possessive adjectives and possessive nouns. ■ I need more practice. ■

For more practice, go to MyEnglishLab.

Read about blended families

1 BEFORE YOU READ

A **CHOOSE.** Complete the sentences with the vocabulary in the box.

divorced	married	step-sister

1. In 2008, Jimmy's parents got _____.

2. In 2016, Jimmy's parents got _____.

3. Jimmy now lives with his mother, step-father, and _____.

B **MAKE CONNECTIONS.** Do you have a big family? Who's in your family?

2 READ

▶ **Listen and read.**

Academic Skill: Make connections

When you read, try to make connections between the article and your own life. Does the article make you think about people you know?

The Blended Family

In 2015, Jimmy Peterson had a small family. He had a mother and a father. He had no brothers or sisters. In 2016, his parents got divorced.

In 2017, Jimmy's mother got married again. In 2018, his
5 father remarried. Now Jimmy lives in two homes. Each home has a blended family. From Monday to Friday, Jimmy lives with his mother, step-father, and step-sister. On weekends, he lives with his father, step-mother, and two step-brothers. Jimmy says, "My life is different now,
10 but I love my big family."

Jimmy's family life isn't simple, but it is common. Today in the U.S., many people marry, divorce, and remarry. Many children live in blended families. Just 46% of

Jimmy with his father, step-mother, and step-brothers

children live with two parents who are married
15 for the first time.

Source: www.pewsocialtrends.org

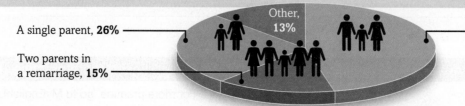

A single parent, **26%**

Other, **13%**

Two parents in a remarriage, **15%**

Two parents in their first marriage, **46%**

3 CLOSE READING

CITE EVIDENCE. Answer the questions. Complete the sentences. Where is the information? Write the line number.

Lines

1. What happened in 2016?

   Jimmy's parents _____. _____

2. What happened in 2017?

   Jimmy's mother _____. _____

3. What happened in 2018?

   Jimmy's father _____. _____

4. Who does Jimmy live with during the week?

   His _____. _____

5. Who does Jimmy live with on weekends?

   His _____. _____

6. What does Jimmy say about his family?

   " _____." _____

4 SUMMARIZE

Complete the summary with the words in the box.

common	divorced	families	remarried	step-father

In 2016, Jimmy Peterson's parents got (1) _____. Later, his mother got married again, and his father (2) _____, too. Now Jimmy has two blended (3) _____. During the week, he lives with his mother, (4) _____, and step-sister. On weekends, he lives with his father, step-mother, and step-brothers. Blended families are (5) _____ in the U.S.

Show what you know!

1. **TALK ABOUT IT.** Do you know someone who is part of a blended family? Who? Talk about the people in his or her family.

2. **WRITE ABOUT IT.** Now write about the person you know and his or her blended family.

   _____ *is part of a blended family. (He/She) has* _____.

I can make connections. ☐   I need more practice. ☐

To read more, go to MyEnglishLab.

Listening and Speaking

Describe people

1 BEFORE YOU LISTEN

A ▶ **READ.** Look at the picture of Pam's parents and brother. Then listen and read.

Pam's father is *average height* and *heavy*. He has a *mustache*. Her mother is *short* and *average weight*. She has *long hair*. Her brother is *tall* and *thin*. He has a *beard*.

B **IDENTIFY.** Answer the questions.

1. Who has a mustache?   _____
2. Who has a beard?   _____
3. Who is average weight?   _____

2 LISTEN

A ▶ **LISTEN.** Look at the picture of Pam and Leo. Listen to the conversation. Check (✓) the correct answer.

Who is Leo talking about?

☐ his father   ☐ his grandfather   ☐ his brother

B ▶ **LISTEN FOR DETAILS.** Check (✓) all the correct answers.

Leo's brother is _____.

☐ a painter   ☐ a carpenter
☐ great   ☐ interesting   ☐ fun   ☐ smart
☐ short   ☐ tall   ☐ heavy   ☐ thin

C ▶ **EXPAND.** Listen to the whole conversation. Check (✓) the correct answers.

1. Which picture shows Leo's brother?
   a. ☐   b. ☐   c. ☐

2. Is Leo's brother married?
   ☐ yes   ☐ no

3 CONVERSATION

A **LISTEN AND READ.** Then listen and repeat.

A: Is your family here in this country?
B: My brother is here. He's a carpenter.
A: Oh. What's he like?
B: He's great. He's a lot of fun.
A: Does he look like you?
B: No. He's tall and thin, and he has long hair.

B **WORK TOGETHER.** Practice the conversation in Exercise A.

C **CREATE.** Make new conversations. Talk about a family member in this country.

A: Is your family here in this country?
B: My ____________ is here.
A: Oh. What's ____________ like?
(he / she)
B: ____________'s great.
(He / She)
____________'s a lot of fun.
(He / She)
A: Does ____________ look like you?
(he / she)
B: Yes/No. ____________'s
(He / She)
____________ and
____________ and
has ____________.

uncle	aunt	cousin
tall	short	average height
thin	heavy	average weight
short hair	long hair	short hair

D **MAKE CONNECTIONS.** Make your own conversations. Student A, ask about your partner's family. Student B, talk about one person.

A: What's your brother like?
B: He's great. He's a lot of fun.
A: Does he look like you?
B: No. He's tall and thin and has short hair.

I can describe people. ☐ I need more practice. ☐

For more practice, go to MyEnglishLab.

Grammar

Have and *be* for descriptions

Descriptions with *have*					
I			He		
You	**have**	long hair.	She	**has**	short hair.
We			Marco		
They					

A **IDENTIFY. Cross out the incorrect words.**

1. My name is Paul. I **have / ~~has~~** short hair.
2. My parents both **have / has** short hair, too.
3. My brother and I both **have / has** mustaches. But I also **have / has** a beard.
4. Our sister looks like our mother. But she **have / has** long hair.

B **DECIDE. Look at the picture in Exercise A. Circle Paul.**

C **APPLY. Look at the pictures. Describe the people. Use *have* or *has*.**

1. Ali _has a mustache._   2. Aya _____   3. Kim and Rita _____

4. Feng _____   5. Karl and Nick _____   6. Max _____

Grammar

Descriptions with *be* and *have*

Be			Have		
I	**am**		I	**have**	
She	**is**	tall.	She	**has**	long hair.
We			We		
They	**are**		They	**have**	

D **IDENTIFY. Read about Donna's family. Cross out the incorrect words.**

Donna's mother **is / has** average height and weight, but her sister **is / are** short and heavy. Her sister and her mother both **has / have** short hair. Donna's father **is / has** a beard, and her brother **is / has** a mustache. Her father and her brother both **are / have** short hair. Her father **is / has** thin, but her brother **is / has** heavy.

E **WORK TOGETHER. Look at the pictures of Donna and her husband. Talk about the differences.**

A: In Picture A, Donna is average
   weight. In Picture B, she's heavy.
B: In Picture A, she has . . .

May 2011

April 2017

Show what you know!

1. **TALK ABOUT IT. Look at your classmates. Complete the chart. Write the number of students. Talk about your classmates.**

Beard	Mustache	Long hair	Short hair	Tall	Short

A: Who has a beard?
B: Carlos and Chen have beards. What about mustaches?

2. **WRITE ABOUT IT. Now write two sentences about two classmates.**

_____   _____

Workplace, Life, and Community Skills

Say and write dates

1 TALK ABOUT MONTHS

A ▶ **LISTEN AND POINT.** Then listen and repeat.

January _____	February _____	March _____
April _____	May _____	June _____
July _____	August _____	September _____
October _____	November _____	December _____

B **USE ABBREVIATIONS.** Look at the calendar. Write the abbreviations for the months in Exercise 1A.

C **WORK TOGETHER.** Student A, say a month. Student B, repeat the month and say the next month. Student C, continue. Then Student B, say a new month.

A: March.
B: March, April.
C: March, April, May.
B: August.

2019 ⚙ ⑦

JAN FEB MAR APR MAY JUN
JUL AUG SEP OCT NOV DEC

SUN	MON	TUE	WED	THU	FRI	SAT
30	31	1	2	3	4	5
6	7	8	9	10	11	12
13	14	15	16	17	18	19
20	21	22	23	24	25	26
27	28	29	30	31	1	2

TODAY   ❷ NOTIFICATIONS

2 TALK ABOUT AND WRITE DATES

A ▶ **LISTEN AND POINT.** Then listen and repeat.

1st	2nd	3rd	4th	5th	6th
7th	8th	9th	10th	11th	12th
13th	14th	15th	16th	17th	18th
19th	20th	21st	22nd	23rd	24th
25th	26th	27th	28th	29th	30th
31st					

B ▶ **LISTEN AND POINT.** Look at the calendar for January. Listen and point to the dates.

Workplace, Life, and Community Skills

C **APPLY.** Look at the calendars. Write the dates. Use this year.

| JAN FEB MAR APR MAY JUN | JAN FEB MAR APR MAY JUN | JAN FEB MAR APR MAY JUN | JAN FEB MAR APR MAY JUN |
| JUL AUG SEP OCT NOV DEC | JUL AUG SEP OCT NOV DEC | JUL AUG SEP OCT NOV DEC | JUL AUG SEP OCT NOV DEC |

February 24, _____   _____   _____   _____

D **REWRITE.** Look at the calendars in Exercise 2C. Write the dates in numbers.

1. 2/24/ _____   2. _____   3. _____   4. _____

E ▶ **CHOOSE.** Circle the dates you hear.

1. **a.** 3/4/87   **(b.)** 3/14/87   4. **a.** 8/30/05   **b.** 8/31/05
2. **a.** 10/2/11   **b.** 2/10/11   5. **a.** 12/17/69   **b.** 12/7/69
3. **a.** 6/28/98   **b.** 5/28/98   6. **a.** 9/2/72   **b.** 9/22/62

F ▶ **LISTEN AND READ.** Then listen and repeat.

A: When is your birthday?
B: My birthday is July 29. When is your birthday?

G **MAKE CONNECTIONS.** Ask three classmates for their birthdays. Write the names and dates.

Name	Birthday
Han	7/29

H **PRESENT.** Tell your class about your classmates' birthdays.

I GO ONLINE. Find the date of the next holiday on your calendar.

I can say and write dates. ▢   I need more practice. ▢

For more practice, go to MyEnglishLab.

Lesson 8

Give a child's age and grade in school

1 BEFORE YOU LISTEN

INTERPRET. Look at the picture. Answer the questions.

1. How old is the little girl?
2. What grade is she in?

How old are you?

I'm ten. I'm in the fourth grade.

2 LISTEN

A **PREDICT.** Look at the pictures. Ellen is babysitting for her friend's kids. What do you see?

Ellen

B ▶ **LISTEN.** Where is Ellen?

a. at school   b. at home   c. at a friend's house

C ▶ **LISTEN FOR DETAILS.** Complete the sentences.

1. The boy is in the _____ grade.
   a. fourth   b. fifth   c. sixth

2. The girl is in the _____ grade.
   a. first   b. third   c. fourth

D ▶ **EXPAND.** Listen to the whole conversation. Answer the questions.

1. Who says Terry is friendly?
   a. Ellen   b. Ellen's friend   c. Ken

2. Who calls Terry "Terry the Terrible"?
   a. Ellen   b. Ellen's friend   c. Ken

Listening and Speaking

3 PRONUNCIATION

A ▶ **PRACTICE. Listen. Then listen and repeat.**

Her son is eleven.

He's in the fifth grade.

Where are you?

Linking words together: consonant to vowel

We connect a consonant sound at the end of a word to a vowel sound at the beginning of the next word.

B ▶ **APPLY. Practice saying the sentences. Then listen and repeat.**

1. How old are they?
2. She's in the first grade.

4 CONVERSATION

A ▶ **LISTEN AND READ. Then listen and repeat.**

A: Hi, Ellen. Where are you?
B: I'm at my friend's house. I'm babysitting for her kids.
A: Oh. How old are they?
B: Well, her son is in the fifth grade. I think he's eleven. And her daughter is six. She's in the first grade.

B **WORK TOGETHER. Practice the conversation in Exercise A.**

12 (years old)
6th grade

8 (years old)
3rd grade

C **CREATE. Make new conversations. Use the information in the boxes.**

A: Hi! Where are you?
B: I'm at my friend's house. I'm babysitting for her kids.
A: Oh. How old are they?
B: Well, her son is ▩▩▩▩. He's in the ▩▩▩▩. And her daughter is ▩▩▩▩. She's in the ▩▩▩▩.

14 (years old)
8th grade

13 (years old)
7th grade

D **MAKE CONNECTIONS. Make your own conversations. Talk about children you know.**

A: My sister has two children.
B: Oh, really? How old are they?

7 (years old)
2nd grade

10 (years old)
4th grade

I can give a child's age and grade in school. ▩   I need more practice. ▩

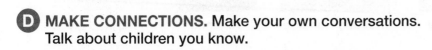

For more practice, go to MyEnglishLab.

Questions with *How old*

Questions with *How old*					
How old	**are**	you?			he?
		they?	**How old**	**is**	she?
		your friend's children?			Terry?

A COMPLETE. Ask about age.

Date of birth:
Jan. 4, 1985

Date of birth:
May 6, 2014

Date of birth:
Oct. 4, 1997

1. **A:** How old ___is___
   Dean's son?
   B: He's _____.

2. **A:** How old _____
   Eric's cousins?
   B: They're _____.

3. **A:** _____ Marco's
   sisters?
   B: _____.

Date of birth:
Aug. 11,1936

Date of birth:
June 2, 2010

Date of birth:
Sept. 30, 2013

You
Date of birth:

4. **A:** _____ Barry's
   grandmother?
   B: _____.

5. **A:** _____ Eva's kids?
   B: Her son _____ and her
   daughter _____.

6. **A:** How old _____ you?
   B: I'd rather not say!

B WORK TOGETHER. Look at these photos of famous people. Guess. How old are they?

Zhang Ziyi

George Clooney

Cristiano Ronaldo

Rihanna

A: How old is Zhang Ziyi?
B: I don't know. I think she's (around) thirty.
A: Oh, no. I think she's (around) forty.

I can ask questions with *How old*. ■   I need more practice. ■

For more practice, go to MyEnglishLab.

Write about a family member

1 STUDY THE MODEL

READ. Answer the questions.

Ana Montes

My Sister

My sister's name is Betta. She's 40 years old. Her birthday is in March. She's tall and thin. She has long hair. She's fun and smart.

1. Who is Betta?
2. How old is she?
3. When is her birthday?
4. What does she look like?
5. What is she like?

2 PLAN YOUR WRITING

WORK TOGETHER. Ask and answer the questions.

1. Who is one of your family members?
2. How old is he/she?
3. When is his/her birthday?
4. What does he/she look like?
5. What is he/she like?

Writing Skill: Use a capital letter for months

Months always begin with a capital letter.
For example:
March

3 WRITE

Now write about a family member. Use the frame, the model, the Writing Skill, and your ideas from Exercise 2 to help you.

My ____'s name is ____. He's/She's ____ years old. His/Her birthday is in ____. He's/She's ____ and ____. He/She has ____ hair. He/She is ____ and ____.

4 CHECK YOUR WRITING

WORK TOGETHER. Read your writing aloud with a partner.

WRITING CHECKLIST

☐ The writing answers the questions in Exercise 2.

☐ Each sentence begins with a capital letter.

☐ The month begins with a capital letter.

☐ Each sentence ends with a period.

I can use a capital letter for months. ■   I need more practice. ■

For more practice, go to MyEnglishLab.

Separate work and home life

1 MEET HANI

Read about one of her workplace skills.

> I can separate work and home life. When I am at work, I think about my work. I don't make personal phone calls at work.

2 HANI'S PROBLEM

READ. Circle *True* or *False*.

Hani is an accountant. She works in a busy office. The office has many rules. One rule is "Work calls only."

Her father lives alone in another city. He calls Hani at work every day, but Hani can't talk on the phone at work.

1. Hani is busy at work.	True	False
2. Hani lives with her father.	True	False
3. Hani's father likes to talk to Hani on the phone.	True	False

3 HANI'S SOLUTION

WORK TOGETHER. Hani separates work and home life.
What is the right thing to do? Explain your answer.

1. Hani answers the phone and talks quietly.
2. Hani doesn't answer the phone. She texts her father at work.
3. Hani calls her father during the break and says, "I can't talk on the phone at work. Please call me at home."
4. Hani says, "_____."

Show what you know!

1. THINK ABOUT IT. How do you separate work and home life? Give examples.

2. WRITE ABOUT IT. Now write your example in your Skills Log.

I don't text friends or family members at work.

I can give an example from my life of separating work and home life. ■

Unit Review: Go back to page 65. Which goals can you check off?

5 Shop, Shop, Shop

PREVIEW

Look at the picture. What do you see?
Where are the people?

UNIT GOALS

- ☐ Name colors and clothes
- ☐ Talk about things you need or want
- ☐ Identify U.S. money
- ☐ Talk about money and prices and read receipts
- ☐ Ask for sizes and colors

- ☐ Return something to a store
- ☐ **Academic skill:** Make inferences
- ☐ **Writing skill:** Use commas between words in a list
- ☐ **Workplace soft skill:** Be professional

Lesson 1

A **PREDICT.** Look at the pictures. What do you see? What are the clothes and colors?

Number 1 is a dress. Number 4 is orange.

B ▶ **LISTEN AND POINT.** Then listen and repeat.

Vocabulary

Colors and clothes

1. a blue dress
2. a green shirt
3. a purple skirt

4. an orange blouse
5. a pink sweater
6. black jeans

7. a red jacket
8. a yellow T-shirt
9. khaki pants

10. gray socks
11. white sneakers
12. brown shoes

C **IDENTIFY.** Look at the pictures and the list of clothes. Which clothes come in pairs? Write the words.

_____pants_____   _____   _____

_____   _____

D **WORK TOGETHER.** Ask and answer questions about the pictures.

A: What's number 12?
B: Shoes.
A: What color are they?
B: Brown. What's number 3?
A: A skirt.
B: What color is it?
A: Purple.

Study Tip

Use an online dictionary

Look up three words about clothes on the Longman Online Dictionary. Listen to and repeat the pronunciation of the words.

Show what you know!

1. **IDENTIFY.** Student A, look around the room. Say what a classmate is wearing. Student B, guess the classmate.

   A: Who's wearing gray pants and a red sweater?
   B: Paul.
   A: Right!
   B: Who's wearing . . . ?

2. **TALK ABOUT IT.** Talk about your clothes.

   A: I'm wearing a green T-shirt, blue jeans, and black sneakers.
   B: And I'm wearing . . .

3. **WRITE ABOUT IT.** Now write a sentence about your clothes.

   I'm wearing _____.

I can name colors and clothes. ☐   I need more practice. ☐

For more practice, go to MyEnglishLab.

Listening and Speaking

Talk about things you need or want

1 BEFORE YOU LISTEN

CHOOSE. Complete the sentences with the words in the box.

wants   needs

She _____ a sweater.   She _____ those shoes.

2 LISTEN

A ▶ **LISTEN. Look at the picture. Listen to the conversation. What's the conversation about?**

a. a birthday gift   **b.** a shirt

Carlos

Meg

B ▶ **LISTEN FOR DETAILS. Read the sentences. Circle *True* or *False*.**

1. Meg's birthday is next week.	True	False
2. Meg's brother needs clothes.	True	False
3. Meg's brother wants clothes.	True	False

C ▶ **EXPAND. Listen to the whole conversation. Complete the sentence.**

Carlos wants a _____.

a.

b.

c.

Listening and Speaking

3 CONVERSATION

A ▶ **LISTEN AND READ.** Then listen and repeat.

A: I need a gift for my brother. It's his birthday next week.
B: How about clothes?
A: Well, he needs clothes, but he wants a backpack!

B **WORK TOGETHER.** Practice the conversation in Exercise A.

C **CREATE.** Make new conversations.
Use the information in the boxes.

A: I need a gift for my _____.

It's _____ birthday next
      (his / her)
week.

B: How about clothes?

A: Well, _____ needs
       (he / she)

clothes, but _____
        (he / she)

wants _____!

friend

mother

father

a wallet

a handbag

a watch

D **MAKE CONNECTIONS.** Make your own conversations.
Use different people and gifts.

A: I need a gift for my friend. It's her birthday tomorrow.
B: How about a handbag?
A: That's a good idea.

I can talk about things I need or want. ■   I need more practice. ■

For more practice, go to MyEnglishLab.

Grammar

Simple present affirmative

Simple present affirmative						
I	**need**		He	**needs**	
You	**want**	new clothes.	She	**wants**	new clothes.
They	**have**		Bob	**has**	

Grammar Watch

- With **he**, **she**, or **it**, the simple present verb ends in **-s**.
- Remember: The verb **have** is irregular. Use **has** with *he*, *she*, or *it*.

A IDENTIFY. Cross out the incorrect words.

1. Mr. Garcia ~~have~~ / **has** an orange shirt.
   He **want** / **wants** a green shirt.

2. Amy and Jeff **have** / **has** black sneakers.
   I **want** / **wants** black sneakers, too.

3. Our teacher **need** / **needs** a new jacket.
   He **need** / **needs** new pants, too.

B COMPLETE. Use the verbs in parentheses.

1. My sister ___needs___ a skirt.
   (need)
   She _____ a pink skirt.
   (want)

2. My brothers _____ new shoes.
   (have)
   Now they _____ new socks.
   (need)

3. Allen _____ brown jeans.
   (have)
   We _____ brown jeans, too.
   (want)

4. You _____ a nice new wallet.
   (have)
   I _____ a new wallet, too.
   (want)

Grammar

C **WORK TOGETHER. Look at the picture. What do they need? What do they want? There is more than one correct answer.**

A: What does he need?
B: He needs new shoes. He also needs . . .
A: Yes. But he really wants . . .

D **WRITE. Complete the sentences.**

He needs _____
_____
_____ .

He wants _____
_____
_____ .

She needs _____
_____
_____ .

She wants _____
_____
_____ .

Show what you know!

1. THINK ABOUT IT. Complete the chart.

2. TALK ABOUT IT. Talk about your clothes.

A: I have a blue T-shirt. I need a white T-shirt, and I want a blue jacket.
B: I have a blue T-shirt, too, and I want blue pants.

Clothes I have	Clothes I need	Clothes I want

3. WRITE ABOUT IT. Now write three sentences about your partner. What does he or she have, need, and want?

My partner has blue pants. She needs _____. She _____.

I can use the simple present affirmative. ■   I need more practice. ■

For more practice, go to MyEnglishLab.

Workplace, Life, and Community Skills

Talk about money and prices and read receipts

1 IDENTIFY U.S. MONEY

A **MAKE CONNECTIONS.** Where do you shop for clothes? Do you pay with cash?

B ▶ **LISTEN AND POINT.** Then listen and repeat.

1. one dollar ($1.00)

2. five dollars ($5.00)

3. ten dollars ($10.00)

4. twenty dollars ($20.00)

C ▶ **LISTEN AND POINT.** Then listen and repeat.

1. a penny (1¢)　**2.** a nickel (5¢)　**3.** a dime (10¢)　**4.** a quarter (25¢)

D **CALCULATE.** Count the money. Write the amount.

1. _____65¢_____

2. _____

3. _____

4. _____

E ▶ **SELF-ASSESS.** Listen and check your answers. Then listen and repeat.

| I can identify U.S. money. ☐ | I need more practice. ☐ |

For more practice, go to MyEnglishLab.

Workplace, Life, and Community Skills

2 TALK ABOUT PRICES

A ▶ **LISTEN AND READ.** Then listen and repeat.

Customer:	Excuse me. How much is this **skirt**?
Assistant:	It's **$15.99**.
Customer:	And how much are these **jeans**?
Assistant:	They're **$17.99**.

B ▶ **LISTEN.** Write the prices.

1.    2.    3.    4.

C **ROLE-PLAY.** Ask about prices. Use the pictures in Exercise 2B.

D **INTERPRET.** Look at the receipt. Answer the questions.

1. What is the date on the receipt?

   Write it in words. _____

2. How much are the jeans? _____

3. How much is the tax? _____

4. How much are the clothes before tax? _____

5. How much are the clothes after tax? _____

6. How much is the change? _____

E GO ONLINE. Find the tax rate in your city and calculate the total on the receipt in Exercise 2D.

_____

```
            IMAGINE
    Los Angeles, CA 90027
      (213) 555-6111

    08-06-18
                        2:25 P.M.

    WOMEN'S JEANS
    WOMEN'S SWEATERS        18.99
    WOMEN'S T-SHIRTS        13.99
                            7.99
    SUBTOTAL
    TAX 8% ON 40.97         40.97
                            3.28
    TOTAL
                            44.25
    CASH AMOUNT PAID
    CHANGE DUE              45.00
                            .75
    Please keep receipt for
    returns.
    Thank you for shopping
    at IMAGINE.
```

I can talk about money and prices and read receipts. ■	I need more practice. ■

For more practice, go to MyEnglishLab.

Lesson 5

Ask for sizes and colors

1 BEFORE YOU LISTEN

A **LABEL.** Look at the pictures. Write the sizes under the shirts.

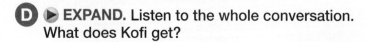

| extra large | extra small | medium | large | small |

_____ _____ _____ _____ _____

B **IDENTIFY.** Some clothes come in sizes with letters, and some clothes come in sizes with numbers. Check (✓) the clothes that come in sizes with numbers.

☐ shoes ☐ socks ☐ sweaters ☐ jeans ☐ T-shirts

2 LISTEN

A **PREDICT.** Look at the picture. Where are they? What do you see?

B ▶ **LISTEN.** Complete the sentence.

Kofi wants clothes for his _____.
a. mother **b.** sister **c.** wife

C ▶ **LISTEN FOR DETAILS.** Complete the sentences.

1. Kofi wants a _____.
   a. sweater **b.** blouse **c.** jacket

2. His sister needs a _____.
   a. small **b.** medium **c.** large

D ▶ **EXPAND.** Listen to the whole conversation. What does Kofi get?

a. **b.** **c.**

Kofi

Listening and Speaking

3 PRONUNCIATION

A ▶ **PRACTICE. Listen. Then listen and repeat.**

Do you have this sweater in a ~~large~~?

It's a gift for my ~~sister~~.

I have a ~~jacket~~.

How much is this ~~skirt~~?

B ▶ **APPLY. Listen. Put a dot (•) on the word with the most stress.**

1. Do you like ~~green~~?

2. Do you need a small?

3. He wants a watch.

4. Does she like blue?

5. Here you go.

6. I'm sorry.

4 CONVERSATION

A ▶ **LISTEN AND READ. Then listen and repeat.**

A: Do you have this sweater in a large?
B: No, I'm sorry. We don't.
A: Too bad. It's for my sister, and she needs a large.

B **WORK TOGETHER. Practice the conversation in Exercise A.**

C **CREATE. Make new conversations. Use the pictures.**

A: Do you have this ▭▭▭▭ in a(n) ▭▭▭▭?
B: No, I'm sorry. We don't.
A: Too bad. It's for my sister, and she needs a(n) ▭▭▭▭.

D **ROLE-PLAY. Make your own conversations. Use different clothes and sizes.**

I can ask for sizes and colors. ▢   I need more practice. ▢

For more practice, go to MyEnglishLab.

Grammar

Simple present: *Yes/no* questions and short answers

Simple present: *Yes/no* questions and short answers								
Do	I we you they	**need** new shoes?	**Yes,**	you we I they	**do.**	**No,**	you we I they	**don't.**
Does	he she			he she	**does.**		he she	**doesn't.**

A MATCH.

1. Do you have this shirt in gray? __d__
2. Does your son like his new jeans? ____
3. Does Ms. Cho have a backpack? ____
4. Do your sisters want new clothes? ____

    a. Yes, he does.
    b. No, she doesn't.
    c. Yes, they do.
    d. Yes, we do.

> ### Grammar Watch
>
> Use the base form of the verb in questions with *do* or *does*. In the chart, *need* is the base form.
>
> **Contractions**
> **don't** = do not
> **doesn't** = does not

B COMPLETE. Use *do, does, don't,* or *doesn't*.

1. **A:** _____Do_____ you have this jacket in blue?
   B: Yes, we _____do_____. Here you go.

2. **A:** _____ Cindy want a new watch?
   B: No, she _____. She likes her old watch.

3. **A:** _____ you need these jeans in a size 14?
   B: No, I _____. I need a size 12.

4. **A:** _____ you have this shirt in an extra small?
   B: No, we _____. But we have it in a small.

5. **A:** _____ the customer like that green sweater?
   B: No, he _____. He likes the blue sweater.

C WORK TOGETHER. Practice the conversations in Exercise B.

Grammar

D **WRITE.** Complete the questions. Use *do* or *does* and the verbs in parentheses. Then look at the pictures. Answer the questions.

1. **A:** _____Does_____ Ben _____have_____ an extra-large white T-shirt?
   (have)

   B: Yes, he does. _____

2. **A:** _____ Ben and Tina _____ blue shirts?
   (have)

   B: _____

3. **A:** _____ Tina _____ a large red jacket?
   (need)

   B: _____

4. **A:** _____ Ben and Tina _____ red sweaters?
   (need)

   B: _____

5. **A:** _____ Tina _____ a small green sweater?
   (have)

   B: _____

6. **A:** _____ Ben and Tina _____ blue jeans.
   (have)

   B: _____

BEN'S CLOTHES

TINA'S CLOTHES

Show what you know!

1. **TALK ABOUT IT.** Ask and answer *yes/no* questions. Use the words in the box.

like / red ties	have / a favorite color
need / new clothes	want / new jeans

A: Do you like red ties?
B: Yes, I do. Do you like red ties?
A: No, I don't.

2. **WRITE ABOUT IT.** Now write a new question to ask about a classmate's clothes.

Does _____?

I can ask and answer *yes/no* questions in the simple present. ☐   I need more practice. ☐

Read about credit cards and debit cards

1 BEFORE YOU READ

A **LABEL.** Write the vocabulary words under the pictures.

cash	a credit card bill	plastic

1. _____

2. _____

3. _____

B **MAKE CONNECTIONS.** When you go to the store, how do you pay for things? What are some other ways to pay?

2 READ

▶ Listen and read.

> **Academic Skill: Make inferences**
>
> You make inferences about things the writer is thinking but doesn't say. For example, this writer says, "That is expensive!" You can infer that the writer thinks, "Paying interest is a bad idea."

SHOPPING WITHOUT CASH

Do you have cash in your wallet? Maybe you do, and maybe you don't. Some people almost never use cash.

In 2011, 36% of Americans used cash for shopping most or all of the time. Today, that number is down. People are using other ways to pay. The most common ways are debit cards and credit cards.

5 Let's say you are buying a new jacket at a store. You use a debit card. That card is connected to your account at a bank. When you use the card, the money comes out of your account that same day.

Let's say you buy the jacket with a credit card instead. A credit card lets you borrow money from the credit card company. Later, the company sends you a bill. You need to pay the money back. It is better to pay it all back on time. After the payment due date, the company charges interest on the
10 money. That is expensive!

Some people never use credit cards. They like using cash. In the U.S., people often spend more money when they shop with a credit card. Why? A credit card is a piece of plastic. Maybe it doesn't seem like real money.

Most Americans Have Credit Cards

An average of 3.7 credit cards, **71%**

No credit cards, **29%**

Source: Gallup

Reading

3 CLOSE READING

A **CITE EVIDENCE. Complete the sentences. Where is the information? Write the line number.**

Lines

1. Debit cards and credit cards are _____ in the U.S.
   a. common   **b.** new   **c.** hard to find   _____

2. When you use a debit card in a store, you _____.
   a. borrow money   **b.** use money you   **c.** pay more money   _____
   from your bank   have in the bank

3. When you use _____, sometimes you need to pay interest.
   a. a credit card   **b.** a debit card   **c.** cash   _____

4. Credit card companies charge you interest when you pay your bill _____.
   a. before the payment **b.** on time   **c.** late   _____
   due date

5. When Americans shop with credit cards, not cash, they often _____.
   a. get better prices   **b.** don't pay tax   **c.** spend more money   _____

B **INTERPRET. Complete the sentences about the pie chart.**

1. The pie chart shows that most Americans have _____.
   a. cash   **b.** debit cards   **c.** credit cards

2. _____ of Americans don't have a credit card.
   a. 19%   **b.** 29%   **c.** 69%

3. An American with credit cards usually has _____.
   a. 1 card   **b.** 3 or 4 cards   **c.** 71 cards

4 SUMMARIZE

Complete the summary with the words in the box.

bank account	cash	credit card	due date	interest

Many Americans don't shop with (1) _____. They often use debit cards or credit

cards. A debit card takes money out of your (2) _____. But when you use

a (3) _____, you are borrowing money. Pay it back by the payment

(4) _____ , or you will need to pay (5) _____.

Show what you know!

1. **TALK ABOUT IT. Ask your partner, "Do you like to shop with cash? Debit cards? Credit cards?" Ask why or why not.**

2. **WRITE ABOUT IT. Now write about how you like to pay when you shop and why.**

   I (like/don't like) to shop with _____ because _____.

I can make inferences. ■   I need more practice. ■

To read more, go to MyEnglishLab.

1 BEFORE YOU LISTEN

CHOOSE. Look at the pictures. Write the sentence under the correct picture.

The zipper doesn't work.   ~~It doesn't look good.~~   They don't fit.   They don't match.

Reasons People Return Clothes

a. _It doesn't look good._
I don't like it.

b. _____
They're too big.

c. _____
The colors don't look good together.

d. _____
It's broken.

2 LISTEN

A ▶ **LISTEN.** Two customers are talking to a sales assistant. Why are they at the store?

They want to _____ something.
a. buy
b. return

B ▶ **LISTEN FOR DETAILS.** Complete the sentences.

1. The _____ pants are the wrong size.
   a. woman's
   b. man's

2. You need a _____ to get your money back at this store.
   a. credit card
   b. receipt

a receipt

a credit card

3 CONVERSATION

A **PREDICT.** Look at the picture. A customer is returning a shirt. What is she looking for?

a. her money   **b.** her receipt   **c.** her credit card

B ▶ **LISTEN AND READ.** Then listen and repeat.

Assistant: May I help you?
Customer: Yes. I need to return this shirt.
Assistant: OK. What's the problem?
Customer: It doesn't fit.
Assistant: Do you have your receipt?
Customer: Yes, I do.

C **WORK TOGETHER.** Practice the conversation in Exercise B.

D **CREATE.** Make new conversations. Use the information in the boxes.

Assistant: May I help you?
Customer: Yes. I need to return
　　　　　　　 .

Assistant: OK. What's the problem?
Customer: .
Assistant: Do you have your receipt?
Customer: Yes, I do.

E **ROLE-PLAY.** Make your own conversations. Use different clothes and problems.

these shoes
They're too small.

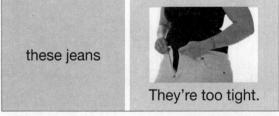

these jeans
They're too tight.

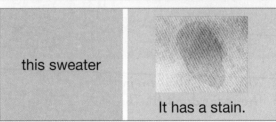

this sweater
It has a stain.

I can return something to a store. ■   I need more practice. ■

For more practice, go to MyEnglishLab.

9

Grammar

Simple present negative

Simple present negative				
I You We They	**don't**	**like**	this color.	
He She The customer			**doesn't**	**like**	this color.

A **IDENTIFY.** Cross out the incorrect words.

1. The zipper on my jacket ~~don't~~ / **doesn't** work.
2. Your new jeans **don't** / **doesn't** fit.
3. I **don't** / **doesn't** have my receipt.
4. The customers **don't** / **doesn't** like their new shoes.
5. Ms. Wong **don't** / **doesn't** like her new skirt.
6. The manager **don't** / **doesn't** need a tie.

> ### Grammar Watch
>
> Use the base form of the verb after *don't* or *doesn't*.

B **WORK TOGETHER.** Look at the picture. Find the problems. Tell your partner. There is more than one correct answer.

A: What's the problem in A?
B: The jeans don't fit. They're too big.

C **WRITE.** Write three problems from Exercise B.

I can make negative statements in the simple present. ■   I need more practice. ■

For more practice, go to MyEnglishLab.

Lesson 10

Write about clothes

1 STUDY THE MODEL

READ. Answer the questions.

> Sue Wong
> My Clothes
>
> At work, I wear a black skirt, a white blouse, and black shoes. At home, I wear jeans, a T-shirt, and sneakers. At school, I wear nice pants, a blouse, and a sweater.

1. What does Sue wear at work?
2. What does Sue wear at home?
3. What does Sue wear at school?

2 PLAN YOUR WRITING

WORK TOGETHER. Ask and answer the questions.

1. What do you wear at work?
2. What do you wear at home?
3. What do you wear at school?

Writing Skill: Use commas in a list

Use commas between words in a list. For example:

I wear a black skirt, a white blouse, and black shoes.

3 WRITE

Now write about the clothes you wear. Use the frame, the model, the Writing Skill, and your ideas from Exercise 2 to help you.

At work, I wear _____, _____, and _____.
At home, I wear _____, _____, and _____. At school, I wear _____, _____, and _____.

4 CHECK YOUR WRITING

WORK TOGETHER. Read your writing aloud with a partner.

WRITING CHECKLIST

☐ The writing answers the questions in Exercise 2.

☐ Each sentence begins with a capital letter.

☐ There are commas between words in a list.

☐ Each sentence ends with a period.

I can use commas between words in a list. ■   I need more practice. ■

For more practice, go to MyEnglishLab.

Lesson 11

Be professional

1 MEET LOC

Read about one of his workplace skills.

> I'm professional. For example, I take care of customers. When a customer is angry, I'm calm.

2 LOC'S PROBLEM

READ. Circle *True* or *False*.

Loc works at a store. He is a cashier. He helps customers every day. He wants the customers to be happy.

One day, there are many customers. They are waiting in line to check out. One customer is angry. The customer says, "Why is there only one cashier? I don't want to wait!"

1.	Loc is a manager at a store.	True	False
2.	Two customers are waiting in line.	True	False
3.	A customer is angry.	True	False

3 LOC'S SOLUTION

A **WORK TOGETHER.** Loc is professional. What is the professional thing to do? Explain your answer.

1. Loc asks the customer, "Do you want to talk to the manager?"
2. Loc tells the customer, "I'm sorry. We're very busy now. I'll be with you in a minute."
3. Loc tells the customer, "If you can't wait, you can come back later."
4. Loc says, "_____."

B **ROLE-PLAY.** Look at your answers to 3A. Role-play Loc's conversation.

Show what you know!

1. **THINK ABOUT IT.** How are you professional at work? Give examples.

2. **WRITE ABOUT IT.** Now write your example in your Skills Log.

   I say "Please" and "Thank you" at work.

3. **PRESENT IT.** Give a short presentation to show how you are professional.

I can give an example from my life of being professional. ▪

Unit Review: Go back to page 85. Which goals can you check off?

6 Home, Sweet Home

PREVIEW

Look at the picture. Where are the people?
Why are they there?

UNIT GOALS

- [ ] Name the rooms and things in a home
- [ ] Talk about a house for rent
- [ ] Ask about an apartment for rent
- [ ] Read, write, and give addresses
- [ ] Read housing ads

- [ ] Give directions
- [ ] **Academic skill:** Read again and again to understand a reading better
- [ ] **Writing skill:** Use details in your writing
- [ ] **Workplace soft skill:** Find information

Vocabulary

Rooms and things in a home

A **PREDICT.** Look at the pictures. What do you see? What are the rooms and things in a home?

D is a bedroom.
Number 14 is a bathtub.

B ▶ **LISTEN AND POINT.** Then listen and repeat.

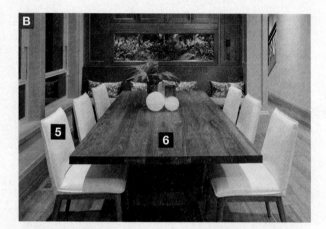

Vocabulary

Rooms and things in a home

A. kitchen	**B. dining room**	**C. living room**	**D. bedroom**	**E. bathroom**
1. refrigerator	5. chair	7. lamp	10. closet	13. shower
2. microwave	6. table	8. sofa	11. bed	14. bathtub
3. stove		9. coffee table	12. dresser	15. toilet
4. sink				

C **GIVE EXAMPLES.** Student A, look at the pictures on page 106. Name the things in a room. Student B, guess the room.

A: A table and chairs.
B: Is it the living room?
A: No.
B: Is it the dining room?
A: Yes.

D **DRAW A PICTURE.** Student A, look at the pictures and the list of things in a home. Draw a picture of one thing. Students B and C, guess.

B: A dresser.
A: No.
C: A refrigerator.
A: Right.

> **Study Tip**
>
> **Use sticky notes**
> Write words on sticky notes. Put the notes on the things in your home. Look at the notes and say the words.

Show what you know!

1. **THINK ABOUT IT.** Think about your dream home. Write a list of rooms.

> My dream home
> two bathrooms
> a living room
> a dining room

2. **TALK ABOUT IT.** Talk about your dream home.

My dream home has two bathrooms. It has a living room, a dining room, a kitchen, and three bedrooms.

3. **WRITE ABOUT IT.** Now write a sentence about your dream home.

My dream home has _____.

I can name the rooms and things in a home. ■   I need more practice. ■

For more practice, go to MyEnglishLab.

1 BEFORE YOU LISTEN

CHOOSE. Write the words under the pictures.

new	old

a _new_ kitchen   an _____ kitchen

large	small

a _____ bathroom   a _____ bathroom

dark	sunny

a _____ bedroom   a _____ bedroom

expensive	inexpensive

House for Rent!
$3,000/month
3-BR, 2 BA, Large
kitchen, new apps

House for Rent!
$800/month
1-BR, 1 BA, small
kitchen, a/c, heat

an _____ house   an _____ house

2 LISTEN

A **PREDICT.** Look at the picture. Dan and Emily are looking at an ad for a house. What are they talking about?

Dan

Emily

B ▶ **LISTEN.** Complete the sentence.

Dan says the house looks _____.

a. inexpensive   **b.** great   **c.** large

C ▶ **LISTEN FOR DETAILS.** Complete the sentence.

The house has two bedrooms and a _____.

a. large kitchen   **b.** dining room

D ▶ **EXPAND.** Listen to the whole conversation. What's wrong with the house?

It's _____.

a. old   **b.** very expensive   **c.** not in the U.S.

Listening and Speaking

3 CONVERSATION

A ▶ **LISTEN AND READ. Then listen and repeat.**

A: Oh, wow! This house looks great!
B: Really?
A: Yes. There are two bedrooms and a large kitchen.
B: What about a dining room?
A: Well, no. There's no dining room.

B **WORK TOGETHER. Practice the conversation in Exercise A.**

C **CREATE. Make new conversations. Use the information in the boxes.**

A: Oh, wow! This house looks great!
B: Really?
A: Yes. There are two bedrooms and a ▮▮▮▮▮▮▮▮▮▮▮.
B: What about a ▮▮▮▮▮▮▮▮▮▮?
A: Well, no. There's no ▮▮▮▮▮▮▮▮▮.

new bathroom

garage

sunny kitchen

laundry room

nice living room

yard

D **ROLE-PLAY. Make your own conversations about a home.**

I can talk about a house for rent. ■   I need more practice. ■

For more practice, go to MyEnglishLab.

Grammar

There is/There are

There is/There are						Grammar Watch
There is **There's**	a one	bathroom.	**There is** **There's**	no	dining room.	**Contraction** ***There's*** = *There is*
There are	two	bedrooms.	**There are**		closets.	

A **INTERPRET.** Read the apartment ad. Cirlce *True* or *False*. Correct the false sentences.

○ ○ ○

FOR RENT

Large one-bedroom apartment with dining room, new bathroom, and new kitchen. Five closets! Garage. $700/month.

email Tom at tom@apartments4rent.com

There's one bedroom.

1. ~~There are two bedrooms.~~   True   (False)

2. There's one bathroom.   True   False

3. There's no dining room.   True   False

4. There's a new kitchen.   True   False

5. There's one closet.   True   False

6. There's no garage.   True   False

B **COMPLETE.** Look at the picture on page 111. Complete the conversation. Use the words in the box. Use some words more than once.

there's a	there are two	there's no

A: So, tell me about your new house!

B: Well, ____*there are two*____ bedrooms.
                    1.

A: Nice! What about bathrooms?

B: _____ bathrooms.
                2.

A: Great. And a dining room?

B: _____ dining room, but _____ table and chairs in the
            3.   **4.**

   kitchen. _____ large yard, too. We love it!
                        5.

Grammar

C **WRITE.** Look at the picture of the house. What's in each room? What's *not* in each room? Write sentences. Use *there is*, *there are*, *there's no*, and *there are no*.

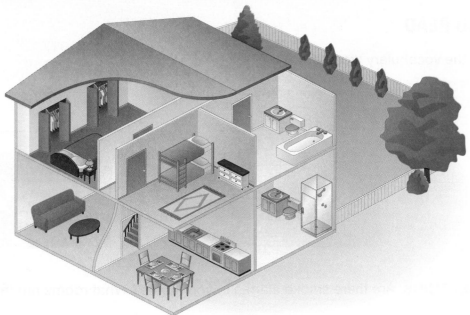

In the parents' bedroom, there's a bed, a table, and a lamp. There are no pictures.

In the children's bedroom, _____

In the upstairs bathroom, _____

In the living room, _____

In the kitchen, _____

In the downstairs bathroom, _____

Show what you know!

1. TALK ABOUT IT. Talk about things in the rooms of your home.

A: In my bedroom, there's a bed and a dresser.
B: What about closets?
A: No, there are no closets.
C: In my bathroom . . .

2. WRITE ABOUT IT. Now write two sentences about a room in your home.

In my bedroom, there is a _____.
There is no _____.

I can use *there is/there are*. ■   I need more practice. ■

For more practice, go to MyEnglishLab.

Read about smoke alarms

1 BEFORE YOU READ

A **LABEL.** Write the vocabulary words from the box on the lines.

| the ceiling | a landlord | a smoke alarm | renters |

3. _____

2. _____

4. _____

1. _____

B **MAKE CONNECTIONS.** Are there smoke alarms in your home? What rooms are they in?

2 READ

▶ Listen and read.

Academic Skill: Read again and again

Read the article. Then read it again and again. Every time you read it, you learn more. One time is not enough.

Smoke Alarms

Home fires are dangerous. Every year in the U.S., about 2,500 people die from home fires. Smoke alarms save lives. They make a loud noise when a fire starts. Smoke alarms give people time to leave their homes before a fire gets too big.

5 *Which parts of the home need smoke alarms?*
Every bedroom needs a smoke alarm. Every floor of a home needs a smoke alarm. When there is no bedroom on a floor, the living room needs a smoke alarm. It is good to have a smoke alarm near the stairs, too. Smoke alarms go on or near the ceiling.

10 *Which parts of the home do not need smoke alarms?*
Most kitchens do not need smoke alarms. A smoke alarm should not be close to the stove or microwave. Then it will go off when someone cooks! A smoke alarm should never be near a window or door.

15 *Who buys the smoke alarms?*
People who own a home need to buy smoke alarms. But renters do not need to buy them. The law says their landlord needs to put smoke alarms in their home to make sure they are safe.

A smoke alarm going off

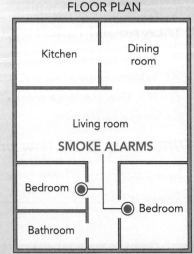

FLOOR PLAN

Kitchen | Dining room

Living room

SMOKE ALARMS

Bedroom ⦿

⦿ Bedroom

Bathroom

3 CLOSE READING

CITE EVIDENCE. Answer the questions. Where is the information? Write the line numbers.

Lines

1. How do smoke alarms help people?
   a. They stop fires from starting.
   b. They pour water on fires.
   c. They let people know when a fire starts. _____

2. What's a good place for a smoke alarm?
   a. near a door
   b. near stairs
   c. near a window _____

3. Which place needs a smoke alarm?
   a. the kitchen
   b. the bedroom
   c. the yard _____

4. What can make the smoke alarm go off?
   a. a refrigerator
   b. a stove
   c. a sink _____

5. Who needs to buy smoke alarms for an apartment or a house?
   a. the person who owns it
   b. the person who rents it
   c. any person with children _____

4 SUMMARIZE

Complete the summary with the words in the box.

bedroom	fire	landlords	smoke alarms

Every home needs (1) _____. A smoke alarm can save your life when there is a
(2) _____. There needs to be a smoke alarm in every (3) _____ of a
house or apartment. Renters do not need to buy them. All (4) _____ need to put
them in the right places in their buildings.

Show what you know!

1. **DRAW A PICTURE.** Draw a floor plan of your home. Draw your smoke alarms on the plan.

2. **TALK ABOUT IT.** Show your plan to your partner. Are the smoke alarms in good places? Explain.

3. **WRITE ABOUT IT.** Now write about your floor plan.

   One smoke alarm is in the _____. *Another smoke alarm is in the*
   _____.

I can read again and again to understand a reading better. ■   I need more practice. ■

To read more, go to MyEnglishLab.

Lesson 5

Ask about an apartment for rent

1 BEFORE YOU LISTEN

IDENTIFY. Look at the pictures. Complete the sentences with the words from the box. You will not use every word.

Studio apartments for rent

furnished   unfurnished

appliances	furnished	unfurnished

1. The _____ room has a sofa, two armchairs, and a coffee table.

2. The two kitchen areas have new _____.

2 LISTEN

A **PREDICT.** Look at the picture. Amy and Lei are talking to a building manager. What are they talking about?

B ▶ **LISTEN.** Complete the sentence.

There's a _____ apartment for rent.
a. one-bedroom   **b.** two-bedroom

C ▶ **LISTEN FOR DETAILS.** Cross out the incorrect words.

1. The apartment is on the **second / seventh** floor.

2. The apartment has **beds / a dresser**.

3. The apartment has a **stove / refrigerator**.

D ▶ **EXPAND.** Listen to the whole conversation. Complete the sentences.

1. Amy _____ interested in the apartment.
   a. is   **b.** is not

2. Lei _____ interested in the apartment.
   a. is   **b.** is not

Listening and Speaking

3 PRONUNCIATION

A ▶ **PRACTICE. Listen. Then listen and repeat.**

floor lamp   There's a floor lamp.

dining room   It's in the dining room.

Stress in compound nouns

In two-word nouns, the first word is stressed.

B ▶ **APPLY. Listen to the sentences. Mark (•) the stress.**

1. There's a <u>coffee table</u>.

2. There are two <u>desk lamps</u>.

3. There's a <u>smoke alarm</u>.

4. It's in the <u>living room</u>.

4 CONVERSATION

A ▶ **LISTEN AND READ. Then listen and repeat.**

A: Excuse me. Is there an apartment for rent in this building?
B: Yes, there is. There's a one-bedroom apartment on the second floor.
A: Oh, great. Is it furnished?
B: Well, yes and no. There's a dresser, but no beds.
A: Oh. Well, are there appliances?
B: Uh, yes and no. There's a stove, but no refrigerator.

B **WORK TOGETHER. Practice the conversation in Exercise A.**

C **CREATE. Make new conversations. Use the words in the boxes.**

A: Excuse me. Is there an apartment for rent in this building?
B: Yes, there is. There's a _____ apartment on the second floor.
A: Oh, great. Is it furnished?
B: Well, yes and no. There's a _____, but no _____.

studio	sofa	coffee table
two-bedroom	desk	lamp
three-bedroom	table	chairs

D **ROLE-PLAY. Make your own conversations. Student A, you are looking for an apartment. Student B, you are the building manager.**

I can ask about an apartment for rent. ■   I need more practice. ■

For more practice, go to MyEnglishLab.

Is there/Are there

Is there/Are there						
Is there	a table?	Yes,	there is.	No,	there isn't.
Are there	lamps?		there are.		there aren't.

A **IDENTIFY. Cross out the incorrect words.**

1. **A:** **Is there / ~~Are there~~** a bathtub in the bathroom?
   B: No, **there is / there isn't**. There's a shower.

2. **A:** **Is there / Are there** closets in the bedrooms?
   B: Yes, **there is / there are**. There's a closet in each bedroom.

3. **A:** **Is there / Are there** table lamps in the living room?
   B: No, **there are / there aren't**. There are floor lamps.

4. **A:** **Is there / Are there** a coffee table in the living room?
   B: Yes, **there is / there isn't**. There's a small coffee table and a sofa.

5. **A:** **Is there / Are there** a dining room in the apartment?
   B: No, **there isn't / there aren't**.

6. **A:** **Is there / Are there** a sunny kitchen?
   B: Yes, **there is / there are**. The kitchen is very sunny.

7. **A:** **Is there / Are there** a table in the kitchen?
   B: Yes, **there is / there are**. There's a table and four chairs.

B ▶ **SELF-ASSESS. Listen and check your answers.**

C **WORK TOGETHER. Practice the conversations in Exercise A.**

Grammar

D **WRITE. Make questions. Then look at the picture and write short answers.**

1. there / two / are / tables
   A: _Are there two tables?_
   B: _Yes, there are._

2. lamps / are / on the tables / there
   A: _____
   B: _____

3. a sofa / in the room / there / is
   A: _____
   B: _____

4. book / on the sofa / is / there / a
   A: _____
   B: _____

5. pictures / there / are / in the room
   A: _____
   B: _____

Show what you know!

1. **THINK ABOUT IT.** Write three questions about your partner's home.
   Use *Is there* and *Are there*.

   Is there a lamp in your living room?
   _____
   _____
   _____

2. **TALK ABOUT IT.** Ask your questions. Answer your partner's questions.

   A: _Is there a lamp in your living room?_
   B: _Yes, there is. There's a lamp near the sofa._

3. **WRITE ABOUT IT.** Now write about your partner's home.

   There's a lamp near the sofa in Ed's living room.
   _____
   _____

I can ask and answer questions with *Is there* and *Are there*. ☐   I need more practice. ☐

For more practice, go to MyEnglishLab.

7 Workplace, Life, and Community Skills

Read addresses and housing ads

1 SAY ADDRESSES

A ▶ **LISTEN AND READ.** Then listen and repeat.

- ★ 6103 Lake Drive, Apartment 27
- ★ 98 East High Street
- ★ 45720 Foothill Road
- ★ 3095 Sunset Boulevard
- ★ 1463 2nd Avenue, Apartment 10
- ★ 852 Mission Street, Apartment 903

B **WORK TOGETHER.** Ask about addresses. Use the addresses in Exercise 1A.

A: What's the address, please?
B: It's 6103 Lake Drive, Apartment 27.

2 WRITE ADDRESSES

A **LOCATE.** Find the words in Exercise 1A for each abbreviation below.

1. St. _Street_   **3.** Dr. _____   **5.** Blvd. _____

2. Ave. _____   **4.** Rd. _____   **6.** Apt. _____

B **USE ABBREVIATIONS.** Write the addresses in Exercise 1A with abbreviations.

1. _____   **4.** _____

2. _____   **5.** _____

3. _____   **6.** _____

C **WORK TOGETHER.** Ask three classmates for an address in their neighborhood. Write the addresses. Use abbreviations.

1451 Pine St., Apt. 3

A: What's the address?
B: It's 1451 Pine Street, Apartment 3.

D **GO ONLINE.** Find the address of a home for rent in or near your neighborhood.

I can read, write, and give addresses. ■   I need more practice. ■

3 READ HOUSING ADS

A LABEL. Write the words under the pictures.

air conditioning   cable   heat   Internet   parking   pets

1. _____   2. _____   3. _____

4. _____   5. _____   6. _____

B INTERPRET. Read the housing ads. Answer the questions.

A

New 3 bedroom 2 bathroom apartment
Air conditioning and heat included. In unit laundry. High speed internet. Pets. 2 parking spaces.

● **$3,000**/mo

B

Large 3 bedroom 1 bathroom apartment
Large closets. Laundry in the building. Cable and Internet ready. No pets. Street parking.

● **$2,000**/mo

Which apartment . . .

1. has two bathrooms? ____
2. has good closets? ____
3. has air conditioning? ____
4. is $2,000 a month? ____

5. has laundry in the apartment? ____
6. has no parking? ____
7. has cable? ____
8. is pet friendly? ____

C TALK ABOUT IT. Which apartment do you like?

A: Which apartment do you like?
B: I like A.
A: Why?
B: It is new. It has two bathrooms.

D PRESENT. Tell your class which apartment your partner likes and why.

I can read housing ads. ■   I need more practice. ■

For more practice, go to MyEnglishLab.

Lesson 8

Give directions

1 BEFORE YOU LISTEN

A **MAKE CONNECTIONS.** How do you get directions to a store?
Do you use a GPS, call the store, or look at a map?

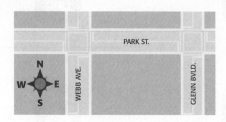

a. I use a GPS.   **b.** I call the store.   **c.** I look at a map.

B **LOCATE.** Look at the map in Exercise A. Point to North, South, East, and West.

2 LISTEN

A ▶ **LISTEN.** A couple wants to go to Joe's
Furniture Store. What are they talking about?

a. the prices at Joe's
b. the directions to Joe's
c. the furniture at Joe's

B ▶ **LISTEN FOR DETAILS.** Complete the
directions to Joe's Furniture Store.

1. Go _____ on Route 1.
   a. north   **b.** south

2. Turn _____ on Fifth Avenue.
   a. right   **b.** left

3. Continue for one _____.
   a. block   **b.** mile

4. It's _____ a park.
   a. across from   **b.** next to

C ▶ **EXPAND.** Listen to the whole conversation. Complete the sentence.

Joe's Furniture Store is _____.
a. closed on Sundays
b. open on Sundays until 5:00
c. open on Sundays until 7:00

3 CONVERSATION

A ▶ **LISTEN AND READ. Then listen and repeat.**

A: How do we get to Joe's Furniture Store?
B: Let me check on my phone. OK. First, go north on Route 1 for three miles.
A: North?
B: Uh-huh. Then turn left on Fifth Avenue. Continue for one block. It's on the left, across from a park.
A: That sounds easy!

B **WORK TOGETHER. Practice the conversation in Exercise A.**

C **CREATE. Make new conversations. Use the words in the boxes.**

A: How do we get to
_____ ?

B: Let me check on my phone.
OK. First, go _____
on Route 1 for three miles.

A: _____ ?

B: Uh-huh. Then turn left on Fifth
Avenue. Continue for one block.
It's on the left, across from a
_____ .

A: That sounds easy!

Sam's Appliances	south	computer store
Ali's Air Conditioners	east	school
Ken's Kitchen	west	hospital

D **MAKE CONNECTIONS. Make your own conversations. Ask for directions from your school to your partner's favorite store.**

A: What's your favorite store?
B: I like Computer World.
A: How do you get there from here?
B: Go north on . . .

I can give directions. ☐   I need more practice. ☐

For more practice, go to MyEnglishLab.

Prepositions of direction and location

You're coming	**from**	home.
You're going	**to**	Joe's Furniture Store.

The store is	**in**	Riverside.
Turn left	**at**	the second light.
The store is	**on**	Fifth Avenue.
It's	**at**	231 Fifth Avenue.
It's	**on**	the corner.

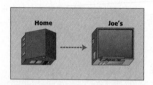

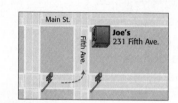

A IDENTIFY. Cross out the incorrect words.

Directions to Our New Apartment

- Our apartment is **on / ~~in~~** Tenth Avenue **in / at** Greenville.
- If you're coming **from / to** the school, go **from / to** the first light.
- Turn right **at / on** the light. You're now **on / in** Tenth Avenue.
- Our apartment is **on / to** the corner of Tenth Avenue and Elm Street.
  It's **in / at** 3245 Tenth Avenue.

B COMPLETE. Use the words in the box.

~~at~~	at	from	in	on	to

A: Where is Eric's office?

B: It's _____*at*_____ 649 Second Avenue _____ Greenville.
　　　　　　1.　　　　　　　　　　　　　　　2.

A: OK. How do I get there _____ here?
　　　　　　　　　　　　　　　　3.

B: It's easy. Go _____ First Street and turn right _____ the light.
　　　　　　　　　4.　　　　　　　　　　　　　　5.

Continue for three blocks. Eric's office is on the right.

A: Is there a coffee shop near his office?

B: Yes. There's a nice coffee shop _____ Second Avenue.
　　　　　　　　　　　　　　　　　　6.

I can use prepositions of direction and location. ■　　　I need more practice. ■

For more practice, go to MyEnglishLab.

Write about your favorite room at home

1 STUDY THE MODEL

READ. Answer the questions.

Amy Krupin
My Favorite Room

My favorite room at home is the living room. It's large and sunny. There are three big windows. There's a new sofa and a coffee table. There's a lamp next to the sofa. There's a large TV. The best part is the wall with all my family photos.

1. What is Amy's favorite room?
2. What's the room like?
3. What furniture is in the room?
4. What does Amy think is the best part?

2 PLAN YOUR WRITING

WORK TOGETHER. Ask and answer the questions.

1. What's your favorite room at home?
2. What's the room like?
3. What furniture is in the room?
4. What's the best part?

Writing Skill: Use details

Put details in your writing. For example:
No details: There are windows.
With details: There are three big windows.

3 WRITE

Now write about your favorite room at home. Use the frame, the model, the Writing Skill, and your ideas from Exercise 2 to help you.

My favorite room at home is the ____.
It's ____ and ____. There are ____.
There's a ____ and a ____. There's a ____
next to the ____. The best part is ____.

4 CHECK YOUR WRITING

WORK TOGETHER. Read your writing aloud with a partner.

WRITING CHECKLIST

☐ The writing answers the questions in Exercise 2.

☐ There are details.

I can use details in my writing. ☐   I need more practice. ☐

For more practice, go to MyEnglishLab.

Find information

1 MEET MILOS

Read about one of his workplace skills.

> I'm good at finding information. When I can't answer a question, I find an answer. For example, I go online or I ask a co-worker.

2 MILOS'S PROBLEM

READ. Circle *True* or *False*.

Milos is an assistant building manager. He takes care of problems in the building. Sometimes he shows apartments to renters.

One day a family looks at an apartment. They ask about the neighborhood schools and stores. Milos doesn't live in the neighborhood. He can't answer their question.

1. Milos shows apartments to renters every day.	True	False
2. Milos lives in the building.	True	False
3. Milos knows the answer to the family's questions.	True	False

3 MILOS'S SOLUTION

A **WORK TOGETHER.** Milos is good at finding information. What is the right thing to say? Explain your answer.

1. Milos says, "I'm sorry. I don't know. I don't live in the neighborhood."
2. Milos says, "Ask the building manager. He knows the neighborhood."
3. Milos says, "I'm sorry. I don't know. Let me ask the building manager."
4. Milos says, "_____."

B **ROLE-PLAY.** Look at your answer to 3A. Role-play Milos's conversation.

Show what you know!

1. **THINK ABOUT IT.** What do you do when you don't know the answer to a question at school? At work? At home? Give examples.

2. **WRITE ABOUT IT.** Now write your example in your Skills Log.

   Sometimes I don't know a new word. I ask my teacher.

I can give an example from my life of finding information. ■

Unit Review: Go back to page 105. Which goals can you check off?

7 Day After Day

PREVIEW

Look at the picture. What do you see?
Where are the people?

UNIT GOALS

- [ ] Name daily activities
- [ ] Make plans with someone
- [ ] Talk about work schedules
- [ ] Read and complete a time sheet
- [ ] Talk about weekend activities
- [ ] Talk about ways to relax
- [ ] **Academic skill:** Make predictions
- [ ] **Writing skill:** Use a capital letter for days of the week
- [ ] **Workplace soft skill:** Be a team player

Vocabulary

Daily activities

A **PREDICT.** Look at the pictures. What do you see? What are the activities?

Number 4 is "eat breakfast."

B ▶ **LISTEN AND POINT.** Then listen and repeat.

C ▶ **LISTEN AND POINT.** Listen and point to the time in each picture.
Then listen and repeat.

Vocabulary

Daily activities

1. get up
2. take a shower
3. get dressed
4. eat breakfast
5. go to work
6. get home
7. exercise
8. cook dinner
9. eat dinner
10. wash the dishes
11. do homework
12. watch TV
13. go to bed

D **WORK TOGETHER.** Look at the pictures on page 126. Student A, ask about an activity. Student B, say the time.

A: What time does he go to work?
B: At 8:00.
A: Right!
B: What time does he . . . ?

E **ACT IT OUT.** Student A, look at the pictures and the word list. Act out an activity. Student B, guess.

B: Wash the dishes?
A: No.
B: Cook dinner?
A: Right!

> **Study Tip**
>
> **Write personal sentences**
> Write sentences about your daily activities. Include a time for each activity.

Show what you know!

1. THINK ABOUT IT. Think about your daily activities. Write the activities in the chart.

Morning	Afternoon	Evening

2. TALK ABOUT IT. Talk about your daily activities.

A: What do you do in the morning?
B: I get up at 5:30, and I go to work at 7:00.
A: What do you do in the afternoon?

3. WRITE ABOUT IT. Now write a sentence about your daily activities.

I _____ at _____.

I can name daily activities. ■   I need more practice. ■

For more practice, go to MyEnglishLab.

Listening and Speaking

Make plans with someone

1 BEFORE YOU LISTEN

GIVE EXAMPLES. What do you do in your free time? Check (✓) the activities. What other activities do you do?

☐ go to the movies   ☐ go to the mall   ☐ play soccer   ☐ go to the park

2 LISTEN

A PREDICT. Look at the picture. What are they doing?

B ▶ LISTEN. Complete the sentence.

The women are making plans for _____.
a. tomorrow   b. tonight   c. Sunday

C ▶ LISTEN FOR DETAILS. Complete the sentences.

1. On Saturdays, Mia _____.
   a. works   b. goes to school   c. babysits for
                                              her cousin

2. Mia gets home at _____ on Saturdays.
   a. 6:00   b. 7:00   c. 8:00

D ▶ EXPAND. Listen to the whole conversation. What does Sue want to do on Saturday?

a.    b.

3 PRONUNCIATION

A ▶ **PRACTICE. Listen. Then listen and repeat.**

When do you get home?   Where do you work?
What do you mean?   What do you do?

B ▶ **COMPLETE. Listen. Complete the sentences.**

1. ___What do you___ do in your free time?
2. _____ have English class?
3. _____ go to work?
4. _____ exercise?

4 CONVERSATION

A ▶ **LISTEN AND READ. Then listen and repeat.**

A: Are you free tomorrow? How about a movie?
B: Sorry, I'm busy. I work on Saturdays.
A: Oh. Well, when do you get home?
B: At 8:00.

B **WORK TOGETHER. Practice the conversation in Exercise A.**

C **CREATE. Make new conversations. Use the information in the boxes.**

A: Are you free tomorrow?
   How about a movie?
B: Sorry, I'm busy.
   I ▓▓▓▓▓▓▓▓
   on ▓▓▓▓▓▓▓▓.
A: Oh. Well, when do you get home?
B: At ▓▓▓▓▓▓▓▓.

D **MAKE CONNECTIONS. Make your own conversations. Use different activities, days, and times.**

take a computer class — Fridays — 9:00

babysit — Thursdays — 7:00

visit my grandparents — Sundays — 7:30

I can make plans with someone. ☐   I need more practice. ☐

For more practice, go to MyEnglishLab.

Grammar

Simple present: *When* and *What time*; Prepositions of time

Simple present: Questions with *When* and *What time*				
When	**does**	he		**work?**
What time	**do**	you		

Prepositions of time
He works **on** Mondays.
He works **from** 9:00 **to** 5:00.
He gets home **at** 6:00.

Grammar Watch

- *on Mondays* = *every Monday*
- Use *from . . . to . . .* with days and times. This shows when an activity starts and ends.
- For more prepositions of time, see page 259.

A COMPLETE. Use *on*, *at*, *from*, or *to*.

1. Ava starts work ___at___ 8:00 ___on___ Mondays.
2. She works _____ Monday _____ Friday.
3. _____ Fridays, she has dinner with her father. They eat _____ 7:00.
4. Ava has English class _____ 10:00 _____ 12:00 _____ Saturdays.
5. She meets her friends at the mall _____ 3:00.
6. _____ Sundays, she plays soccer _____ 11:00.
7. She watches TV _____ 9:00 _____ 11:00, and she goes to bed _____ 11:30.

B COMPLETE. Read the answers. Then complete the questions.

1. **A:** When ___do___ Paul and Ella ___go___ to work?
   B: They go to work at 9:00. They work from Monday to Friday.

2. **A:** What time _____ Paul _____ _____?
   B: He gets home at 6:00. Ella gets home at 6:30.

3. **A:** And when _____ they _____ dinner?
   B: They have dinner together at 7:00. It's their favorite time of the day.

Grammar

C **INTERPRET.** Look at Ben's schedule. Write questions about his activities. Use the words in parentheses.

○○○	Day	Week	Month	Year	🔍

Fri	Sat	Sun
work—8:00	soccer game—9:00 study with Maria—1:00–3:00	exercise—2:00–3:00 dinner with Mom—6:00

1. _What time does Ben start work on Fridays?_
   (What time / Ben / start work on Fridays)

2. _____
   (What time / he / play soccer on Saturdays)

3. _____
   (What time / he and Maria / study on Saturdays)

4. _____
   (When / he / exercise)

5. _____
   (When / he and his mother / have dinner)

D **WORK TOGETHER.** Ask and answer the questions in Exercise C.

Show what you know!

1. THINK ABOUT IT. What time do you do each activity? Complete the "You" columns.

	Friday			Saturday		
	get up	eat dinner	watch TV	get up	eat dinner	watch TV
You						
Partner						

2. TALK ABOUT IT. What time does your partner do each activity? Complete the chart.

A: What time do you get up on Fridays?
B: I get up at 7:00. What about you?

3. WRITE ABOUT IT. Now write about the time you and your partner do the activities.

I get up at 7:00 on Fridays. Paul gets up at 7:30.

_____

I can ask questions with *when* and *what time* and use prepositions of time. ■   I need more practice. ■

For more practice, go to MyEnglishLab.

Lesson 4

Read work schedules and time sheets

1 TALK ABOUT WORK SCHEDULES

A MAKE CONNECTIONS. Look at the calendar. Which days do you work? Which days do you go to school?

Mon 3	Tue 4	Wed 5	Thu 6	Fri 7	Sat 8	Sun 9

Calendar — Calendars + — Day | Week | Month | Year

December

B LOCATE. Write the abbreviations for the days.

Monday _Mon_   Tuesday _____   Wednesday _____   Thursday _____

Friday _____   Saturday _____   Sunday _____

C WORK TOGETHER. Look at the work schedules. Ask and answer questions. Take turns.

A: When does Ming work?
B: She works from Tuesday to Saturday, from 11:00 to 5:00.

The Computer Store
Work Schedule: December 3–9

Schedule | My Account | Help?

Employee	12/3 MON	12/4 TUE	12/5 WED	12/6 THU	12/7 FRI	12/8 SAT	12/9 SUN
Ming Chu		11:00 A.M.–5:00 P.M.	11:00 A.M.–5:00 P.M.	11:00 A.M.–5:00 P.M.	11:00 A.M.–5:00 P.M.	11:00 A.M.–5:00 P.M.	
Pedro Molina	2:30 P.M.–8:30 P.M.	2:30 P.M.–8:30 P.M.	2:30 P.M.–8:30 P.M.	2:30 P.M.–8:30 P.M.	2:30 P.M.–8:30 P.M.		
Maya Kabir		7:00 A.M.–4:00 P.M.		7:00 A.M.–4:00 P.M.		7:00 A.M.–4:00 P.M.	
Danny Costa			6:30 A.M.–10:30 A.M.	6:30 A.M.–10:30 A.M.	6:30 A.M.–10:30 A.M.		
Dawit Alemu			3:00 P.M.–10:00 P.M.	3:00 P.M.–10:00 P.M.	3:00 P.M.–10:00 P.M.	3:00 P.M.–10:00 P.M.	3:00 P.M.–10:00 P.M.

I can talk about work schedules. ■   I need more practice. ■

For more practice, go to MyEnglishLab.

2 READ AND COMPLETE A TIME SHEET

A **MATCH.** Look at Nancy's time sheet. Match the words and definitions. Write the letter.

_____ **1.** employee

_____ **2.** ID #

_____ **3.** Time In

_____ **4.** Time Out

a. identification number

b. the time you finish work

c. worker

d. the time you start work

TIME SHEET

❶ EMPLOYEE NAME   ❷ EMPLOYEE I.D. # 987-65-4321

Last	First		
Johnson	Nancy		

Week ending 7/15

DAY ❸	TIME IN	❹ TIME OUT	HOURS
Mon	8:30 A.M.	1:00 P.M.	4.5
Tue	9:00 A.M.	5:00 P.M.	8
Wed	8:30 A.M.	3:30 P.M.	7
Thu			
Fri			
Sat	12:00 P.M.	5:00 P.M.	5
Sun			

TOTAL HOURS: 24.5

B **INTERPRET.** Look at the time sheet in Exercise 2A. Complete the sentences.

1. Nancy worked on _Monday, Tuesday, Wednesday, and Saturday_.

2. On Tuesday, she started work at _____.

3. On _____, she finished work at 3:30.

4. She didn't work on _____.

5. She worked _____ hours on Monday.

C **APPLY.** Read the information. Complete your time sheet for the week.

You work from 7:00 A.M. to 3:00 P.M. from Tuesday to Saturday. Your employee I.D. number is 00312. Today is Monday, March 11.

D **GO ONLINE.** Find the next event on your calendar. What day is it?

_____

_____

TIME SHEET

EMPLOYEE NAME   EMPLOYEE I.D. _____

First	Last		

Week ending _____

DAY	TIME IN	TIME OUT	HOURS
Mon			
Tue			
Wed			
Thu			
Fri			
Sat			
Sun			

TOTAL HOURS:

I can read and complete a time sheet. ☐   I need more practice. ☐

For more practice, go to MyEnglishLab.

5 Lesson

Talk about weekend activities

1 BEFORE YOU LISTEN

GIVE EXAMPLES. In the U.S. and Canada, many people work from Monday to Friday. They are free on the weekend (Saturday and Sunday). Are you free on the weekend? What do you do? Check (✓) the activities. What other activities do you do?

☐ clean

☐ spend time with my family

☐ shop for food

2 LISTEN

A ▶ **LISTEN.** Look at the picture. Ling and Tony are leaving work. Listen to the conversation. What are they talking about?

a. homework   b. weekend activities   c. work

B ▶ **LISTEN FOR DETAILS.** Complete the schedules.

Tony

Ling

EMPLOYEE ENTRANCE

Ling	Saturday	Sunday
	_____	_____

Tony	Saturday	Sunday
	_____	_____

C ▶ **EXPAND.** Listen to the whole conversation. Complete the sentence.

In Tony's home, they call Sunday _____.
a. "work day"   b. "play day"   c. "fun day"

3 CONVERSATION

A ▶ **LISTEN AND READ.** Then listen and repeat.

A: Gee, I'm so glad it's Friday!
B: Me, too. What do you usually do on the weekend?
A: Well, I always clean the house on Saturdays, and I always spend time with my family on Sundays. What about you?
B: I usually shop for food on Saturdays, and I sometimes go to the park on Sundays.

B **WORK TOGETHER.** Practice the conversation in Exercise A.

C **CREATE.** Make new conversations. Use the pictures.

A: Gee, I'm so glad it's Friday!
B: Me, too. What do you usually do on the weekend?
A: Well, I always ▢▢▢ on Saturdays, and I always ▢▢▢ on Sundays. What about you?
B: I usually ▢▢▢ on Saturdays, and I sometimes ▢▢▢ on Sundays.

cook	ride my bike	stay home	play basketball	read	go dancing

do the laundry	go to the beach	wash my car	play cards	play video games	go swimming

D **MAKE CONNECTIONS.** Make your own conversations. Talk about your weekend activities.

I can talk about weekend activities. ▢   I need more practice. ▢

For more practice, go to MyEnglishLab.

Grammar

Adverbs of frequency

Adverbs of frequency		
I	always	clean on Saturdays.
	usually	
	sometimes	
	never	

Grammar Watch	
always	100%
usually	
sometimes	
never	0%

A **INTERPRET.** David is a student at Greenville Adult School. Look at his schedule. Complete the email with *always, usually, sometimes,* or *never,* and the correct form of the verb.

	Mon	Tue	Wed	Thu	Fri	Sat	Sun
7:00	exercise	exercise	exercise	exercise	exercise		
8:00–12:00	class	work	class	work	class		
12:30	lunch	lunch	lunch	lunch	lunch	lunch	lunch
1:00–5:00	work		work		work	work	soccer?

Hi Nicole,

How are you? I'm fine. My new job is great. I ___*usually*___ ___*work*___ in
1. (work)

the afternoon, but I _____ _____ in the morning, too. In my free
2. (work)

time, I do a lot of things. I _____ _____ at 7:00 A.M. Then on
3. (exercise)

Mondays, Wednesdays, and Fridays, I _____ _____ class. I
4. (have)

_____ _____ lunch at 12:30. I _____ _____
5. (have)   6. (work)

on Sundays. It's my only day off! I _____ _____ soccer in the
7. (play)

afternoon. I love Sundays!

Write soon,

David

Grammar

B **WRITE.** Look at the pictures. Write about David's Sunday activities.

1. _David always visits his family on Sundays._
   (David / always / on Sundays)

2. _____
   (They / always / at 12:30)

3. _____
   (He and his brothers / sometimes / in the park)

4. _____
   (His father and his sister / usually)

5. _____
   (His mother / usually / after lunch)

6. _____
   (His mother / never / on Sundays)

Show what you know!

1. TALK ABOUT IT. Tell your partner two things you always do and one thing you never do on Sundays.

A: I always eat a big breakfast on Sundays. I always visit my mother on Sundays.
   I never work on Sundays.
B: I always . . .

2. WRITE ABOUT IT. Now write what you and your partner *always do* and *never do* on Sundays.

I always _____ on Sundays.
My partner always _____ on Sundays.
I never _____ .
My partner never _____ .

I can use adverbs of frequency. ☐   I need more practice. ☐

For more practice, go to MyEnglishLab.

Read about how Americans spend their free time

1 BEFORE YOU READ

A **MATCH.** Find the meanings for the vocabulary words. Write the letters.

_____ **1.** chores

_____ **2.** communicate

_____ **3.** on average

_____ **4.** relax

_____ **5.** socialize

a. usually

b. jobs you do at home (like cleaning, cooking)

c. talk to other people

d. spend time with other people for fun

e. do something fun or just rest

B **TALK ABOUT IT.** How much free time do you have? What do you do in your free time?

2 READ

Academic Skill: Make predictions

Before you read an article, guess what it will say. Then read to find out: Were your predictions correct?

▶ **Listen and read.**

FREE TIME

What do American men and women do with their free time? Here are four common activities.

They spend time with family and friends. This is common for
5 both men and women in the U.S. On average, men spend about 38 minutes a day with their family and friends. Women spend about 40 minutes a day with theirs.

10 **They communicate.** Many people spend time texting, using email, and talking on the phone. Men spend about 44 minutes a day on these activities. Women spend about 47
15 minutes a day on them.

They exercise. On average, men exercise or play sports for about 23 minutes a day. Women exercise only 15 minutes a day.

20 **They watch TV.** Men watch about 3 hours of TV a day. Women watch less TV. They watch about 2 hours and 30 minutes.

On average, American men have about 5 hours and
25 30 minutes of free time a day. American women have about 4 hours and 48 minutes. What's one reason American men have more free time? They don't do as many chores at home. They cook and clean for only 36 minutes a day. Women cook and
30 clean for 1 hour and 41 minutes a day!

Source: U.S. Bureau of Labor Statistics

Free Time on an Average Day

Other (12 minutes)

Relaxing and thinking (17 minutes)

Sports, games, and exercise (18 minutes)

Reading (19 minutes)

Computer games and other computer activities (25 minutes)

Communicating and socializing (41 minutes)

Watching TV (2 hours and 47 minutes)

Total free time = 4 hours 59 minutes

*Americans age 15 and older

Source: U.S. Bureau of Labor Statistics

3 CLOSE READING

A **CITE EVIDENCE. Complete the sentences. Where is the information? Write the line number.**

Lines

1. On average, American men _____ for about 3 hours a day.
   a. have free time   **b.** watch TV   **c.** spend time with their families   _____

2. On average, women _____ more than men in the U.S.
   a. watch TV   **b.** exercise or play sports   **c.** communicate by phone and computer   _____

3. On average, American men have more _____ than American women.
   a. free time   **b.** ways to relax   **c.** hours at work   _____

4. On average, American women spend more time _____ than American men.
   a. doing chores   **b.** sleeping   **c.** working   _____

B **INTERPRET. Complete the sentences about the chart.**

1. On an average day, Americans watch TV for _____.

2. On an average day, Americans spend _____ communicating and socializing.

3. On an average day, Americans spend 17–19 minutes on each of these activities:
   _____; _____; and _____.

4 SUMMARIZE

Complete the summary with the words in the box.

| chores | communicate | on average | sports |

Americans often use their free time in these four ways: (a) they spend it with family and friends, (b) they (1) _____ by phone or by computer, (c) they exercise or play (2) _____, and (d) they watch TV. (3) _____, American men have more free time than American women. The men don't do as many (4) _____ at home.

Show what you know!

1. **TALK ABOUT IT.** Talk about the four common activities in the reading. How much time do you spend doing these things?

2. **WRITE ABOUT IT.** Now write about how you spend your free time.

   In my free time, I sometimes _____. I spend about _____ (a day/a week) doing this.

I can make predictions. ☐   I need more practice. ☐

To read more, go to MyEnglishLab.

1 BEFORE YOU LISTEN

MAKE CONNECTIONS. Look at ways to relax. Which activities do you do? How often?

Ways to Relax

☐ take a hot bath   ☐ do puzzles   ☐ go running

☐ knit   ☐ listen to music   ☐ take a long walk

2 LISTEN

A ▶ **IDENTIFY.** Listen to Dr. Sue Miller's podcast about relaxing. Look at the pictures in Exercise 1. Check (✓) the four activities she talks about.

B ▶ **LISTEN FOR DETAILS.** Complete the sentence. Check (✓) all the correct answers.

Sue Miller says we need to relax. It helps us be better _____.

☐ runners   ☐ students   ☐ teachers

☐ friends   ☐ workers   ☐ family members

3 PRONUNCIATION

Extra syllable in -es endings

Sometimes the **-es** ending on verbs adds an extra syllable.

A ▶ PRACTICE. Listen. Then listen and repeat.

wash	I **wash** the dishes after dinner.
washes	He **washes** the dishes in the morning.
relax	We **relax** at night.
relaxes	She **relaxes** on Sundays.
watch	They **watch** TV every night.
watches	He never **watches** TV.

B ▶ APPLY. Practice saying the sentences. Then listen and repeat.

I **use** a laptop at work.
My brother **uses** a laptop at school.

They **exercise** on the weekend.
He **exercises** in the park.

4 CONVERSATION

A ▶ LISTEN AND READ. Then listen and repeat.

A: You look stressed.
B: I *am* stressed. I really need to relax.
How do *you* relax?
A: Well, I listen to music.
B: Really? How often?
A: Every day.
B: That's great.

B WORK TOGETHER. Practice the conversation in Exercise A.

C CREATE. Make new conversations. Use the activities on page 140.

D ROLE-PLAY. Make your own conversations. Tell your partner how you relax and how often.

I can talk about ways to relax. ▪

I need more practice. ▪

For more practice, go to MyEnglishLab.

Grammar

Questions with *How often*; expressions of frequency

Simple present: Questions with *How often*			
		you	
How often	**do**	we	
		they	**play** soccer?
	does	he	
		she	

Expressions of frequency
Every day.
Once a week.
Twice a week.
Three times a week.

A **WRITE.** Look at Adam's schedule. Write questions. Use *How often* and the activities in the schedule.

Sun	Mon	Tue	Wed	Thu	Fri	Sat
ride my bike	have class	ride my bike	have class	ride my bike	have class	ride my bike
play soccer	ride my bike	see friends	ride my bike	see friends	ride my bike	play soccer
		go food shopping		do laundry		

1. *How often does Adam ride his bike?*
2. *How often does he . . . ?*
3. _____
4. _____
5. _____
6. _____

B **WORK TOGETHER.** Ask and answer the questions in Exercise A. Give two answers for every question.

A: *How often does Adam play soccer?*
B: *Twice a week. Every Saturday and Sunday.*
A: *Right.*
B: *How often does Adam . . . ?*

I can ask questions with *How often* and use expressions of frequency. ■   I need more practice. ■

For more practice, go to MyEnglishLab.

Write about a favorite day of the week

1 STUDY THE MODEL

READ. Answer the questions.

> Ahmed Ali
> My Favorite Day
>
> My favorite day of the week is Sunday. I never work on Sundays. On Sundays, I spend time with my friends and family. We usually go to the park. We bring a lot of food. We sit and talk. We play soccer. It's a lot of fun.

1. What is Ahmed's favorite day of the week?
2. Why is it his favorite day?
3. Who does he spend time with on his favorite day?
4. What does he do on his favorite day?

2 PLAN YOUR WRITING

WORK TOGETHER. Ask and answer the questions.

1. What's your favorite day of the week?
2. Why is it your favorite day?
3. Who do you spend time with on your favorite day?
4. What do you do on your favorite day?

Writing Skill: Use a capital letter for days of the week

Days of the week begin with a capital letter. For example:
My favorite day of the week is Sunday.

3 WRITE

Now write about your favorite day of the week. Use the frame, the model, the Writing Skill, and your ideas from Exercise 2 to help you.

> My favorite day of the week is _____. I _____ on _____. On _____, I spend time with _____. We usually go to _____. We _____. We _____. It's a lot of fun.

4 CHECK YOUR WRITING

WORK TOGETHER. Read your writing aloud with a partner.

WRITING CHECKLIST

☐ The writing answers all the questions in Exercise 2.

☐ Each day of the week begins with a capital letter.

I can use a capital letter for days of the week. ■   I need more practice. ■

For more practice, go to MyEnglishLab.

Be a team player

1 MEET RITA

Read about one of her workplace skills.

> I'm a team player. For example, I help my co-workers when they need help. I help them when I finish my work.

2 RITA'S PROBLEM

READ. Circle *True* or *False*.

Rita is an office assistant. She makes a lot of copies. Sometimes the copy machine doesn't work. Rita can fix it.

One day, she sees her co-worker at the copy machine. Her co-worker says, "I need these copies now, but the machine doesn't work!" Rita wants to leave. She is meeting her friend after work.

1. Rita works in an office.	True	False
2. The copy machine sometimes doesn't work.	True	False
3. Rita's co-worker can fix the copy machine.	True	False

3 RITA'S SOLUTION

A WORK TOGETHER. Rita is a team player. What is the right thing to say? Explain your answer.

1. Rita says, "I need to leave now, but I can help you tomorrow."
2. Rita says, "Sorry. I can't help you now. Ask Tom."
3. Rita says, "I can help you. Let me show you."
4. Rita says, "_____."

B ROLE-PLAY. Look at your answer to 3A. Role-play Rita's conversation.

Show what you know!

1. **THINK ABOUT IT.** How are you a team player at school? At work? At home? Give examples.

2. **WRITE ABOUT IT.** Now write your example in your Skills Log.

   Sometimes my classmates and I study together after class. I help them. They help me.

3. **PRESENT IT.** Give a short presentation to show how you are a team player.

I can give an example from my life of being a team player. ■

Unit Review: Go back to page 125. Which goals can you check off?

8 From Soup to Nuts

PREVIEW
Look at the picture. Who are the people?
Where are they?

UNIT GOALS

- [ ] Name common foods
- [ ] Talk about foods you like and don't like
- [ ] Order a meal in a restaurant
- [ ] Compare food prices
- [ ] Talk about healthy food
- [ ] Plan a healthy meal
- [ ] **Academic skill:** Read captions before reading an article
- [ ] **Writing skill:** Choose the correct verb
- [ ] **Workplace soft skill:** Take action

145

Common foods

A **PREDICT.** Look at the pictures. What do you see? What are the foods?

Number 14 is eggs.

B ► **LISTEN AND POINT.** Then listen and repeat.

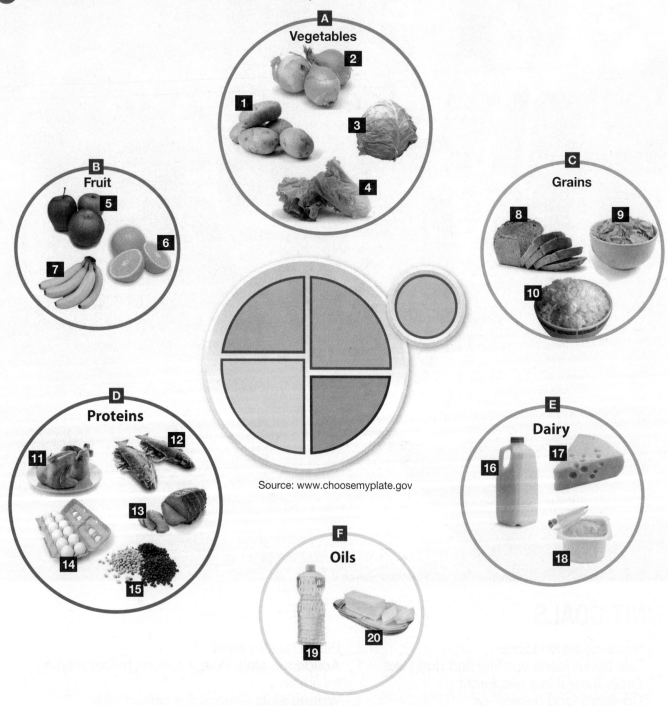

Source: www.choosemyplate.gov

Vocabulary

Common foods

A. Vegetables
1. potatoes
2. onions
3. cabbage
4. lettuce

B. Fruit
5. apples
6. oranges
7. bananas

C. Grains
8. bread
9. cereal
10. rice

D. Proteins
11. chicken
12. fish
13. beef
14. eggs
15. beans

E. Dairy
16. milk
17. cheese
18. yogurt

F. Oils
19. vegetable oil
20. butter

C **GIVE EXAMPLES.** Student A, say a food group. Student B, say two foods in the group.

A: Vegetables.
B: Cabbage and lettuce.

D **ASK AND ANSWER.** Student A, look at the pictures and the list of foods. Choose a food, but don't say it. Students B, C, and D, ask *yes/no* questions and guess the food.

B: Do you eat it for breakfast?
A: Sometimes.
C: Is it a fruit?
A: Yes.

D: Is it red?
A: No.
B: Is it a banana?
A: Yes!

> **Study Tip**
>
> **Practice online**
> Use the flashcards in MyEnglishLab.

Show what you know!

1. **THINK ABOUT IT.** Look at page 146. Write a food you usually eat on each part of the plate. Write how often you eat the food outside the plate.

2. **TALK ABOUT IT.** Talk about the foods you eat and how often you eat them. Write your partner's information.

A: What vegetables do you eat?
B: Potatoes.
A: How often do you eat potatoes?
B: Twice a week.

3. **WRITE ABOUT IT.** Now write a sentence about a food you eat and how often you eat it.

I eat a banana every day.

I can name common foods. ☐   I need more practice. ☐

For more practice, go to MyEnglishLab.

Listening and Speaking

Talk about foods you like and don't like

1 BEFORE YOU LISTEN

A LABEL. Write the words under the pictures.

hamburger	~~hungry~~	pizza	taco

a. ___hungry___   b. _____   c. _____   d. _____

B MAKE CONNECTIONS. Check (✓) the foods you like.

☐ pizza   ☐ tacos   ☐ hamburgers

2 LISTEN

A ▶ LISTEN. Look at the picture. Listen to the conversation. Answer the question.

What are they talking about?
a. breakfast   b. lunch   c. dinner

B ▶ LISTEN FOR DETAILS. Answer the questions.

1. Who is hungry?
   a. Mark   b. Rosa   c. Mark and Rosa

2. What does Mark want for lunch?
   a. pizza   b. tacos   c. a hamburger

3. What does Rosa want for lunch?
   a. pizza   b. tacos   c. a hamburger

C ▶ EXPAND. Listen to the whole conversation. Complete the sentence.

Rosa says, "Let's have pizza and tacos for _____."
a. breakfast   b. lunch   c. dinner

3 CONVERSATION

A ▶ **LISTEN AND READ.** Then listen and repeat.

A: Wow, I'm hungry!
B: Yeah, me too. What do you want for lunch?
A: Pizza. I love pizza! What about you?
B: I don't really like pizza, but I love tacos!

B **WORK TOGETHER.** Practice the conversation in Exercise A.

C **CREATE.** Make new conversations. Use the information in the boxes.

A: What do you want for ▭ ?
B: ▭ . I love ▭ ! What about you?
A: I don't really like ▭ , but I love ▭ !

breakfast	scrambled eggs	pancakes
lunch	salad	wraps
dinner	steak	pasta

D **MAKE CONNECTIONS.** Make your own conversations.
Use different foods.

I can talk about foods I like and don't like. ☐   I need more practice. ☐

For more practice, go to MyEnglishLab.

Grammar

Count and non-count nouns

Count nouns		Non-count nouns	
Rosa wants	**a potato.**	I want	**rice.**
She loves	**potatoes.**	I love	**rice.**

Grammar Watch

- **Count nouns** are nouns you can count: *one apple, two apples.*
- **Non-count nouns** are nouns you can't count: ~~one rice, two rices~~
- For a list of more non-count nouns, see page 260.
- For spelling rules for plural count nouns, see page 260.

A **IDENTIFY. Complete the shopping list.**

TO BUY

4 _oranges_

6 _____

black _____

apple _____

2 large _____

banana _____

3 _____

5 green _____

Grammar

B **COMPLETE. Look at the pictures. Complete the conversations.**

1. **A:** _____Apples_____ are good for you.

   B: I know. I eat an _____ every day.

2. **A:** I love _____.

   B: Me, too! I often have two _____ for breakfast.

3. **A:** Do you have _____?

   B: Of course! I always have _____ in the house. It's in the refrigerator.

4. **A:** I eat _____ every day.

   B: Me, too. I love _____!

Show what you know!

1. **THINK ABOUT IT. Name foods of the same color.**

   yellow: _bananas_____

   white: _____

   red: _____

   green: _____

2. **WRITE ABOUT IT. Now write 2 sentences about foods and colors.**

   _Bananas are yellow._____

   _____ green.

   _____

I can use count and non-count nouns. ■   I need more practice. ■

For more practice, go to MyEnglishLab.

Reading

Read about food safety

1 BEFORE YOU READ

A **LABEL.** Write the words under the pictures.

| a cabinet | a counter | a freezer | a refrigerator |

1. _____

2. _____

3. _____

4. _____

B **MAKE CONNECTIONS.** In your kitchen, where do you keep these foods?

canned beans, oranges, cereal, milk, chicken, eggs, ice cream, potatoes, frozen vegetables, bananas

Academic Skill: Read captions

The words you see above or below a picture are **captions**. They often add important information about the picture. Before you read an article, look at any pictures and read their captions.

2 READ

▶ Listen and read.

Eat Fresh!

A careful shopper always checks the date on food.

Do you buy fresh food? Are you sure it is fresh? Be careful! Stores sometimes sell old food. Check the date on food before you buy it.

How long can you keep your food at home?

Milk is usually safe to drink for two to ten days after its sell-by date. Be
5 sure to keep it cold.

Eggs are good for three to five weeks after their sell-by date. Keep them in the refrigerator, too.

Chicken is different. You cannot keep chicken in your refrigerator for weeks after the sell-by date.
10 The refrigerators in stores are very cold. Your home refrigerator isn't as cold. Freeze chicken or cook it a day or two after you buy it. You can keep chicken in the freezer for twelve months. You can keep cooked chicken in the refrigerator for a week.

15 Some food, like **canned food**, doesn't have a sell-by date. But it isn't good forever. Keep canned food in a cool, dry place. Try to use it in twelve months.

Sometimes canned food or **frozen food** has a best-before date or a use-by date. The food will
20 taste better before that date.

SELL BY OCT 14 08:53

Stores cannot sell food after its sell-by date.

Reading

3 CLOSE READING

CITE EVIDENCE. Complete the sentences. Where is the information? Write the line number.

Lines

1. When you go food shopping, don't buy _____.
   a. canned food   **b.** frozen chicken   **c.** food after its   _____
                                                            sell-by date

2. You can usually drink milk for 2 to _____ days after its sell-by date.
   a. 3   **b.** 10   **c.** 14   _____

3. It is important to keep _____ in the refrigerator.
   a. frozen foods   **b.** canned foods   **c.** milk and eggs   _____

4. When you buy fresh chicken, _____ in the next 1 to 2 days.
   a. cook it or freeze it **b.** put it in the refrigerator **c.** eat it   _____

5. _____ doesn't have a sell-by date.
   a. Canned food   **b.** Chicken   **c.** Milk   _____

6. It is a good idea to _____.
   a. eat food before its   **b.** keep canned food   **c.** keep canned food   _____
   use-by date   for many years   in a warm place

4 SUMMARIZE

Complete the summary with the words in the box.

buy	canned foods	safe	sell-by date	use-by date

Most food in the supermarket has a (1) _____. Don't (2) _____
food after that date. Food is (3) _____ to eat after its sell-by date, but every
food is different. Some foods are safe for a few weeks but others for only a day or two.
(4) _____ don't have a sell-by date, but they have a best-before or
(5) _____.

Show what you know!

1. **THINK ABOUT IT.** How do you make sure your food is fresh?

2. **WRITE ABOUT IT.** Now write about how you make sure your food is fresh.

   I always check the _____ on _____. I keep _____
   in the _____.

I can read captions before reading an article. ■   I need more practice. ■

Lesson 5

Order a meal in a restaurant

1 BEFORE YOU LISTEN

MAKE CONNECTIONS. Look at the pictures. Check (✓) the foods you eat or drink.

tomato soup

coffee

turkey sandwich

fries

soda

baked potato

hamburger

iced tea

salad

fruit cup

apple pie

ice cream

2 LISTEN

A ▶ **LISTEN. Look at the picture. Listen to the conversation. What is Greg doing? Complete the sentence.**

He's _____ a meal.
a. ordering   **b.** eating   **c.** serving

B ▶ **LISTEN FOR DETAILS. What does Greg want? Complete the sentence.**

Greg wants a hamburger, _____.
a. a small soda, and a large order of fries
b. a large soda, and a large order of fries
c. a large soda, and a small order of fries

C ▶ **EXPAND. Listen to the whole conversation. Complete the sentence.**

For fruit, Greg orders _____.
a. an apple   **b.** apple juice   **c.** apple pie

Listening and Speaking

3 PRONUNCIATION

A ▶ **PRACTICE. Listen. Then listen and repeat.**

Is that a large soda or a small soda?

Would you like coffee or tea?

> **Intonation of choice questions with *or***
>
> In choice questions with *or*, the voice goes up ⤴ on the first choice and down ⤵ on the last choice.

B ▶ **APPLY. Practice saying the sentences. Then listen and repeat.**

Do you want steak or pasta?
Would you like pizza or tacos?

4 CONVERSATION

A ▶ **LISTEN AND READ. Then listen and repeat.**

Server:	Can I help you?
Customer:	Yes. I'd like a hamburger and a soda.
Server:	Is that a large soda or a small soda?
Customer:	Large, please.
Server:	OK, a large soda. Anything else?
Customer:	Yes. A small order of fries.

B **WORK TOGETHER. Practice the conversation in Exercise A.**

C **CREATE. Make new conversations. Use the menu.**

A: Can I help you?

B: Yes. I'd like _____ and _____.
        (food)   (drink)

A: Is that a large _____ or a small
                         (drink)

_____?
(drink)

B: Large, please.

A: OK, a large _____. Anything else?
                      (drink)

B: Yes. _____.
             (food)

❧ Starters ❧	❧ Sides ❧	❧ Desserts ❧
tomato soup	baked potato	apple pie
onion soup	fries	ice cream
green salad	rice	fruit cup
	vegetables	

❧ Sandwiches ❧	❧ Drinks ❧
turkey sandwich	soda
cheese sandwich	iced tea
hamburger	coffee
black bean taco	orange juice

D **ROLE-PLAY. Make your own conversations. Use the menu.**

I can order a meal in a restaurant. ☐   I need more practice. ☐

For more practice, go to MyEnglishLab.

6 Grammar

Choice questions with *or*

Choice questions with *or*			
Would you like **coffee**	**or**	**tea**?	Tea, please.
Do you want **an apple**		**a banana**?	An apple, please.

Grammar Watch

Questions with *or* give choices. Answer with your choice. Do not say *yes* or *no*.

A **COMPLETE.** Use the words in parentheses with *or*.

1. Do you want _____chicken soup or salad_____?
   (chicken soup / salad)

2. Would you like _____?
   (a fish sandwich / a hamburger)

3. Do you want _____?
   (fries / a baked potato)

4. Do you want _____?
   (soda / juice)

5. Would you like _____?
   (ice cream / apple pie)

B ▶ **SELF-ASSESS.** Listen and check your answers. Then listen and repeat.

Show what you know!

1. **WRITE ABOUT IT.** Student A, you're a server. Student B, you're a customer. Student A, write two choice questions for your partner.

   Would you like meat or fish?

   _____

   _____

2. **ROLE-PLAY.** Ask your questions from Exercise 1. Write your partner's order.

   A: *Would you like meat or fish?*
   B: *Fish, please.*

3. **PRESENT IT.** Now report to the class.

   Maria wants fish.

I can ask choice questions with *or*. ■   I need more practice. ■

For more practice, go to MyEnglishLab.

Compare food prices; Talk about healthy food

1 COMPARE FOOD PRICES

A ▶ **LISTEN.** Look at the ad for Farmer Tom's. Listen and repeat the prices and amounts.

B ▶ **APPLY.** Look at the ad for Country Market. Listen and fill in the prices.

C **COMPARE.** Look at the prices in the ads again. Where is each food cheaper? Circle the cheaper price.

D ▶ **LISTEN AND READ.** Then listen and repeat.

  A: Where are **onions** cheaper, Farmer Tom's or Country Market?
  B: Farmer Tom's. They're **79 cents a pound**.
  A: Where is **bread** cheaper, Farmer Tom's or Country Market?
  B: Country Market. It's **$2.59**.

E **ROLE-PLAY.** Make new conversations. Use different foods from the ads.

Farmer Tom's
$2.99/lb. 69¢/lb.
YUM YUM YOGURT 32 oz. $2.79
$1.49/lb.
79¢/lb.
$3.19

COUNTRY MARKET
$3.29/lb. _____/lb.
Sunny Farms Yogurt 32 oz _____
_____/lb.
_____/lb.
_____

I can compare food prices. ■   I need more practice. ■

2 TALK ABOUT HEALTHY FOOD

A **TALK ABOUT IT.** Read the tips. Do you eat healthy food?

Tips to Stay Healthy

Don't eat a lot of fat.

Don't eat a lot of sodium.

Don't eat a lot of sugar.

12 calories

300 calories

Eat the right number of calories. How many calories can you eat? Every person is different. Talk to a doctor or nurse.

B **ASSESS.** Look at the pictures. Check (✓) the foods that you think are healthy.

C **WORK TOGETHER.** Talk about your answers in Exercise 2B.

A: Green beans are good for you.
B: Why?
A: Because they don't have fat.

A: Ice cream isn't good for you.
B: Why not?
A: Because it has a lot of fat and sugar.

D **MAKE CONNECTIONS.** Which healthy foods do you usually eat?

A: I eat a lot of beans.
B: Really? Well, I eat rice every day.
C: I eat...

Workplace, Life, and Community Skills

E **MATCH.** Look at this label for bread. Match the words and definitions. Write the letter.

Nutrition Facts
Serving Size: 1 slice
Servings per Container: 18

Calories	90
Total Fat	1 g
Sodium	180 mg
Sugar	3 g
Net Wt. =	1 lb. 8 oz.

_____ **1.** g   **a.** how much you eat at one time

_____ **2.** mg   **b.** gram(s)

_____ **3.** Net Wt.   **c.** milligram(s)

_____ **4.** Serving size   **d.** how much food is in the container

F **LOCATE.** Look at the label in Exercise 2E. Answer the questions.

1. How much is one serving? _____ *1 slice* _____

2. How many servings are in the package? _____

3. How many calories are in one serving? _____

4. How much fat is in one serving? _____

5. How much sodium is in one serving? _____

6. How much sugar is in one serving? _____

G **INTERPRET.** Look at the labels. Which drink is better for your health? Why?

Nutrition Facts
Serving Size: 12 oz.
Servings per Container: 1

Calories	140
Total Fat	0 g
Sodium	50 mg
Sugar	33 g

Nutrition Facts
Serving Size: 12 oz.
Servings per Container: 1

Calories	75
Total Fat	0 g
Sodium	0 mg
Sugar	16 g

_____ is better for your health because _____

_____.

H **GO ONLINE.** Look up the number of calories in your favorite food.

I can talk about healthy food. ■	I need more practice. ■

For more practice, go to MyEnglishLab.

Lesson 8

Plan a healthy meal

1 BEFORE YOU LISTEN

GIVE EXAMPLES. Look at the pictures. What other foods are steamed, grilled, or fried?

steamed vegetables

grilled chicken

fried fish

2 LISTEN

A ▶ **LISTEN FOR DETAILS. Listen to the radio talk show. Check (✓) all the correct answers.**

1. What does Greg like to eat?
   ☐ fruit and vegetables   ☐ meat and potatoes   ☐ chicken

2. What does Greg's wife think is good for Greg?
   ☐ meat   ☐ fruit   ☐ vegetables

3. What does Hanna think is good for Greg?
   ☐ meat   ☐ fruit   ☐ vegetables

B ▶ **LISTEN FOR DETAILS. Complete the chart.**

Fried chicken	_____ calories
Grilled chicken	_____ calories
Fries (small)	_____ fat (in grams)
Baked potato	_____ fat (in grams)

C **WORK TOGETHER. Look at the pictures. Plan a healthy meal for Greg. Choose from the pictures.**

A: How about salad, a hamburger, and fruit?
B: The hamburger isn't really healthy. It has a lot of fat! How about...?

Listening and Speaking

3 CONVERSATION

A **MAKE CONNECTIONS.** Look at the pictures. Which of these foods do you like?

shrimp

tomatoes

B ▶ **LISTEN AND READ.** Then listen and repeat.

A: Let's have **chicken** for dinner.
B: OK. How much **chicken** do we need?
A: Two pounds.
B: OK. And let's have salad with it.
A: Good idea. We have lettuce, but we need **onions**.
B: How many **onions** do we need?
A: Just one.

turkey

red peppers

C **WORK TOGETHER.** Practice the conversation in Exercise B.

salmon

cucumbers

D **CREATE.** Make new conversations. Use the pictures in Exercise A.

E **DECIDE.** Plan an interesting salad.

roast beef

avocados

A: Let's put nuts in the salad.
B: OK. And how about an avocado?
A: Oh, I don't like avocados. Let's put a mango in it.

F **PRESENT.** Tell your classmates about the salad.

Our salad has nuts, mango. . . .

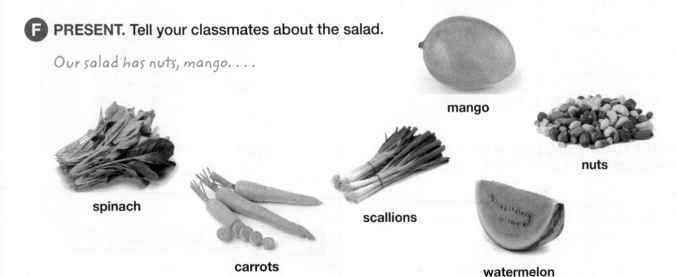

mango

nuts

spinach

scallions

carrots

watermelon

I can plan a healthy meal. ■

I need more practice. ■

For more practice, go to MyEnglishLab.

Lesson 9

Questions and short answers with *How many* and *How much*

Questions and short answers with *How many* and *How much*					
How many	**eggs**	do we have?	**A lot.**		**Not many.**
How much	**milk**	is there?	**A lot.**		**Not much.**

Grammar Watch

- Use *how many* with plural count nouns.
- Use *how much* with non-count nouns.

A **COMPLETE.** Look at the picture. Read the answers. Complete the questions with *How many* or *How much* and a noun.

1. **A:** _____How many oranges_____ do we have?
   B: Not many. We only have three.

2. **A:** _____ do we have?
   B: Not much. Just one container.

3. **A:** _____ are there?
   B: Twelve. We don't need more.

4. **A:** _____ is there?
   B: There is no cheese! Put it on the shopping list.

5. **A:** _____ are there?
   B: Six. And they're big!
   A: Great. Let's have them tonight.

B **WORK TOGETHER.** Look at the picture again. Ask about other food in the refrigerator.

A: How much orange juice do we have?
B: There's a lot. We don't need orange juice.
A: How many apples . . . ?

I can use questions and short answers with *How many* and *How much*. ■   I need more practice. ■

For more practice, go to MyEnglishLab.

Lesson 10 — Write about food

1 STUDY THE MODEL

READ. Answer the questions.

> Maya Black
>
> <u>My Food</u>
>
> I always have cereal and a large coffee for breakfast. I usually eat a sandwich and a salad for lunch. In the afternoon, I usually have a cookie and a glass of milk for a snack. I sometimes eat pasta or rice for dinner.

1. What does Maya have for breakfast?
2. What does she usually eat for lunch?
3. What does she usually have for a snack?
4. What does she sometimes eat for dinner?

2 PLAN YOUR WRITING

WORK TOGETHER. Ask and answer the questions.

1. What do you have for breakfast?
2. What do you usually eat for lunch?
3. What do you usually have for a snack?
4. What do you eat for dinner?

Writing Skill: Choose the correct verb

Use the verb *eat* when you talk about food. Use the verb *drink* when you talk about drinks. You can use *have* with food or drinks. For example:

I eat scrambled eggs for breakfast.
I drink coffee for breakfast.
I have scrambled eggs and coffee for breakfast.

3 WRITE

Now write about the food you usually eat. Use the frame, the model, the Writing Skill, and your ideas from Exercise 2 to help you.

> I always have _____ for breakfast. I usually eat _____ for lunch. I usually have _____ for a snack. I sometimes eat _____ for dinner.

4 CHECK YOUR WRITING

WORK TOGETHER. Read your writing aloud with a partner.

WRITING CHECKLIST

☐ The writing answers all the questions in Exercise 2.

☐ Each sentence has a verb.

☐ The verbs *eat, drink,* and *have* are used correctly.

I can choose the correct verb. ■   I need more practice. ■

For more practice, go to MyEnglishLab.

11

Soft Skills at Work

Take action

1 MEET NASIR

Read about one of his workplace skills.

I take action. When I see a problem, I do something.

2 NASIR'S PROBLEM

READ. Circle *True* or *False*.

Nasir works in a restaurant. He is a dishwasher. He washes dishes and cleans the restaurant.

One day, the restaurant is very busy. The cooks make a lot of food. Nasir sees there are not many onions or potatoes on the shelves. There is not much milk in the refrigerator. There is no bread.

1. Nasir is a server.	True	False
2. The restaurant is very busy.	True	False
3. There is a lot of milk in the refrigerator.	True	False

3 NASIR'S SOLUTION

WORK TOGETHER. Nasir takes action. What does Nasir do? Explain your answer.

1. Nasir writes a note for the manager with the food they need.
2. Nasir tells the cooks that they need to order food.
3. Nasir says nothing. It is not his job to order food.
4. Nasir _____.

Show what you know!

1. **THINK ABOUT IT.** How do you take action at school? At work? At home? Give examples.

2. **WRITE ABOUT IT.** Now write your example in your Skills Log.

   I tell my manager when something doesn't work.

I can give an example from my life of taking action. ☐

Unit Review: Go back to page 145. Which goals can you check off?

9 Rain or Shine

PREVIEW
Look at the picture. What do you see?

UNIT GOALS

- [ ] Name seasons and weather
- [ ] Talk about what you are doing now
- [ ] Plan for an emergency
- [ ] Ask what someone is doing now
- [ ] Understand a weather report

- [ ] **Academic skill:** Focus on details
- [ ] **Writing skill:** Use *because* to give a reason
- [ ] **Workplace soft skill:** Be ready to learn new skills

Vocabulary

Seasons and weather

A **PREDICT.** Look at the pictures. What are the seasons and weather words?

C is spring. Number 8 is sunny.

B ▶ **LISTEN AND POINT.** Then listen and repeat.

Vocabulary

Seasons and weather			
A. Fall	**B. Winter**	**C. Spring**	**D. Summer**
1. cool	**3.** cold	**5.** warm	**7.** hot
2. cloudy	**4.** snowy	**6.** rainy	**8.** sunny

C **ASK AND ANSWER.** Student A, point to a picture and ask about the weather. Student B, answer.

A: How's the weather?
B: It's hot and sunny.

D **TALK ABOUT IT.** Look at the pictures and the list of weather words. Talk about the weather in your native country.

A: I'm from Colombia. It's usually cool and cloudy in spring.
B: Oh, really? In Korea, it's usually . . .

> **Study Tip**
>
> **Write and spell**
> Write the words. Spell the words aloud when you write.

Show what you know!

1. SURVEY. Ask three classmates about their favorite season here. Write their answers in the chart.

Name	Favorite Season	Reason
Paul	spring	warm, not hot

A: What's your favorite season?
B: I like spring.
A: Why?
B: Because it's warm but not hot.

2. PRESENT IT. Tell your class about your classmates' favorite seasons.

Paul likes spring because it is warm but not hot.

3. WRITE ABOUT IT. Now write a sentence about your favorite season.

I like _____ because _____.

I can name seasons and weather. ■	I need more practice. ■

For more practice, go to MyEnglishLab.

Lesson 2

Talk about what you are doing now

1 BEFORE YOU LISTEN

READ. Then answer the question.

Green Bay, Wisconsin, is in the north of the United States. Winter is usually cold and snowy there. Tampa, Florida, is in the south of the United States. Winter there is usually warm and sunny.

How is winter in your area?

2 LISTEN

A ▶ **LISTEN.** Laura is in Tampa, Florida. She is calling her friend David in Green Bay, Wisconsin. Complete the sentence.

Laura is _____ in Tampa.
a. working **b.** studying **c.** visiting family

B ▶ **LISTEN FOR DETAILS.** Complete the sentences.

1. Laura's family is _____ now.
   a. at home **b.** at work **c.** at school

2. The weather in Tampa is _____.
   a. warm and sunny **b.** warm and rainy **c.** cold and rainy

C ▶ **EXPAND.** Listen to the whole conversation. Complete the sentences.

1. The weather in Green Bay is _____.
   a. warm and sunny
   b. cold and rainy
   c. sunny, but not warm

2. Laura is watching _____.
   a. her friend
   b. the rain
   c. TV

3. Laura sounds _____.
   a. happy
   b. unhappy
   c. stressed

Listening and Speaking

3 CONVERSATION

A ▶ **LISTEN AND READ.** Then listen and repeat.

A: Hello?
B: Hi! It's me. How are you doing?
A: I'm fine, thanks. Where are you?
B: I'm in Tampa. I'm visiting family, but they're at work now.
A: Tampa! That's great! How's the weather there?
B: Well, it's cold and rainy.

B **WORK TOGETHER.** Practice the conversation in Exercise A.

C **CREATE.** Make new conversations. Use the information in the boxes.

A: Hello?
B: Hi! It's me. How are you doing?
A: I'm fine, thanks. Where are you?
B: I'm in _____. I'm visiting _____, but they're at work now.
A: _____! That's great! How's the weather there?
B: Well, it's _____ and _____.

Dallas	San Francisco	Boston
friends	my aunt and uncle	my cousins
hot	cool	cold
humid	foggy	windy

D **ROLE-PLAY.** Make your own conversations. Use different cities, people, and weather.

I can talk about what I am doing now. ■   I need more practice. ■

Present continuous: Statements

Present continuous: Statements			
Affirmative			
I	**am**		
You			
We	**are**		
They		reading.	
He	**is**		
She			
It	**is**	raining.	

Negative			
I	**am**		
You			
We	**are**		
They		**not**	**working.**
He	**is**		
She			
It	**is**	**not**	**snowing.**

Grammar Watch

- Use the present continuous for things that are happening now.
- Remember: We usually use contractions with *be* in conversations.
- For spelling rules for the present continuous, see page 260.

A COMPLETE. Use contractions.

A: What are you doing?

B: I <u>'m watching</u> TV. What are *you* doing?
       1. (watch)

A: I _____ to you!
      2. (talk)

B: Very funny. How's the weather there?

A: Well, it _____, but it's cold. How's the weather in Chicago?
      3. (not rain)

B: It _____ here.
      4. (snow)

A: Oh. Is it cold?

B: Yes. I _____ two sweaters.
      5. (wear)

A: Is Jason home?

B: Yes. He _____ today.
      6. (not work)

A: What about the kids? What are they doing?

B: They're outside. They _____ a snowman!
      7. (make)

Grammar

B COMPARE. Look at the pictures. Find 10 differences. Talk about them.

A: In Picture 1, a woman is eating an apple.
B: Right. But in Picture 2, she isn't eating an apple. She's eating a banana.

Show what you know!

1. **THINK ABOUT IT.** Find a photo of yourself.

2. **TALK ABOUT IT.** Show your photo to your partner. What are you doing? Tell your partner.

   A: I'm visiting my cousin. We're eating dinner.
   B: That's a nice picture.

3. **WRITE ABOUT IT.** Now write a sentence about your photo.

   My cousin and I are eating dinner.

   _____

I can make statements in the present continuous. ■   I need more practice. ■

For more practice, go to MyEnglishLab.

Lesson **4**

Plan for an emergency

1 TALK ABOUT BAD WEATHER AND EMERGENCIES

A **LABEL.** Which words for bad weather and emergencies do you know? Write the words under the pictures.

an earthquake	a snowstorm
a flood	a thunderstorm
a landslide	a tornado
a hurricane	a wildfire

1. _a landslide_

2. _____

3. _____

4. _____

5. _____

6. _____

7. _____

8. _____

B ▶ **SELF-ASSESS.** Listen and check your answers. Then listen and repeat.

C ▶ **LISTEN AND READ.** Then listen and repeat.

A: What do you do in a flood?
B: I leave my home.

D **ROLE-PLAY.** Make new conversations. Use the information in the chart.

Emergency	What to do
fire, flood, landslide	leave your home
snowstorm, thunderstorm, hurricane	stay home
tornado	go downstairs
earthquake	go under a piece of furniture

2 PLAN FOR AN EMERGENCY

A **TALK ABOUT IT.** Read the email. What information do employees need to know for an emergency?

TO: employees@smbus.com
FROM: Management
SUBJECT: Emergency plan

All Employees,

We have a new emergency system.
- New exit maps: Know the exit doors.
- New alarm system: We will test the system on Friday, 10/28 at 10:00 A.M.
- Put emergency numbers in your phone: Police, Fire

In an emergency:
- Leave quickly. Be calm.
- Listen for instructions from your emergency leader.
- Do not use elevators.
- Go to an exit near you.
- Go to safe areas.
  - Parking lot next to office
  - Sidewalk in front of office
- Do not go back in the building.

B **INTERPRET.** Read the sentences about the email in Exercise 2A.
Circle *True* or *False*.

1. There are new exit doors.	True	False
2. The alarm system test is on October 25.	True	False
3. Go out of the building quickly.	True	False
4. Use an exit near you.	True	False
5. Use the elevators in an emergency.	True	False

C **REWRITE.** Correct the false sentences in Exercise 2B.

D ▶ **LISTEN AND READ.** Then listen and repeat.

A: Where is the emergency exit near our classroom?
B: It's next to the restrooms.

E **ROLE-PLAY.** Make new conversations. Use the emergency exit maps at your school.

F GO ONLINE. Add emergency phone numbers to your phone.

I can plan for an emergency. ■   I need more practice. ■

Ask what someone is doing now

1 BEFORE YOU LISTEN

LABEL. What do you need in an emergency? Write the words under the pictures.

| batteries | a first aid kit | a flashlight | matches |

1. _____   2. _____   3. _____   4. _____

2 LISTEN

A ▶ **LISTEN.** Look at the picture. Ron is calling his wife Emma. Why is Ron at the supermarket?

B ▶ **LISTEN FOR DETAILS.** Read the sentences. Circle *True* or *False*.

1. Emma is watching TV.   True   False
2. Emma is doing the laundry.   True   False
3. Ron is working late.   True   False
4. A big storm is coming.   True   False

C ▶ **EXPAND.** Listen to the whole conversation. Complete the sentences. Check (✓) the correct answers.

1. Ron is buying _____. (Check more than one answer.)

   ☐ water   ☐ food   ☐ a flashlight   ☐ batteries   ☐ clothes

2. Emma wants _____.

   ☐ candles   ☐ matches   ☐ a first-aid kit

3. Emma and Ron need _____.

   ☐ good friends   ☐ a good TV   ☐ good weather

3 CONVERSATION

A ▶ **LISTEN AND READ.** Then listen and repeat.

A: Are you watching the news?
B: No, I'm not. I'm doing the laundry.
A: Turn on the TV. A big storm is coming.
B: Really?
A: Yes. I'm coming home early. I'm at the supermarket now.

B **WORK TOGETHER.** Practice the conversation in Exercise A.

C **CREATE.** Make new conversations. Use the information in the boxes.

A: Are you watching the news?
B: No, I'm not. I'm _____.
A: Well, turn on the TV. A _____ is coming.
B: Really?
A: Yes. I'm coming home early. I'm at the _____ now.

checking email	making lunch	cleaning the apartment
hurricane	thunderstorm	snowstorm

hardware store	grocery store	shopping center

D **ROLE-PLAY.** Make your own conversations. Use different activities and locations.

I can ask what someone is doing now. ☐ | I need more practice. ☐

Grammar

Present continuous: *Yes/no* questions and short answers

Present continuous: *Yes/no* questions and short answers							
Are	you			I **am**.		I'm **not**.
	they	**working**?	Yes,	they **are**.	No,	they**'re not**. / they **aren't**.
Is	he			he **is**.		he**'s not**. / he **isn't**.

A **APPLY.** Look at the picture. Answer the questions. Use short answers.

1. **A:** Are they working?

   B: *No, they're not. (No, they aren't.)*

2. **A:** Is it raining?

   B: _____

3. **A:** Is the man wearing a blue uniform?

   B: _____

4. **A:** Are they reading?

   B: _____

5. **A:** Is the woman listening to music?

   B: _____

6. **A:** Is the man eating a sandwich?

   B: _____

7. **A:** Is the man playing a game?

   B: _____

B **WRITE.** Use the words in parentheses to write *yes/no* questions.

1. (they / eating pizza) _Are they eating pizza?_ _____
2. (they / text) _____
3. (she / wear a hat) _____
4. (he / listen to music) _____
5. (they / wear jackets) _____

C **WORK TOGETHER.** Look at the picture on page 176. Ask and answer the questions in Exercises A and B.

A: Are they eating pizza?
B: No, they're not.

Show what you know!

1. LIST. Make a list of activities.

_____
_____
_____
_____

2. ACT IT OUT. Student A, act out one activity from Exercise 1. Students B and C, guess the activity.

B: Are you checking email?
A: No, I'm not.
C: Are you texting?
A: Yes, I am.

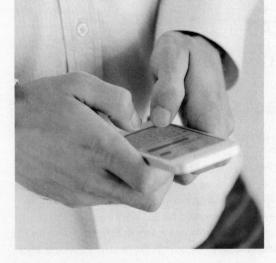

3. WRITE ABOUT IT. Now write two *yes/no* questions from Exercise 2.

_____
_____

I can ask and answer *yes/no* questions in the present continuous. ☐   I need more practice. ☐

For more practice, go to MyEnglishLab.

Read about hurricanes

1 BEFORE YOU READ

A **LABEL.** Write the vocabulary words from the box on the map.

| Northeast | Northwest | Southeast | Southwest |

1. _____

2. _____

3. _____

4. _____

Regions of the U.S.

North

NW   NE

West   East

SW   SE

South

A compass.

B **TALK ABOUT IT.** Where do hurricanes happen? What happens during a hurricane?

2 READ

▶ Listen and read.

Academic Skill: Focus on details

The first time you read an article, read for the main idea. Then read again and focus on the details. The details answer questions such as *who*, *what*, *when*, *where*, *how*, and *why*.

Facts about Hurricanes

Hurricanes are big storms. A hurricane can be 600 miles across! The winds can be as strong as 200 mph (miles per hour). The winds move in a circle. The center of the circle is called the eye.

5 Hurricanes form only over warm ocean water. The water needs to be 80 degrees or higher. Warmer water makes a storm stronger. When the storm hits land, it brings both strong winds and heavy rain.

10 A hurricane also brings a storm surge. It pushes ocean water on land. The water moves at 10 to 15 mph. It can be several feet high. A one-foot storm surge can push a car off the road.

Most big storms happen during hurricane
15 season. In the Atlantic Ocean, it goes from June 1 to November 30. During hurricane season, people listen for news of storms. A hurricane watch means a bad storm might come in the next 36 hours. A hurricane warning means a hurricane is coming in
20 the next 24 hours. On average, hurricane season brings five or six hurricanes, but sometimes there are more. Usually only two are major hurricanes.

In the U.S., hurricanes most often hit the South and the Southeast. They do the most damage in
25 Florida, Texas, and Louisiana. But they cause problems in other states, too.

Source: U.S. National Weather Service Climate Prediction Center

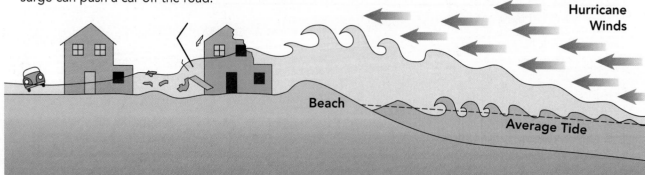

Hurricane Winds

Beach

Average Tide

3 CLOSE READING

CITE EVIDENCE. Complete the sentences. Where is the information?
Write the line number.

Lines

1. A hurricane can be up to _____ miles wide.
   a. 60   **b.** 200   **c.** 600   _____

2. Hurricane winds can blow up to _____ mph (miles per hour).
   a. 100   **b.** 150   **c.** 200   _____

3. Hurricanes get started only _____.
   a. during hurricane   **b.** over warm ocean   **c.** in the Atlantic Ocean   _____
   season   water

4. _____ means that a hurricane is coming in the next 24 hours.
   a. A storm surge   **b.** A hurricane watch   **c.** A hurricane warning   _____

5. A storm surge can be _____ high.
   a. only one foot   **b.** several feet   **c.** over 25 feet   _____

6. In the U.S., hurricanes are most common in _____.
   a. the Southwest   **b.** the South and   **c.** the 14 states on the   _____
   Southeast   Atlantic Ocean

4 SUMMARIZE

Complete the summary with the words in the box.

| Hurricanes | ocean | Southeast | storm surges | winds |

(1) _____ are big storms. They bring dangerous (2) _____ of up
to 200 mph, heavy rain, and (3) _____. Hurricanes form only over warm
(4) _____ water (80° or higher). Hurricane season in the Atlantic Ocean goes
from June to November. In the U.S., hurricanes most often hit places in the South and
(5) _____.

Show what you know!

1. **THINK ABOUT IT.** What do people do when there is a hurricane watch?

2. **WRITE ABOUT IT.** Now write about what people do before a hurricane.

   Before a hurricane, people _____.

I can focus on details. ■   I need more practice. ■

To read more, go to MyEnglishLab.

1 BEFORE YOU LISTEN

LABEL. Write the words under the pictures.

boots	earmuffs	gloves	a hat	~~light clothes~~	a raincoat
a scarf	shorts	sunblock	sunglasses	an umbrella	a bottle of water

Weather! Do you have the right clothes, accessories, and supplies?

1. _light clothes_

2. _____

3. _____

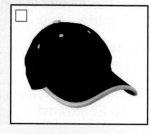

4. _____

5. _____

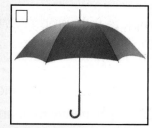

6. _____

7. _____

8. _____

9. _____

10. _____

11. _____

12. _____

2 LISTEN

A ▶ **RECALL.** Listen to the weather report. What clothes, accessories, and supplies do you hear? Check (✓) the pictures on page 180.

B ▶ **LISTEN FOR DETAILS.** Write the temperature for each city on the map.

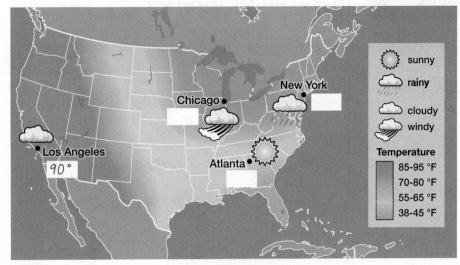

New York

Chicago •

Los Angeles
90°

Atlanta •

☼	sunny
☁	rainy
☁	cloudy
☁	windy

Temperature
	85-95 °F
	70-80 °F
	55-65 °F
	38-45 °F

3 CONVERSATION

A **PREDICT.** Look at the picture. How is the weather?

B ▶ **LISTEN AND READ.** Then listen and repeat.

A: Are you going out?
B: Yes. Why?
A: Well, it's really **cold**, and it's pretty **windy**.
B: That's OK. I have a **scarf** and **gloves**!

C **WORK TOGETHER.** Practice the conversation in Exercise B.

D **CREATE.** Make new conversations. Use different weather words and clothes, accessories, or supplies from page 180.

E **ROLE-PLAY.** Make your own conversations. Talk about today's weather.

I can understand a weather report. ■   I need more practice. ■

For more practice, go to MyEnglishLab.

9 Grammar
Adverbs of degree

Adverbs of degree: *Very, really, pretty*					
	Adverb	Adjective		Adverb	Adjective
	very			very	
It's	really	windy.	He's	really	cold.
	pretty			pretty	

Grammar Watch

Use *very*, *really*, or *pretty* before an adjective to make it stronger.

A APPLY. Write sentences with the words in parentheses. Then match the sentences with the pictures.

1. _It's really cold._   D
   (really / it's / cold)

2. _____ ___
   (pretty / it's / hot)

3. _____ ___
   (very / it's / windy)

4. _____ ___
   (foggy / really / it's)

B APPLY. Read the conversation. Find the three adjectives in blue. Add the word *very*, *really*, or *pretty* before each adjective. Use each word only once.

A: How's the weather?
B: It's nice.
A: Then let's take a walk!
B: OK. But I'm hungry. Let's eat first.
A: Well, there's a good restaurant on Main Street.
B: Great. Let's go there.

C WORK TOGETHER. Perform your conversation for the class.

D WRITE. Now write sentences about today's weather. Use *very*, *really*, or *pretty* in your sentences.

I can use adverbs of degree. ☐   I need more practice. ☐

For more practice, go to MyEnglishLab.

Write about weather

1 STUDY THE MODEL

READ. Answer the questions.

> Pedro Melez
> The Weather in Cuba
>
> I am from Havana, Cuba. In the summer, it is hot and humid. It rains a lot. In the winter, it is sunny and warm. Winter is my favorite season in Cuba because it is warm in the day and cool at night.

1. Where is Pedro from?
2. How is the weather in Cuba in the summer?
3. How is the weather in Cuba in the winter?
4. What is Pedro's favorite season in Cuba? Why?

2 PLAN YOUR WRITING

WORK TOGETHER. Ask and answer the questions.

1. Where are you from?
2. How is the weather in your native country in the summer?
3. How is the weather in your native country in the winter?
4. What is your favorite season in your native country? Why?

Writing Skill: Use *because* to give a reason

The word *because* gives a reason. It explains why. For example:

Why is winter his favorite season? Winter is his favorite season *because* it is warm in the day and cool at night.

3 WRITE

Now write about the weather in your native country. Use the frame, the model, the Writing Skill, and your ideas from Exercise 2 to help you.

> I'm from _____, _____. In the summer, it _____. In the winter, it _____. My favorite season is _____ because it _____.

4 CHECK YOUR WRITING

WORK TOGETHER. Read your writing aloud with a partner.

WRITING CHECKLIST

☐ The writing answers the questions in Exercise 2.

☐ The writer uses *because* to explain why.

I can use *because* to give a reason. ■   I need more practice. ■

For more practice, go to MyEnglishLab.

Be ready to learn new skills

1 MEET YEFIM

Read about one of his workplace skills.

> I am ready to learn new skills. For example, sometimes my work changes. Sometimes, I need to do my work in a different way. I like to learn new things.

2 YEFIM'S PROBLEM

READ. Circle *True* or *False*.

Yefim is a teacher. He learns new things in his job. Sometimes he teaches different classes. Sometimes the school has new technology.

One day he goes to a meeting. He learns about a new mobile app for emergencies at the school. All teachers need to learn the app. He's worried because he isn't good at technology. After the meeting, he talks to a co-worker.

1.	The school has a new app for emergencies.	True	False
2.	Teachers don't have to learn the new app.	True	False
3.	Yefim is good at technology.	True	False

3 YEFIM'S SOLUTION

A **WORK TOGETHER.** Yefim is ready to learn new skills. What is the right thing to say to his co-worker? Explain your answer.

1. Yefim says, "I know the new mobile app is important, but I don't think I can learn it."
2. Yefim says, "I'm not good at technology. Can you help me learn the new mobile app?"
3. Yefim says, "I don't need to learn the new app. I can call 911."
4. Yefim says, "_____."

B **ROLE-PLAY.** Look at your answer to 3A. Role-play Yefim's conversation.

Show what you know!

1. **THINK ABOUT IT.** How are you ready to learn new things at school? At work? At home? Give examples.

2. **WRITE ABOUT IT.** Now write your example in your Skills Log.

   I can learn a new way to do my work from my co-workers.

I can give an example of how I'm ready to learn new skills. ☐

Unit Review: Go back to page 165. Which goals can you check off?

10 Around Town

PREVIEW

Look at the picture. Where are the people?
What are they doing?

UNIT GOALS

- [ ] Name places in the community
- [ ] Give locations of places in the community
- [ ] Talk about kinds of transportation
- [ ] Read traffic signs
- [ ] Read bus signs and schedules
- [ ] Ask about bus routes and costs
- [ ] Talk about weekend plans
- [ ] **Academic skill:** Give your own examples
- [ ] **Writing skill:** Use prepositions
- [ ] **Workplace soft skill:** Be reliable

Places in the community

A **PREDICT.** Look at the pictures. What do you see? What are the places?

Number 3 is a post office.

B ▶ **LISTEN AND POINT.** Then listen and repeat.

Vocabulary

Places in the community

1. a fire station	**5.** a supermarket	**9.** a bank	**13.** a gym
2. a bus stop	**6.** a drugstore	**10.** an ATM	**14.** a clothing store
3. a post office	**7.** a gas station	**11.** a farmers' market	**15.** a café
4. a police station	**8.** a park	**12.** a laundromat	**16.** a salon

C **WORK TOGETHER.** Look at the pictures and the list of places. Student A, choose a place. Say something you do there. Student B, guess the place.

A: I buy fruit there.
B: The supermarket?
A: No.
A: The farmers' market?
B: Right!

D **CATEGORIZE.** Look at the pictures and list of places. Complete the chart. Then compare answers.

Words with *station*	Words with *market*	Words with *store*

Study Tip

Count syllables

Mark the number of syllables in each word. Listen to the audio and check your work.

Show what you know!

1. **DRAW A PICTURE.** Draw a map of the streets near your school. Write the places on the map.

2. **TALK ABOUT IT.** Talk about the places around your school.

   A: Is there a café near here?
   B: Yes, it's across the street.
   C: Right. And there's a bank on King Street, next to the drugstore.

3. **WRITE ABOUT IT.** Now write a sentence about places in your community.

   There is _____ on _____, _____

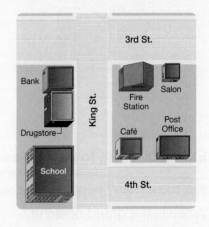

I can name places in the community. ☐   I need more practice. ☐

For more practice, go to MyEnglishLab.

Listening and Speaking

Give locations of places in the community

1 BEFORE YOU LISTEN

IDENTIFY. Look at the ad. Complete the sentences with the words in the box.

~~gas station~~   library   post office

1. Foodsmart is near the ___*gas station*___.
2. It is between the bank and the _____.
3. It is around the corner from the _____.

Foodsmart
Grand Opening

Bank   Library   Gas Station

We are here ★

Post Office

Saturday, October 8

2 LISTEN

A ▶ **LISTEN.** Look at the picture. Listen to the conversation. Brenda is asking a man a question. What does she want?

a. a map
b. a good supermarket
c. directions

Brenda

B ▶ **LISTEN FOR DETAILS.** Where is the new supermarket?

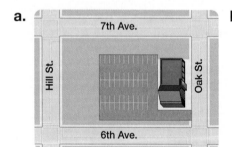
a.
7th Ave.
Hill St.
Oak St.
6th Ave.

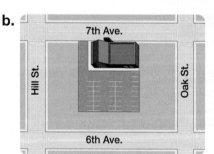
b.
7th Ave.
Hill St.
Oak St.
6th Ave.

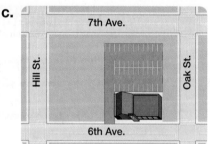
c.
7th Ave.
Hill St.
Oak St.
6th Ave.

C ▶ **EXPAND.** Listen to the whole conversation. Answer the questions.

1. Are there many people at the supermarket?   **a.** no   **b.** yes
2. When is the grand opening?   **a.** today   **b.** tomorrow

3 PRONUNCIATION

A ▶ **PRACTICE. Listen. Then listen and repeat.**

a **round**   **o** pen   to **day**   po **lice**   **sta** tion

B ▶ **APPLY. Listen to the words. Mark (•) the stressed syllable.**

sa lon   be tween   cor ner   se venth

> **Stressed syllable**
>
> In a two-syllable word, one syllable is stressed. The other syllable is not stressed.

4 CONVERSATION

A ▶ **LISTEN AND READ. Then listen and repeat.**

A: Excuse me. Can you help me? I'm looking for Foodsmart.
B: Sure. It's on Seventh between Hill and Oak.
A: Sorry?
B: It's on Seventh Avenue between Hill Street and Oak Street.
A: Thanks.

B **WORK TOGETHER. Practice the conversation in Exercise A.**

C **CREATE. Make new conversations. Use the pictures and map.**

A: Excuse me. Can you help me? I'm looking

for _____ .
               (place)

B: Sure. It's on _____
                       (Avenue)

between _____ and
                   (Street)

_____ .
        (Street)

A: Sorry?

B: It's on _____
                (Avenue)

between _____ and
                   (Street)

_____ .
         (Street)

A: Thanks.

D **MAKE CONNECTIONS. Make your own conversations. Use places and streets near your school.**

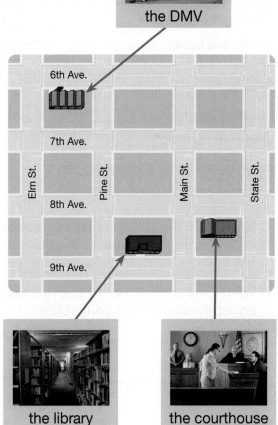

the DMV

the library   the courthouse

> I can give locations of places in the community. ■   I need more practice. ■

For more practice, go to MyEnglishLab.

Grammar

Prepositions of place

Prepositions of place		
	around	the corner from the bank.
	down	the street / the block.
The supermarket is	**between**	Hill and Oak Streets.
	on	the corner of 10th and Pine.
	near	the library.

Grammar Watch
For more prepositions of place, see page 260.

COMPLETE. Use *around*, *down*, *between*, *on*, **or** *near*.

1. The library is _____*on*_____ the corner of Oak and Elm Streets.

2. The police station is _____ Park _____ 9th and 10th Streets.

3. There's a bank _____ the corner from the police station.

4. There's a fire station _____ the street from the police station.

5. There's a post office _____ the library.

6. There's a café _____ the corner of 9th and Elm Streets.

Show what you know!

1. IDENTIFY. Read the sentences above again. Write the names of the places on the map.

2. WRITE ABOUT IT. Now write two sentences about the location of your school.

My school is _____.

It _____.

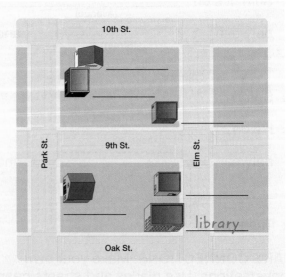

I can use prepositions of place. ■   I need more practice. ■

For more practice, go to MyEnglishLab.

Workplace, Life, and Community Skills

Talk about transportation

1 TALK ABOUT KINDS OF TRANSPORTATION

A ▶ **LISTEN AND POINT.** Then listen and repeat.

a bus

a subway

a train

a car

a bike

a taxi

B **TALK ABOUT IT.** Ask your classmates how they get to work or school. Complete the chart.

A: How do you get to work or school?
B: I take the bus.

Names	Take the bus	Take the train	Walk	Drive	Other
Susan	✓				

C **PRESENT.** Now report to the class.

Susan takes the bus.

| I can talk about kinds of transportation. ■ | I need more practice. ■ |

2 READ TRAFFIC SIGNS

A **LABEL.** Look at the signs. Write the meanings under the signs.

| Don't turn left. | ~~Stop.~~ | Two-way traffic.
Drive on the right. |

1. _Stop._

2. _____

3. _____

| Drive slowly. People often
cross the street here. | Drive slowly.
Wait for other cars. | Right lane ends ahead.
Stay to the left. |

4. _____

5. _____

6. _____

| Be ready to stop for trains. | Don't drive here. | Drive slowly. People often
cross the street here. |

7. _____

8. _____

9. _____

B ▶ **IDENTIFY.** Listen to the conversations. Which signs are the people talking about?
Write the number of the sign.

1. _____

2. _____

3. _____

I can read traffic signs. ■ I need more practice. ■

For more practice, go to MyEnglishLab.

3 READ BUS SIGNS AND SCHEDULES

A WORK TOGETHER. Look at the buses. Ask and answer questions. Take turns.

A: Which bus goes to Pine Street?
B: The Number 51. Which . . . ?

Student A:

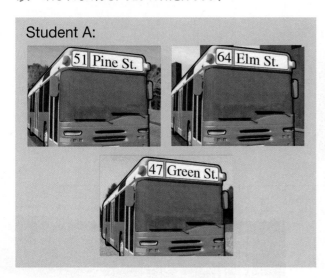

Student B:

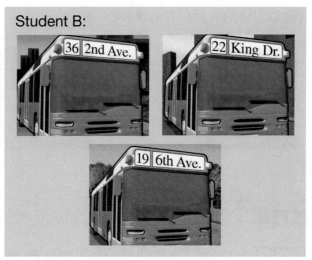

B ▶ COMPLETE. Look at the bus schedules. Listen and fill in the missing times.

GREENVILLE BUS SCHEDULES

BUS 36		BUS 47		BUS 51	
39th Ave.	_____	39th Ave.	8:14	King Dr.	8:15
River Rd.	8:16	Clay St.	8:23	State St.	8:22
16th Ave.	8:24	Park Ave.	_____	Oak St.	8:31
2nd Ave.	8:35	Green St.	8:40	Pine St.	_____

C INTERPRET. Look at the schedules in Exercise 3B. Answer the questions.

1. What time does Bus 36 leave 16th Avenue? _____8:24_____
2. What time does Bus 47 leave 39th Avenue? _____
3. What time does Bus 51 leave State Street? _____

D GO ONLINE. Use a transportation website or app to find public transportation to a supermarket.

I can read bus signs and schedules. ■   I need more practice. ■

For more practice, go to MyEnglishLab.

1 BEFORE YOU LISTEN

LABEL. Write the words under the pictures.

get off	get on	pay the fare

a. _____   b. _____   c. _____

2 LISTEN

A **PREDICT.** Look at the picture. What do you see?

B ▶ **LISTEN.** Where do Matt and Tina want to go?

a. a supermarket
b. Adams College
c. Second Street

C ▶ **LISTEN FOR DETAILS.** Read the sentences. Circle *True* or *False*. Make the false sentences true.

1. They need the Number 5̶ (4) bus.	True	False
2. They get on at Second Street.	True	False
3. The fare is $2.00.	True	False
4. It is OK to give the driver a five-dollar bill.	True	False

D ▶ **EXPAND.** Listen to the second part of the conversation. Complete the sentences.

1. Matt asks the woman for _____.
   a. exact change   b. directions   c. a map

2. The woman _____ directions to Adams College.
   a. gives   b. doesn't give   c. gets

3. The woman says, "_____"
   a. It's over there.   b. It's on Second Street.   c. Study, study, study!

3 PRONUNCIATION

A ▶ **PRACTICE.** Listen. Then listen and repeat.

How **do you** get **to** Adams College?
Take **the** bus, **and** get off **at** Second Street.

B ▶ **APPLY.** Practice saying each sentence. Then listen and repeat.

Here we are at Second Street.
We want to go to Adams College.
How do we get there?

4 CONVERSATION

A ▶ **LISTEN AND READ.** Then listen and repeat.

A: Excuse me. How do you get to Adams College?
B: Take the Number 4 bus, and get off at Second Street. It's not far from there.
A: Thanks. Oh, and how much does the bus cost?
B: Two dollars, but you need exact change.

B **WORK TOGETHER.** Practice the conversation in Exercise A.

C **CREATE.** Make new conversations. Use the information in the boxes.

A: Excuse me. How do you get to
⬚⬚⬚⬚⬚⬚⬚ ?
B: Take the ⬚⬚⬚⬚⬚⬚ , and get off at Second Street. It's not far from there.
A: Thanks. Oh, and how much does the bus cost?
B: ⬚⬚⬚⬚⬚⬚ , but you need exact change.

Pine Hill Park

$2.50

Green's

$3.00

the main post office

$3.50

D **MAKE CONNECTIONS.** Make your own conversations. Ask for directions from school to places in town.

I can ask about bus routes and costs. ▪   I need more practice. ▪

Grammar

Simple present questions with *How*, *How much*, and *Where*

Simple present: Questions with *How*, *How much*, and *Where*			Grammar Watch
How	do you get to Adams College?	Take the Number 4 bus.	Remember: For questions in the simple present, use ***does*** with *he*, *she*, and *it*.
How much	does it cost?	$2.00.	
Where	do you get off?	Second Street.	

A **PUT IN ORDER.** Maria is going shopping. Put the pictures in the correct order (1–4).

B **WRITE.** Unscramble the words to ask questions about Maria.

1. (Maria / does / shop for food / where) *Where does Maria shop for food?*
2. (get there / how / she / does) _____
3. (does / cost / how much / the milk) _____
4. (she / does / get home / how) _____
5. (the bus / where / she / does / wait for) _____

C **WORK TOGETHER.** Ask and answer the questions in Exercise B.

A: *Where does Maria shop for food?*
B: *At Bob's supermarket. How . . . ?*

Grammar

D **COMPLETE.** Use *How, How much,* or *Where* and the words in parentheses. Add *do* or *does*.

A: Excuse me. _____How do you get to_____
1. (you / get to)

Pine Hill Park?

B: Take the Number 4 train.

A: OK. _____ the train?
2. (you / get)

B: The train station is down the block. Do you see it?

A: Oh, yes. And _____ a ticket?
3. (you / buy)

B: In the station.

A: _____?
4. (it / cost)

B $2.00.

A: OK. Sorry, one more question. _____ for the park?
5. (you / get off)

B: Park Avenue. There's a big sign for the park. You can't miss it.

E ▶ **SELF-ASSESS.** Listen and check your answers.

Show what you know!

1. THINK ABOUT IT. Look at the pictures. Where do you buy these things? Write the places.

_____milk—DVS Drugstore_____   _____

_____   _____

chocolate

tissues

2. TALK ABOUT IT. Talk about your answers in Step 1.

A: *Where do you buy milk?*
B: *At DVS Drugstore.*
A: *Oh? How much does it cost there?*

milk   pens

3. WRITE ABOUT IT. Now write a note to your partner. Ask where your partner buys something. Ask how much it costs there.

Where _____?

_____?

I can use simple present questions with *How, How much,* and *Where.* ■	I need more practice. ■

For more practice, go to MyEnglishLab.

Read about public libraries

1 BEFORE YOU READ

A LABEL. Write the words under the pictures.

| an e-book on a tablet | a library card | a receipt with a due date |

1. _____

2. _____

3. _____

B MAKE CONNECTIONS. Where is your public library? What can people do there?

2 READ

▶ Listen and read.

Academic Skill: Give your own examples

Writers often give examples to help the reader understand their ideas, like the examples in this article of library activities for children. Try to think of examples of your own when you read.

Your Public Library

The U.S. has more than 16,000 public libraries. They are open to everyone, and they are free.

You can do many things at a public library. You can read newspapers and magazines. You can study or do
5 homework. You can use Wi-Fi to go online. Many libraries have computer and English classes. Some have information about jobs. All libraries have activities for children. For example, some have summer programs. Some have homework help after school.

An event for children at a public library.

10 With a library card, you can borrow books, tablets, and more! How long can you keep them? Check the due date on your receipt. Don't be late, or you will need to pay a fine. The fine might be only five cents or a lot more. To get a card, fill out an application.
15 You will need to show something with your name and address. For example, show an ID, your driver's license, or a credit card bill.

Your public library has a website. You can find out library hours. You can read about events. You can
20 borrow e-books and watch movies online. You can renew books so you can keep them longer.

These are only a few reasons to use your public library. Go online or visit to learn more.

3 CLOSE READING

**CITE EVIDENCE. Complete the sentences. Where is the information?
Write the line number.**

Lines

1. There are more than _____ public libraries in the U.S.
   a. 1,600   **b.** 16,000   **c.** 16,000,000   _____

2. Public libraries _____.
   a. are open all day every day   **b.** are free to use   **c.** sell books   _____

3. Children can sometimes go to the library for _____ after school.
   a. help with homework   **b.** free child-care   **c.** something to eat   _____

4. Before you can borrow things from the library, you need to _____.
   a. have a school or work ID   **b.** show a credit card   **c.** get a library card   _____

5. When you return something to the library after the due date, you _____.
   a. lose your library card   **b.** need to pay a fine   **c.** fill out an application   _____

6. Go to your public library's website to _____.
   a. take computer classes   **b.** pay a fine   **c.** renew books   _____

4 SUMMARIZE

Complete the summary with the words in the box.

| for free | library card | online | programs | public library |

You can do many things at your (1) _____. You can read, do homework, go

(2) _____, and take classes (3) _____. There are activities and

(4) _____ for children. You can borrow books, tablets, e-books, and movies. You

just need a (5) _____. Visit your public library to get a card and learn more.

Show what you know!

1. **THINK ABOUT IT.** What are some reasons to go to a public library? What are some reasons to visit the library website?

2. **WRITE ABOUT IT.** Now write about good reasons to go to your public library.

   At my public library, I can _____.

I can give my own examples. ☐   I need more practice. ☐

To read more, go to MyEnglishLab.

Talk about weekend plans

1 BEFORE YOU LISTEN

A **MAKE CONNECTIONS.** Look at the pictures. Do you go to events like these in your community?

B **TALK ABOUT IT.** Where do you get information about events in your community? Do you look in the newspaper? Do you look online? Do you watch TV?

grand opening

concert

baseball game

yard sale

2 LISTEN

A **LISTEN FOR DETAILS.** Look at the Greenville Weekend Community Schedule. Listen to the radio show and complete the information.

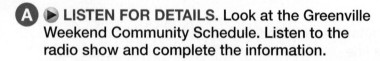

The Greenville Weekend Community Schedule

Grand Opening

Place: Foodsmart

Day: _____

Time: _____

Baseball Game

Place: Greenville _____

Day: _____

Time: 1:00 P.M.

Concert

Place: Greenville Community College

Day: _____

Time: _____

Yard Sale

Place: the Community Center across from the

_____ station

Day: _____

Time: 10:00 A.M. to _____

B ▶ **LISTEN FOR DETAILS.** Which events are free? Check (✓) all the correct answers.

- ☐ the grand opening
- ☐ the concert
- ☐ the baseball game
- ☐ the yard sale

C **GIVE EXAMPLES.** Are there free events in your community? What are some examples?

There are free movies at the library.

3 CONVERSATION

A **PREDICT.** Look at the picture. What are they talking about?

- **a.** the new supermarket
- **b.** a weekend concert
- **c.** the community college

B ▶ **LISTEN AND READ.** Then listen and repeat.

A: What are you doing this weekend?
B: I'm going to **a concert**.
A: Oh? Where's **the concert**?
B: At **the community college**. Do you want to go?
A: Sounds great.

C **WORK TOGETHER.** Practice the conversation in Exercise B.

D **CREATE.** Make new conversations. Use the events in the Greenville Weekend Community Schedule on page 200.

E **MAKE CONNECTIONS.** Make your own conversations.

I can talk about weekend plans. ■   I need more practice. ■

For more practice, go to MyEnglishLab.

Present continuous for future plans					
What	**are** you **doing**	next weekend?	**I'm going**	to a concert.
How	**are** you **getting**	there?	**I'm taking**	the bus.
Who	**are** you **going**	with?	**I'm going**	with Ana.

A **DECIDE.** Read each sentence. Is the sentence about the present or the future? Check (✓) the correct box.

	Present	Future
1. I'm working next weekend.	☐	✓
2. I'm doing my English homework now.	☐	☐
3. Are you coming with us to the movie tomorrow?	☐	☐
4. When are you visiting your grandparents?	☐	☐
5. I'm sorry, but I can't talk now. I'm cooking dinner.	☐	☐

B **COMPLETE.** Use the present continuous form of the verbs in parentheses.

1. **A:** What ___are___ you ___doing___ tomorrow?
   (do)

   B: I _____ my friends at the mall.
   (meet)

   A: How _____ you _____ there?
   (get)

   B: I _____ the bus.
   (take)

2. **A:** Where _____ Sam _____
   (go)
   this weekend?

   B: He _____ to Riverside for a concert.
   (go)

3. **A:** When _____ your children _____ you?
   (visit)

   B: They _____ for dinner next Sunday.
   (come)

I can use the present continuous for future plans. ☐   I need more practice. ☐

For more practice, go to MyEnglishLab.

Write about your street

1 STUDY THE MODEL

READ. Answer the questions.

Lee Chang
My Street

I live on Winter Street. There are many stores near my home. There is a drugstore, a big supermarket, and a café down the block. There is also a bus stop next to my building and a subway station across the street. I like my street because I can walk to the stores.

1. What is the name of Lee's street?
2. What stores are near his home?
3. What transportation is near his home?
4. What does Lee like about his street?

2 PLAN YOUR WRITING

WORK TOGETHER. Ask and answer the questions.

1. What's the name of your street?
2. What stores are near your home?
3. What transportation is near your home?
4. What do you like about your street?

Writing Skill: Use prepositions

Prepositions are very different in every language. Be sure you use the correct preposition in English. For example:
I live (on) Winter Street.

3 WRITE

Now write about your street. Use the frame, the model, the Writing Skill, and your ideas from Exercise 2 to help you.

I live on _____. There are many _____ near my home. There is a _____, a _____, and a _____ down the block. There is also _____. I like my street because _____.

4 CHECK YOUR WRITING

WORK TOGETHER. Read your writing aloud with a partner.

WRITING CHECKLIST

☐ The writing answers all the questions in Exercise 2.

☐ The prepositions are correct.

I can use prepositions. ■   I need more practice. ■

For more practice, go to MyEnglishLab.

11 Soft Skills at Work

Be reliable

1 MEET ANI

Read about one of her workplace skills.

I'm reliable. For example, I always arrive at work on time. My manager knows I will be on time every day.

2 ANI'S PROBLEM

READ. Circle *True* or *False*.

Ani works at a hospital. She is a nurse's assistant. She helps patients. She needs to arrive at work on time. She takes the train to work every day. It takes one hour.

One morning, Ani looks at the train app. She sees the train to work is thirty minutes late.

1. Ani is a nurse at a hospital.	True	False
2. Ani can arrive a little late for work.	True	False
3. Ani's train is one hour late.	True	False

3 ANI'S SOLUTION

WORK TOGETHER. Ani is reliable. What is the reliable thing to do? Explain your answer.

1. Ani calls her supervisor and says, "I'm sorry. I'll be late because the train is late."
2. Ani arrives late for work. Then she says to her supervisor, "I'm sorry I'm late."
3. Ani calls her supervisor and says, "I don't feel well today. I can't come to work."
4. Ani _____.

Show what you know!

1. **THINK ABOUT IT.** How are you reliable at school? At work? At home? Give examples.

2. **WRITE ABOUT IT.** Now write your example in your Skills Log.

   I always finish my homework before class.

I can give an example from my life of being reliable. ☐

Unit Review: Go back to page 185. Which goals can you check off?

11 Health Matters

PREVIEW

Look at the picture. What do you see?
Who are the people?

UNIT GOALS

- [ ] Name parts of the body
- [ ] Call to explain an absence
- [ ] Follow a doctor's instructions
- [ ] Read medicine labels
- [ ] Talk about health problems

- [ ] Give advice
- [ ] **Academic skill:** Apply what you read
- [ ] **Writing skill:** Use a topic sentence
- [ ] **Workplace soft skill:** Make good decisions

A **PREDICT.** Look at the pictures. What do you see? What are the parts of the body?

Number 11 is leg.

B ▶ **LISTEN AND POINT.** Then listen and repeat.

8. hand
7. wrist
1. head
2. face
3. neck
4. shoulder
5. arm
6. elbow
9. chest
10. stomach
11. leg
12. knee
13. ankle
14. foot/feet

19. ear
15. eye
16. nose
17. mouth
18. tooth/teeth
20. back

Vocabulary

Parts of the body

1. head	5. arm	9. chest	13. ankle	17. mouth
2. face	6. elbow	10. stomach	14. foot/feet	18. tooth/teeth
3. neck	7. wrist	11. leg	15. eye	19. ear
4. shoulder	8. hand	12. knee	16. nose	20. back

C **SAY AND SPELL.** Student A, look at the word list. Say a part of the body. Student B, ask for the spelling.

A: Stomach.
B: How do you spell that?
A: S-T-O-M-A-C-H.
B: Thanks.

D **CATEGORIZE.** Look at the pictures and word list. Complete the chart. Then compare answers.

I have one . . .	I have two . . .
head	legs
	.

Study Tip

Type and spell

Type the words in your phone. Spell the words aloud when you type.

Show what you know!

1. **IDENTIFY.** Student A, look at the pictures and word list. Say a part of the body. Student B, point to your body part.

   Ankle.

2. ▶ **LISTEN AND ACT.** Listen and follow the commands.

touch

clap

nod

shake

3. **WRITE ABOUT IT.** Now write sentences about what you do with your body.

   I clap my _____. I nod my _____.
   I point to my _____.

I can name parts of the body. ■   I need more practice. ■

For more practice, go to MyEnglishLab.

1 BEFORE YOU LISTEN

IDENTIFY. Look at the pictures. The children don't feel well. They feel sick. Complete the sentences.

1. Her _____throat_____ hurts.
2. Her _____ hurts.
3. His _____ hurts.
4. His _____ hurts.

1. sore throat

2. stomachache

3. toothache

4. headache

2 LISTEN

A **PREDICT.** Look at the picture. What do you see?

B ▶ **LISTEN.** Complete the sentence.

Mrs. Lee is calling _____.
a. her son's school because he's sick.
b. the doctor because her son is sick.
c. the hospital because she is sick.

C ▶ **LISTEN FOR DETAILS.** Complete the sentences.

1. Ms. Wong is _____.
   a. a teacher
   b. an office assistant
   c. a parent

2. Alex has a sore throat and a _____.
   a. stomachache
   b. headache
   c. toothache

D ▶ **EXPAND.** Listen to the whole conversation. Circle *True* or *False*.

1. Mrs. Lee's other children feel well.   True   False
2. Mrs. Lee needs to call the school again later.   True   False

3 CONVERSATION

A ▶ **LISTEN AND READ. Then listen and repeat.**

A: Good morning. Greenville Elementary.
B: Hello. This is Terry Lee. I'm calling about my son Alex.
A: Is that Alex Lee?
B: Yes. He's sick today. He has a sore throat and a headache.
A: I'm sorry to hear that. What class is he in?
B: He's in Ms. Wong's class.

B **WORK TOGETHER. Practice the conversation in Exercise A.**

C **CREATE. Make new conversations. Use the information in the boxes. Change *he* to *she* when necessary.**

A: Good morning. Greenville Elementary.

B: Hello. This is Terry Lee. I'm calling about my ▭ Alex.

A: Is that Alex Lee?

B: Yes. **He**'s sick today. **He** has ▭ and ▭.

A: I'm sorry to hear that. What class is **he** in?

B: **He**'s in Ms. Wong's class.

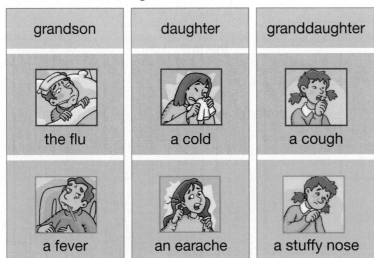

grandson	daughter	granddaughter
the flu	a cold	a cough
a fever	an earache	a stuffy nose

D **ROLE-PLAY. Make your own conversations. Student A, you're sick. Call work.**

A: Hi. This is _____. I can't come to work today. I have a . . .
B: I'm sorry to hear that.

I can call to explain an absence. ■	I need more practice. ■

For more practice, go to MyEnglishLab.

Grammar

Review: Simple present

Review: Simple present			
Information questions and answers		**Yes/no questions and answers**	
How do you **feel**?	My throat **hurts**.	**Do** you **have** a fever?	**Yes**, I **do**.
How does Alex **feel**?	He **doesn't feel** well.	**Does** he **have** a fever?	**No**, he **doesn't**.

COMPLETE. Use the correct form of the verbs in parentheses. Give short answers.

Mom: Doctor, I'm worried about Maria. I think she _____*has*_____ the flu.
(1. have)

Doctor: How _____ you _____, Maria?
(2. feel)

Maria: Terrible. I _____ a cough and a stuffy nose.
(3. have)

Doctor: What about your throat? _____ it _____?
(4. hurt)

Maria: Yes, it _____. But just a little. _____ I
5.

_____ a fever?
(6. have)

Doctor: Let's see, . . . No, you _____.
7.

Mom: _____ she _____ the flu?
(8. have)

Doctor: No. She _____ the flu. It's just a bad cold.
(9. not have)

Mom: That's good. I _____ a lot better now!
(10. feel)

Show what you know!

ROLE-PLAY. Student A, you are sick. Student B, ask questions.

A: I feel terrible.
B: What's wrong?
A: My _____ hurts.
B: Do you have . . . ?

I can use the simple present. ■   I need more practice. ■

For more practice, go to MyEnglishLab.

Lesson 4 Follow a doctor's instructions and read medicine labels

1 SEE THE DOCTOR

A ▶ LISTEN AND READ. Then listen and repeat.

A: City Clinic. Can I help you?

B: This is Viktor Petrov. I'd like to make an appointment for a check-up.

A: Sure. For what day?

B: Can I come in tomorrow?

A: No, I'm sorry. There are no openings this week. How about next Thursday afternoon at 2:00?

B: OK. Next Thursday at 2:00 is good.

A: OK, that's Thursday, March 3rd, at 2:00 P.M. See you then.

B ▶ INTERPRET. Listen to the conversation again. Circle the letter of the correct text message.

a. Please note this new appt for Viktor: 3/2/19 at 2:00 P.M. Text C to confirm. Questions? Call 618-555-6341. City Clinic. Text STOP to Unsubscribe. Thank you.

b. Please note this new appt for Viktor: 3/3/19 at 2:00 P.M. Text C to confirm. Questions? Call 618-555-6341. City Clinic. Text STOP to Unsubscribe. Thank you.

C ROLE-PLAY. Make a new conversation. Use your own name. Use different days, dates, and times. Complete the text message with your partner's information.

Please note this new appt for

_____:

_____ at _____.
Text C to confirm. Questions?
Call 618-555-6341. City
Clinic. Text STOP to
Unsubscribe. Thank you.

D LABEL. Look at the pictures of a check-up. Write the instructions under the pictures.

Lie down.	Open your mouth and say Ahh.	~~Step on the scale.~~
Look straight ahead.	Roll up your sleeve.	Take a deep breath.
Make a fist.	Sit on the table.	

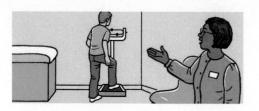

1. <u>Step on the scale.</u>

2. _____

3. _____

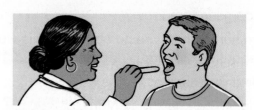

4. _____

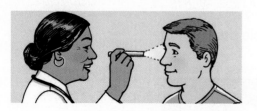

5. _____

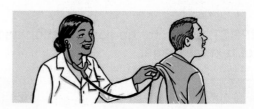

6. _____

7. _____

8. _____

E ROLE-PLAY. Student A, you are a doctor. Give instructions.
Student B, you are a patient. Act out the instructions.

F GO ONLINE. Find the phone number for a clinic in or near your neighborhood.

I can follow a doctor's instructions. ☐   I need more practice. ☐

For more practice, go to MyEnglishLab.

2 READ MEDICINE LABELS

A **LABEL.** Write the words under the pictures.

| operate machinery | ~~orally~~ | out of reach | tablet |

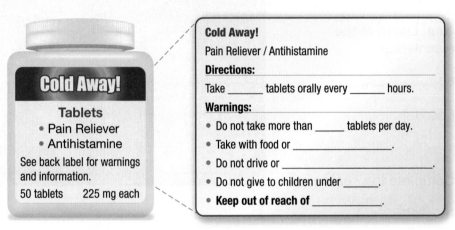

1. ____orally____   2. _____   3. _____   4. _____

B ▶ **SELF-ASSESS.** Listen and check your answers.

C ▶ **LISTEN.** Complete the medicine label.

Cold Away!

Tablets
- Pain Reliever
- Antihistamine

See back label for warnings and information.

50 tablets   225 mg each

Cold Away!

Pain Reliever / Antihistamine

Directions:_____

Take _____ tablets orally every _____ hours.

Warnings:_____
- Do not take more than _____ tablets per day.
- Take with food or _____.
- Do not drive or _____.
- Do not give to children under _____.
- **Keep out of reach of _____.**

D **INTERPRET.** Look at the medicine label. Answer the questions.

1. What is this medicine for? _pain or cold_____

2. How much of the medicine do you take at one time?
   _____

3. How often do you take this medicine? _____

4. How much of this medicine can you take in one day?
   _____

5. What do you take this medicine with? _____

6. What age children cannot take this medicine?
   _____

MAX-COLD AWAY

Pain Reliever / Antihistamine

Directions: Take 1 tablet orally every 4–6 hours

Warnings:
- Do not take more than 6 tablets per day.
- Take with food or milk.
- Do not drive or operate machinery.
- Do not give to children under 12.
- **Keep out of reach of children.**

I can read medicine labels. ☐   I need more practice. ☐

For more practice, go to MyEnglishLab.

Talk about health problems

1 BEFORE YOU LISTEN

**IDENTIFY. Look at the calendar.
Write the words.**

						January
Mon	Tue	Wed	Thu	Fri	Sat	Sun
2	3	4	5	6	7	8
Mon	Tue	Wed	Thu	Fri	Sat	Sun
9	10	11	12	13	14	15

the day before yesterday	last night
yesterday ~~today~~	last week

1. Jan. 12 = _today_

2. Jan. 11 = _____

3. Jan. 11 at night = _____

4. Jan. 10 = _____

5. Jan. 2–8 = _____

2 LISTEN

A ▶ **LISTEN. Look at the picture. Listen to the
conversation. Complete the sentence.**

Luisa wasn't at work because _____.
a. she was sick
b. her daughter was in the hospital
c. her daughter was sick

B ▶ **LISTEN FOR DETAILS. Complete the sentences.**

1. Luisa's daughter was home with _____.

a.    b.    c.

2. Her daughter is now _____.

a.    b.    c.

C ▶ **EXPAND. Listen to the whole conversation. Who is sick now?** _____

3 PRONUNCIATION

A ▶ **PRACTICE. Listen. Then listen and repeat.**

She was **sick**.   She **was**n't in **school**.

It was the **flu**. It **was**n't a **cold**.

They were **ab**sent.   They **were**n't **late**.

B ▶ **CHOOSE. Listen to the sentences. Check (✓) the word you hear.**

1. ☐ was   ☑ wasn't   4. ☐ were   ☐ weren't
2. ☐ were   ☐ weren't   5. ☐ was   ☐ wasn't
3. ☐ was   ☐ wasn't   6. ☐ were   ☐ weren't

4 CONVERSATION

A ▶ **LISTEN AND READ. Then listen and repeat.**

A: You weren't here yesterday.
B: I know. My daughter was home sick. She had a bad cold.
A: Oh, too bad. How is she now?
B: A lot better, thanks. She's back at school.

B **WORK TOGETHER. Practice the conversation in Exercise A.**

C **CREATE. Make new conversations. Use the words in the boxes. Change *she* to *he* when necessary.**

A: You weren't here ▨▨▨▨▨▨.
B: I know. My ▨▨▨▨▨▨▨ was home sick. **She** had a bad ▨▨▨▨▨▨.
A: Oh, too bad. How is **she** now?
B: A lot better, thanks. **She**'s back at school.

Wednesday
last night
the day before yesterday

son
grandson
granddaughter

headache
earache
stomachache

D **ROLE-PLAY. Make your own conversations. Use different times, people, and health problems.**

I can talk about health problems. ☐   I need more practice. ☐

For more practice, go to MyEnglishLab.

Past of *be*: Statements			
Affirmative			
I			
He	**was**		
She		sick yesterday.	
We			
You	**were**		
They			

Negative			
I			
He	**wasn't**		
She		sick last week.	
We			
You	**weren't**		
They			

Grammar Watch
Contractions
wasn't = was not
weren't = were not

A **IDENTIFY.** Cross out the incorrect words.

1. We **are / ~~were~~** here today, but we **are / were** absent yesterday.
2. He **is / was** OK now, but he **is / was** sick last night.
3. They **are / were** in school yesterday, but they **aren't / weren't** here now.
4. She **is / was** at the doctor's office yesterday. Now she **is / was** at home in bed.
5. My brother **isn't / wasn't** here now, but he **is / was** here yesterday.
6. I **am / was** OK last week, but now I **am / was** sick.

B **COMPLETE.** Use *was* or *were*.

Sonia _____was_____ home sick the day before
1.

yesterday. Her sister _____ sick, too.
2.

They _____ both in bed all day.
3.

Sonia's parents _____ worried.
4.

Yesterday, Sonia _____ a lot
5.

better. Her sister _____ better,
6.

too. Sonia's parents _____
7.

very happy!

Grammar

C INTERPRET. Look at yesterday's attendance sheet. Complete the sentences with *was*, *were*, *wasn't*, or *weren't*.

1. Carlos ____wasn't____ in class yesterday.
2. Carla and Min Jung _____ there, but Min Jung _____ late.
3. Tina and Sonia _____ there. They _____ both home sick.
4. Dora _____ there, but Edgar _____ there.

SEMESTER: Fall   H= Here   A= Absent   L= Late

Student Name	Week 1				
	M	T	W	Th	F
Carla Cruz	H				
Carlos Delgado	A				
Min Jung Lee	L				
Sonia Lopez	A				
Dora Moreno	H				
Edgar Vargas	A				
Tina Wong	A				

D WRITE. Look at the pictures. Write two sentences about each picture.

last week

yesterday

1. _The teacher was sick last week._
2. _____

3. _____
4. _____

Show what you know!

1. TALK ABOUT IT. Look at the pictures again. Talk about the differences. Use *was*, *were*, *wasn't*, and *weren't*.

A: Last week it was rainy.
B: Right. But yesterday it was sunny.

2. WRITE ABOUT IT. Now write about two differences in your class.

Last week three students were absent. Yesterday one student was absent.

_____

_____

I can use the past of *be*. ☐	I need more practice. ☐

For more practice, go to MyEnglishLab.

Read about walking and health

1 BEFORE YOU READ

A **CHOOSE.** Complete the sentences with the vocabulary in the box.

energy   getting stronger   losing weight

1. Her bones are _____ _____.

2. He has a lot of _____ _____.

3. She's _____ _____.

B **TALK ABOUT IT.** Do you walk a lot? Do you think walking is good for you? Why or why not?

2 READ

▶ Listen and read.

Academic Skill: Apply what you read

Use what you learn from the reading to think about the world. Does the information change your ideas? Can it be useful to you, your family, or your friends?

Walk Your Way to Good Health!

It's free. It's easy. It's good for you. And guess what? You already do it every day. What is it? Walking.

When you walk every day:
5 You have a lot of energy. Your bones get strong. Your heart gets strong, too. You prevent heart disease and other health problems.

10 For good health, you should walk 10,000 steps a day (about five miles). Taking 10,000 steps a day burns about 2,000 to 3,500 calories

Most people walk 4,000 steps every day.

15 a week. There are 3,500 calories in one pound of body fat. So walking can also help you lose weight.

Most people walk 4,000 steps a day. These 4,000 steps are part of your daily routine. You walk from the bedroom to the kitchen. You walk to your car or 20 the bus stop. You walk from the entrance of your school to your classroom. So you need only 6,000 more steps a day.

Here are some ways to add steps to your daily routine:

25 • Don't take the elevator. Take the stairs.
• Walk when you talk on the phone.
• Get off the bus one stop early. Then walk the rest of the way.
• Don't park near the place you're going.

30 It's easy. So what are you waiting for? Start walking!

Reading

3 CLOSE READING

CITE EVIDENCE. Complete the sentences. Where is the information? Write the line number.

Lines

1. Walking will help you _____.
   a. prevent heart disease
   b. make friends
   c. save time
   _____

2. You need to walk _____ to help your heart and bones get strong.
   a. fast
   b. every day
   c. upstairs
   _____

3. Everyone should walk _____ steps a day for good health.
   a. 2,000
   b. 6,000
   c. 10,000
   _____

4. When you walk 10,000 steps, you are walking _____ miles.
   a. 2
   b. 5
   c. 10
   _____

5. To lose a pound of body fat, you need to use _____ calories.
   a. 2,000
   b. 3,500
   c. 3,000
   _____

6. Add steps to your day! When you take the bus, _____.
   a. don't sit down
   b. get off early and walk
   c. run to the bus stop
   _____

4 SUMMARIZE

Complete the summary with the words in the box.

| energy | health | heart | steps | weight |

Walking is good for your (1) _____. Walking every day gives you a stronger

(2) _____, stronger bones, and more (3) _____. It helps prevent health

problems and helps you lose (4) _____. For good health, walk 10,000

(5) _____ a day (about five miles). It's free and easy to do.

Show what you know!

1. TALK ABOUT IT. How can you add steps to your daily routine?

2. WRITE ABOUT IT. Explain how you can add steps to your daily routine.

To add steps to my daily routine, I can _____.

I can apply what I read. ■   I need more practice. ■

To read more, go to MyEnglishLab.

1 BEFORE YOU LISTEN

MAKE CONNECTIONS. What do you do for a toothache? a backache? the flu? Read the chart in 2A. Are your answers in the chart?

2 LISTEN

A ▶ **IDENTIFY.** Listen to the radio show. Number the problems in the chart in the order you hear them.

Ask the Doctor			
Problem	Advice	The doctor says . . .	
		Do	Don't
☐ A toothache	Put heat on it.	☐	☐
	Eat a piece of onion.	☐	☐
	Drink lime juice.	☐	☐
1 A backache	Use an ice pack.	☑	☐
	Take a hot shower.	☐	☐
	Use a heating pad.	☐	☐
☐ The flu	Stay in bed.	☐	☐
	Drink a lot.	☐	☐
	Take antibiotics.	☐	☐

Important: You should see a doctor or nurse if you don't feel better soon.

B ▶ **LISTEN FOR DETAILS.** What does the doctor say? Check (✓) *Do* or *Don't* in the chart on page 220.

3 CONVERSATION

A **PREDICT.** Look at the pictures. The woman has a sore throat. What does her friend suggest? Do you think it is a good suggestion?

B ▶ **LISTEN AND READ.** Then listen and repeat.

A: I have **a sore throat**.
B: I'm sorry to hear that. Maybe you should **drink tea and honey**.
A: That's a good idea.
B: But call the doctor if you don't feel better soon. You really shouldn't wait too long.

C **WORK TOGETHER.** Practice the conversation in Exercise B.

D **CREATE.** Make new conversations. Use the information from the chart on page 220.

E **ROLE-PLAY.** Make your own conversations. Use different problems and suggestions.

I can give advice. ■   I need more practice. ■

For more practice, go to MyEnglishLab.

Grammar

Statements with *should*

Statements with *should*						
Affirmative			**Negative**			
I			I			
You			You			
He	**should**	**rest.**	He	**shouldn't**	**work.**	
She			She			
We			We			
They			They			

Grammar Watch

Use the base form of the verb after *should* or *shouldn't*.

Contraction

shouldn't = should not

A **IDENTIFY. Cross out the incorrect words.**

1. My sister has a bad back. She ~~should~~ / **shouldn't** lift heavy things.
   She **should / shouldn't** ask a nurse about back exercises.
2. My friend has a stomachache. He **should / shouldn't** drink a lot of tea.
   He **should / shouldn't** eat fries.
3. My uncle has a sore throat and a cough. He **should / shouldn't** talk too much.
   He **should /shouldn't** take medicine.
4. My ankle hurts. I **should / shouldn't** walk. I **should / shouldn't** put ice on it.

B **WORK TOGETHER. Read the labels. What do they mean?**

A: What does this mean: "Take medication on an empty stomach"?
B: It means you shouldn't take it with food.
C: Right. You should take it before you eat.

a. TAKE MEDICATION ON AN **EMPTY STOMACH**

b.  **P.M.**

c.  **DO NOT** REFRIGERATE

d. 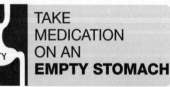 TAKE MEDICATION **WITH FOOD**

e.  **DO NOT** DRINK MILK or EAT DAIRY PRODUCTS WHILE TAKING THIS MEDICATION

I can use *should* and *shouldn't* to give advice. ■   I need more practice. ■

For more practice, go to MyEnglishLab.

10 Writing

Write about healthy habits

1 STUDY THE MODEL

READ. Answer the questions.

> Sam Sousa
> My Healthy Habits
>
> I have many healthy habits. I walk every day. I eat fresh fruit and vegetables every day. I have a check-up with the doctor every year.
> But I should change one habit. I only sleep six hours a night. I should sleep more.

1. What are Sam's healthy habits?
2. What habit should Sam change?
3. How should Sam change that habit?

2 PLAN YOUR WRITING

WORK TOGETHER. Ask and answer the questions.

1. What are your healthy habits?
2. What is one habit you should change?
3. How can you change that habit?

Writing Skill: Use a topic sentence

Start each paragraph with a topic sentence. A topic sentence tells the main idea of the paragraph. For example:

I have many healthy habits. I walk every day. I eat fresh fruit and vegetables every day. I have a check-up with the doctor every year.

3 WRITE

Now write about your healthy habits. Use the frame, the model, the Writing Skill, and your ideas from Exercise 2 to help you.

> I have many healthy habits. I _____ every day. I _____ every day. I _____ every year. But I should change one habit. I _____. I should _____ more.

4 CHECK YOUR WRITING

WORK TOGETHER. Read your writing aloud with a partner.

WRITING CHECKLIST

☐ The writing answers all the questions in Exercise 2.

☐ Each paragraph starts with a topic sentence.

I can use a topic sentence. ■   I need more practice. ■

For more practice, go to MyEnglishLab.

Lesson 11 — Make good decisions

1 MEET AYA

Read about one of her workplace skills.

> I make good decisions. I take care of myself. I know it's important to be healthy.

2 AYA'S PROBLEM

READ. Circle *True* or *False*.

Aya is an office assistant. She works Monday to Friday, 8:00 A.M. to 5:00 P.M. She takes care of herself. She eats healthy food, and she exercises.

Today, Aya is sick. She has a fever, a sore throat, and a headache. The office is very busy today. She has a lot of work to do.

1. Aya works every day from Monday to Friday.   True   False
2. Aya doesn't eat healthy food.   True   False
3. Aya doesn't have a lot of work at the office.   True   False

3 AYA'S SOLUTION

WORK TOGETHER. Aya makes good decisions. What is the right thing to do? Explain your answer.

1. Aya goes to work and goes to the doctor after work.
2. Aya doesn't go to work. She goes to the doctor.
3. Aya takes cold medicine and goes to work.
4. Aya _____.

Show what you know!

1. **THINK ABOUT IT.** How do you make good decisions at school? At work? At home? Give examples.

2. **WRITE ABOUT IT.** Now write your example in your Skills Log.

   I make good decisions about the food I buy and cook for my children. I buy a lot of fruit and vegetables.

3. **PRESENT IT.** Give a short presentation to show how you make good decisions.

I can give an example from my life of making good decisions. ■

Unit Review: Go back to page 205. Which goals can you check off?

12 Help Wanted

PREVIEW

Look at the picture. What do you see?
Where are they?

UNIT GOALS

- [ ] Name job duties
- [ ] Respond to a help-wanted sign
- [ ] Read job postings
- [ ] Talk about hours you can work
- [ ] Talk about work experience

- [ ] **Academic skill:** Mark up a text when reading
- [ ] **Writing skill:** Recognize and use a subject in a sentence
- [ ] **Workplace soft skill:** Respond well to feedback

A PREDICT. Look at the pictures. What do you see? What are the job duties?

Number 2 is "use a computer."

B ▶ LISTEN AND POINT. Then listen and repeat.

Vocabulary

Job duties

1. answer the phone	**5.** serve food	**8.** drive a truck	**12.** use a cash register
2. use a computer	**6.** take care of	**9.** make copies	**13.** supervise workers
3. fix things	children	**10.** help customers	**14.** work on buildings
4. make food	**7.** help patients	**11.** take care of grounds	

C **ASK AND ANSWER.** Student A, point to a picture. Ask, "What is she or he doing?" Student B, answer.

He is using a computer.

D **CATEGORIZE.** Look at the verbs in the list of job duties. Write the words that go with the verbs in the chart. Then compare answers.

Use	Make	Help	Take care of
a computer			

Study Tip

Make connections
Make cards. On one side, write a job duty. On the other side, write one job with that job duty.

Show what you know!

1. SURVEY. Ask four classmates about their job duties. Write their answers in the chart.

A: *Min, what do you do?*
B: *At work, I drive a truck. What about you?*

Name	Duty	Place
Min	*drives a truck*	*at work*

2. PRESENT IT. Tell your class about your classmates' job duties.

Min drives a truck at work.

3. WRITE ABOUT IT. Now write about your job duties.

I _____ at _____.

I can name job duties. ▪   I need more practice. ▪

For more practice, go to MyEnglishLab.

Lesson 2

Respond to a help-wanted sign

1 BEFORE YOU LISTEN

TALK ABOUT IT. Look at the picture of Dino's Diner. What do you see?

2 LISTEN

A ▶ **LISTEN.** Look at the picture. Kofi is in Dino's Diner. Listen to the conversation. Why is he there?

a. He wants a hamburger.
b. He works there.
c. He wants a job.

Kofi

B ▶ **LISTEN FOR DETAILS.** Complete the sentences.

1. Kofi is a _____.

a.    b.    c.

2. He makes great _____.

a.    b.    c.

C ▶ **EXPAND.** Listen to the whole conversation. Read the sentences. Circle *True* or *False*.

1. Dino gives Kofi a job.   True   False
2. Kofi is starting his new job tomorrow.   True   False
3. Kofi answers Dino's phone.   True   False

3 PRONUNCIATION

A ► **PRACTICE. Listen. Then listen and repeat.**

I can **serve**.   I **can't cook**.

She can **make pasta**.   She **can't** make **bread**.

> **Sentence stress: *Can* and *can't* in statements**
>
> *Can* is usually not stressed.
> *Can't* is stressed.

B ► **CHOOSE. Listen to the sentences. Check (✓) the word you hear.**

1. ☐ can   ✓ can't   4. ☐ can   ☐ can't
2. ☐ can   ☐ can't   5. ☐ can   ☐ can't
3. ☐ can   ☐ can't   6. ☐ can   ☐ can't

4 CONVERSATION

A ► **LISTEN AND READ. Then listen and repeat.**

A: I noticed the Help Wanted sign. I'd like to apply for a job.
B: OK. Which job?
A: Well, I'm a cook. I can make great hamburgers.
B: Can you make pizza?
A: No. I can't make pizza, but I can learn.

B **WORK TOGETHER. Practice the conversation in Exercise A.**

C **CREATE. Make new conversations. Use the information in the boxes.**

A: I noticed the Help Wanted sign. I'd like to apply for a job.
B: OK. Which job?
A: Well, I'm ▭▭▭▭▭. I can ▭▭▭▭▭.
B: Can you ▭▭▭▭▭?
A: No. I can't ▭▭▭▭▭, but I can learn.

a sales assistant	 use a cash register	take returns
an office assistant	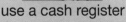 use a computer	take inventory
a carpenter	 make cabinets	fix furniture

D **ROLE-PLAY. Make your own conversations. Use different jobs and skills.**

I can respond to a help-wanted sign. ☐   I need more practice. ☐

For more practice, go to MyEnglishLab.

Grammar

Can: Statements

Can: Statements					
Affirmative			**Negative**		
I			I		
He			He		
She			She		
We	**can**	drive.	We	**can't**	cook.
You			You		
They			They		

Grammar Watch

Use the base form of the verb after *can* or *can't*.
Contraction
can't = can not

A INTERPRET. Read Olga's job skills. Complete the sentences with *can* or *can't*.

Name: _Olga Popova_

Office Jobs 4U

Check the skills you have.

☑ use a computer   ☑ make copies   ☐ work with numbers
☑ answer phones   ☐ write reports   ☑ help customers
☐ create presentations   ☑ organize things   ☐ supervise workers

1. Olga ____can____ use a computer, and she _____ answer phones.
2. She _____ create presentations, and she _____ write reports.
3. She _____ work with numbers, but she _____ organize things.
4. She _____ supervise workers, but she _____ help customers.
5. She _____ make copies.

B WORK TOGETHER. Look at the job skills in Exercise A. What can you do? What can't you do?

A: I can use a computer, but I can't write reports.
B: I can't organize things, but I can work with numbers.

Grammar

C COMPLETE. Look at the pictures. Complete the sentences with *can* or *can't* and the verbs in the box.

cook	drive	~~make~~
speak	take	take care of

1.

He ___can't make___ furniture.

2.

She _____ a taxi.

3.

How are you?

OK, thanks.

They _____ English.

4.

We _____.

5.

I _____ messages.

6.

He _____ children.

Show what you know!

1. TALK ABOUT IT. Look at the picture. What can the people do? What can't they do?

A: The man in the green shirt can't fix the light.
B: Right. The woman in the red shirt can use a cash register.

We're open until 9.

Customer Service

Sorry. No.

Do you speak Spanish?

2. WRITE ABOUT IT. Now write two sentences about the people's job skills.

The woman in the blue shirt can answer the phone.

_____

_____

I can use *can* in affirmative and negative statements. ■   I need more practice. ■

For more practice, go to MyEnglishLab.

Lesson 4 — Read job postings

1 READ JOB POSTINGS

A **MAKE CONNECTIONS. Read the information. Do you work? Do you work full-time or part-time?**

Full-time = 35–40 hours a week
Part-time = less than 35 hours a week

A: I work full-time in an office. What about you?
B: I have two part-time jobs.

B **MATCH. Find the words in the job postings. Match the words and definitions.**

____ 1. experience   **a.** to fill out or give papers to ask for a job

____ 2. apply   **b.** written information about your past jobs and education

____ 3. résumé   **c.** when you go to a place and meet a person

____ 4. in person   **d.** skills you have from a job or jobs you did before

A.
DRIVERS
Deliveries Now is looking for full-time drivers
Drive a truck and deliver packages
One year of experience
$12.00/hour
Apply Now

B.
CHILD-CARE WORKER
Part-time child-care needed for two children after school
Monday to Friday 3 P.M. to 6 P.M
Help with homework and play with children
$10.00/hour

Email résumé to Ina ina.gibbs@igibbs.com

C.
COOK
Aunt Kay's Restaurant. No experience needed
Part-time: evenings
$15.00/hour

Apply in person. Monday to Friday 2:00 P.M. to 4:00 P.M.: 409 Market St., San Francisco, CA

C **INTERPRET. Look at the job postings in Exercise 1B. Write the letter of the posting.**

1. Job _A_ is full-time.
2. Job ____ pays $10 an hour.
3. Job ____ is evenings only.
4. You don't need experience for Job ____.
5. You need to go to the place to apply for Job ____.
6. You need to apply online for Job ____.
7. You can send an email for Job ____.

D **MAKE CONNECTIONS.** Read the information. Which shift do you work?

> The first shift is usually from 7:00 A.M. to 3:00 P.M.
>
> The second shift is usually from 3:00 P.M. to 11:00 P.M.
>
> Third shift is usually from 11:00 P.M. to 7:00 A.M.

E ▶ **IDENTIFY.** Look at the job listings. Listen to the conversation. Which job listing are they talking about?

A.

MANAGER
IMAGINE is looking for a full-time manager for the first shift. You will supervise workers and make schedules. You need 2 years' experience.

APPLY NOW

B.

SECURITY GUARDS
SAFE PLACES is looking for part-time security guards for all shifts. We pay $12.00/hour. You don't need experience.

APPLY NOW

C.

NURSE'S ASSISTANTS   NEW
Greenville General Hospital

We're looking for full-time nurse's assistants for second and third shifts. You will take care of patients and help nurses. You need one year's experience. We pay $15.00/hour.

Email résumé to:
wendy.miller@greenvillehospital.org

F **TALK ABOUT IT.** Talk about the job you want. Why do you want this job?

A: I want a job as a security guard. The pay is good, and I can work the day or night shift. What about you?

B: I want a job as . . .

G GO ONLINE. Find a job listing for a job you want.

I can read job postings. ▢   I need more practice. ▢

Lesson 5

Talk about hours you can work

1 BEFORE YOU LISTEN

LABEL. Look at the picture. Label the people. Use the words in the box.

customer	repair person	sales assistant

2 LISTEN

A ▶ **LISTEN.** Look at the picture below. Listen to the conversation. Who is the woman?

a. a customer
b. an employee at the store
c. a repair person

B ▶ **LISTEN FOR DETAILS.** Which questions does the woman ask the man? Check (✓) the correct questions.

☐ Can you work this Saturday?
☐ Can you work from 2:00 to 6:00?
☐ Can you work this evening?
☐ Can you work from 2:00 to 7:00?

C ▶ **EXPAND.** Listen to the whole conversation. Answer the questions.

1. Who is the man?
   a. a new sales assistant
   b. an elevator repair person

2. Who does the woman think the man is?
   a. a new sales assistant
   b. an elevator repair person

3. What does the woman want the man to do?
   a. work her shift on Saturday
   b. fix the elevator on Saturday

Listening and Speaking

3 PRONUNCIATION

▶ **PRACTICE. Listen. Then listen and repeat.**

> **Sentence stress:** *Can* and *can't* in short answers
>
> In short answers, *can* and *can't* are stressed.

A: Can you start tomorrow?
B: Yes, I **can**.

A: Can you work Saturday?
B: No, I **can't**.

4 CONVERSATION

A ▶ **LISTEN AND READ. Then listen and repeat.**

A: This store is really busy.
B: I know. Listen, I need a favor. Can you work this Saturday?
A: Uh, well, yes, I can.
B: Oh, great, thanks, because I can't. Can you work from 2:00 to 7:00?
A: Um, yes. I guess so.

B **WORK TOGETHER. Practice the conversation in Exercise A.**

C **CREATE. Make new conversations. Use the words in the boxes.**

A: This _____ is really busy.

B: I know. Listen, I need a favor. Can you work _____?

A: Uh, well, yes, I can.

B: Oh, great, thanks, because I can't. Can you work from _____?

A: Um, yes. I guess so.

restaurant	tomorrow	6:00–11:00

hospital	Monday	8:00–3:00

hotel	June 11	4:00–10:00

D **ROLE-PLAY. Make your own conversations. Ask someone you work with to change shifts with you.**

A: Listen, I need a favor. Can you work _____?
B: _____? Yes, I can.
A: Oh, great. And can you work _____?
B: _____? Sure.
A: Thanks!

I can talk about hours I can work. ▪   I need more practice. ▪

For more practice, go to MyEnglishLab.

Can	you	**work**	this Saturday?	**Yes,**	I		**can**.	**No,**	I	**can't**.
	he				he				he	
	she				she				she	
	they				they				they	

A **APPLY.** Write questions with *can*. Use the words in parentheses. Give short answers.

Can you work nights?

1. A: _____ Can you work nights? _____
   (you / work nights)

   B: ___ Yes, I can. ___ I'm free every night.

2. A: _____
   (you / work weekends)

   B: _____ I can only work weekdays. I'm busy on weekends.

3. A: _____
   (you / come to work early tomorrow)

   B: _____ What time should I come in?

4. A: _____
   (she / start tomorrow)

   B: _____ She can be here at 9:00.

5. A: _____
   (your sister / fix the car)

   B: _____ She's good with cars.

6. A: _____
   (Bill / drive a truck)

   B: _____ He doesn't have a driver's license.

B ▶ **SELF-ASSESS.** Listen and check your answers.

C **WORK TOGETHER.** Practice the conversations in Exercise A.

Grammar

D **INTERPRET.** Look at the job posting. Write job interview questions with *can*. Ask about a job applicant's skills and work hours.

1. _Can you answer phones?_
2. _____
3. _____
4. _____
5. _____

E **WORK TOGETHER.** Student A, ask the questions in Exercise D. Student B, answer the questions and add information.

A: Can you answer phones?
B: Yes, I can. I can take messages, too.

---

jobs.com

Office Assistant
General Hospital, Dallas Texas

Job Skills:
Answer phones
Use a computer
Organize files
Write reports

Job Type: Full-Time

Salary: $15.00/hr

APPLY NOW

Show what you know!

1. **THINK ABOUT IT.** Think of a job. Write the name of the job. _____

2. **TALK ABOUT IT.** Student A, ask, "What's my job?" Other students, ask *yes/no* questions with *can* about Student A's job skills. You can ask 10 questions.

A: What's my job?
B: Can you use a cash register?
A: No, I can't.
C: Can you drive a truck?
A: No, I can't.
D: Can you make furniture?
A: Yes, I can.
E: Are you a carpenter?
A: Yes, I am.
B: OK, my turn. Guess my job.

3. **WRITE ABOUT IT.** Now write two questions about job skills. Use *can*.

Can you fix things?
Can you _____?
_____?

I can use *can* in *yes/no* questions and short answers. ■   I need more practice. ■

For more practice, go to MyEnglishLab.

1 BEFORE YOU READ

A **CHOOSE. Complete the sentences with the vocabulary in the box.**

| leaning forward | making eye contact | on her lap |

1. They're _____
   _____.

2. She has her hands _____
   _____.

3. He's _____
   _____.

B **TALK ABOUT IT.** Your body language is the way you stand, sit, or move. All three say something about you. Why is body language important during a job interview?

Academic Skill: Mark up a text

When you read an article for the second time, use a pencil, pen, or highlighter to mark it up. Circle important words. Underline sentences. Try using different colors.

---

2 READ

▶ Listen and read.

MAKING A GOOD FIRST IMPRESSION IN A JOB INTERVIEW

When you meet someone for the first time, you quickly form an opinion about him or her. This opinion is your first impression of the person. That person forms a first impression of you, too. You want to
5 make a good impression. This is very important in a job interview.

Before Your Interview
Choose the right clothes to wear. Your clothes and hair should look
10 clean and neat. Be sure you smell good, but don't wear much perfume or cologne.

During Your Interview
When you meet the interviewer, make
15 eye contact and smile. Shake hands

firmly. Stand about three feet away. When you sit down, try to look relaxed but sit up in your chair. Lean forward a little and look at the interviewer. This shows you are listening. Put your hands on
20 your lap, not in your pockets. Don't touch your face or hair.

At the End of Your Interview
When the interview is finished, shake hands again. Remember that in the
25 U.S., most people like a strong handshake. Make eye contact and smile. Say thank you.

In a job interview, the right clothes and good body language can help you
30 make a good first impression.

A good job interview starts with good body language.

3 CLOSE READING

CITE EVIDENCE. Complete the sentences. Where is the information? Write the line number.

Lines

1. Your first impression of someone is _____.
   a. the first words you say to the person
   b. the opinion you form of the person when you meet
   c. your first interview with the person
   _____

2. When you use the right body language in a job interview, it _____.
   a. helps you make a good impression
   b. means you don't need to talk
   c. saves time
   _____

3. Make eye contact, smile, and give the interviewer a _____ handshake.
   a. fast
   b. relaxed
   c. firm
   _____

4. During the interview, keep your hands _____.
   a. on the interviewer's desk
   b. on your lap
   c. moving
   _____

5. Look at the interviewer and lean forward in your chair to _____.
   a. be friendly
   b. show you are listening
   c. look excited and happy
   _____

6. At the end of your interview, _____.
   a. say you need the job
   b. ask if you can have the job
   c. say thank you
   _____

4 SUMMARIZE

Complete the summary with the words in the box.

| clean | eye contact | forward | impression | interviewer |

In a job interview, you want to make a good (1) _____. Before the interview, make sure you look (2) _____ and neat. When you meet the (3) _____, shake hands firmly and make (4) _____. Sit leaning (5) _____ with your hands on your lap. At the end, say thank you and shake hands again.

Show what you know!

1. **TALK ABOUT IT.** Talk about what you should and should not do when you have a job interview. Make a list of all your ideas.

2. **WRITE ABOUT IT.** Now write about what to do—and what not to do—when you have a job interview.

   When you have a job interview, you should _____. Don't _____.

I can mark up a text when reading. ■   I need more practice. ■

To read more, go to MyEnglishLab.

Talk about work experience

1 BEFORE YOU LISTEN

PREDICT. Look at the picture in the *Greenville Reporter*. What do you see?

2 LISTEN

A ▶ **LISTEN.** Why is Tina Martins interviewing Dinh Tran and Mai Lam?

a. They have a new restaurant.　　b. They were students in Greenville.

B ▶ **LISTEN FOR DETAILS.** Complete the sentences. Choose the correct words from the box.

a hospital	a hotel	people's homes	a restaurant

1. Dinh was a cook in _____.
2. Mai was a cook in _____.

C ▶ **LISTEN AND RECALL.** Complete the newspaper article. Use words from the radio interview.

People in the News　　　　　　　Greenville Reporter

Meet Dinh Tran and Mai Lam. They are the owners of Saigon, Greenville's first

Vietnamese _restaurant_ . Many people here know Dinh and Mai. Dinh was a
　　　　　　　 1.

_____, a server, and a _____ at the Greenville Café for
　　　　 2.　　　　　　　　　　　　 **3.**

Mai Lam (left)　　_____ years, and Mai worked in many people's homes as a cook. Dinh
and Dinh Tran　　　　 **4.**

and Mai were also _____ at the Greenville Adult School. Their first teacher, Emily Reed,
　　　　　　　　　　 5.

says: "They were very good _____, but they were great _____. Our class parties were
　　　　　　　　　　　 6.　　　　　　　　　　　 **7.**

always wonderful because of Dinh and Mai's _____. I'm sure their restaurant will be a big
　　　　　　　　　　　　　　　　　 8.

success." Everyone in Greenville wishes the couple lots of luck.

D **COMPARE.** Look at your answers. Compare with a partner.

Listening and Speaking

3 CONVERSATION

A ▶ **LISTEN AND READ.** Then listen and repeat.

A: Congratulations! This place looks great!
B: Thanks.
A: So, is this your first café?
B: Yes, it is. But I worked in a café before.
A: Oh. What did you do?
B: I was a server.
A: How long were you there?
B: Two years.

B **WORK TOGETHER.** Practice the conversation in Exercise A.

C **CREATE.** Make new conversations.
Use the information in the boxes.

A: Congratulations! This place looks great!
B: Thanks.
A: So, is this your first ⬚⬚⬚⬚?
B: Yes, it is. But I worked in a
⬚⬚⬚⬚ before.
A: Oh. What did you do?
B: I was a ⬚⬚⬚⬚.
A: How long were you there?
B: ⬚⬚⬚⬚ years.

salon   hair stylist   three

grocery store   cashier   four

D **ROLE-PLAY.** Make your own
conversations. Use different stores,
jobs, and times.

clothing store   sales assistant   five

I can talk about work experience. ■   I need more practice. ▢

For more practice, go to MyEnglishLab.

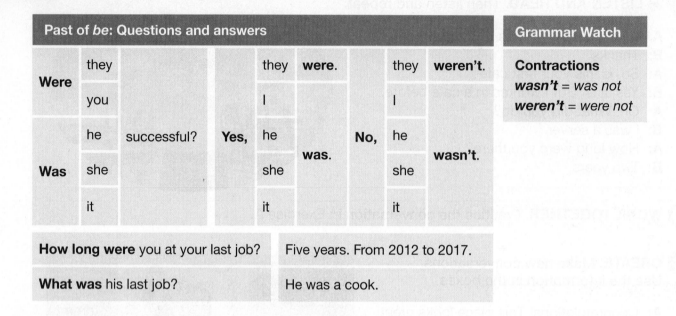

									Grammar Watch
Past of *be*: Questions and answers									
Were	they			they	**were.**		they	**weren't.**	**Contractions**
	you			I			I		***wasn't*** = was not
	he	successful?	**Yes,**	he		**No,**	he		***weren't*** = were not
Was	she			she	**was.**		she	**wasn't.**	
	it			it			it		

How long were you at your last job?	Five years. From 2012 to 2017.
What was his last job?	He was a cook.

A APPLY. Write questions. Use *was* or *were*.

1. What / your last job *What was your last job?*
2. the job / full-time _____
3. How long / you / there _____
4. you / happy there _____

B ▶ SELF-ASSESS. Listen and check your answers.

C ROLE-PLAY. Student A, you are a store manager. Student B, you need a job. Student B, read your job history. Student A, interview Student B.

A: What was your last job?
B: I was a cashier.

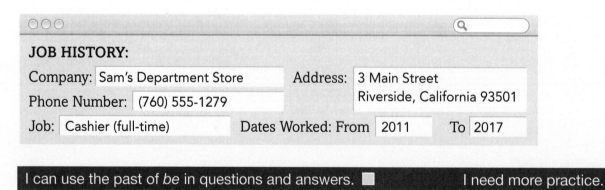

○○○	🔍
JOB HISTORY:	

Company: Sam's Department Store	Address: 3 Main Street
Phone Number: (760) 555-1279	Riverside, California 93501
Job: Cashier (full-time)	Dates Worked: From 2011 To 2017

I can use the past of *be* in questions and answers. ■   I need more practice. ■

For more practice, go to MyEnglishLab.

Lesson 10 · Writing

Write about job skills

1 STUDY THE MODEL

READ. Answer the questions.

> Kim Song
> An Office Assistant
>
> I want a job as an office assistant.
> I have some of the skills for the job.
> I can use a computer. I can make
> copies. I can't write reports in English,
> but I can learn!

1. What job does Kim want?
2. What skills does Kim have for the job?
3. What skill does Kim need to learn?

2 PLAN YOUR WRITING

WORK TOGETHER. Ask and answer the questions.

1. What job do you want?
2. What skills do you have for the job?
3. What skill do you need to learn?

Writing Skill: Recognize and use subjects

In English, every sentence has a subject.
For example:
(He) wants to be a taxi driver.
(I) can make copies.

3 WRITE

Now write about a job you want. Use
the frame, the model, the Writing Skill,
and your ideas from Exercise 2 to
help you.

> I want a job as a/an _____. I have some
> of the skills for the job. I can _____. I can
> _____. I can't_____, but I can learn!

4 CHECK YOUR WRITING

**WORK TOGETHER. Read your writing
aloud with a partner.**

WRITING CHECKLIST

☐ The writing answers all the questions in
Exercise 2.

☐ Each sentence has a subject.

☐ Each sentence has a verb.

I can recognize and use a subject in a sentence. ■   I need more practice. ■

For more practice, go to MyEnglishLab.

11 Lesson

Respond well to feedback

1 MEET KAI

Read about one of his workplace skills.

> I respond well to feedback. When I make a mistake, I listen and learn. The next time I can do a better job.

2 KAI'S PROBLEM

READ. Circle *True* or *False*.

Kai has a new job at a hospital. He is a custodian. He cleans the rooms and halls.

Today is his first day at the new job. Kai is cleaning a room. He is using a new machine. His co-worker comes in the room and says, "You are not cleaning the floor right. This isn't safe."

1. Kai is cleaning a room with his co-worker.	True	False
2. Kai knows how to use the machine.	True	False
3. Kai's co-worker tells Kai he made a mistake.	True	False

3 KAI'S SOLUTION

A **WORK TOGETHER.** Kai responds well to feedback. What is the right thing to say? Explain your answer.

1. Kai says, "I can do it my way. You can do it your way."
2. Kai says, "This is my first day. Can you show me how to do it?"
3. Kai says, "It's OK. I can do it."
4. Kai says, "_____"

B **ROLE-PLAY.** Look at your answer to 3A. Role-play Kai's conversation.

Show what you know!

1. **THINK ABOUT IT.** How do you respond well to feedback at school? At work? At home? Give examples.

2. **WRITE ABOUT IT.** Now write your example in your Skills Log.

   When my teacher corrects my writing, I write it again.

I can give an example from my life of responding well to feedback. ☐

Unit Review: Go back to page 225. Which goals can you check off?

MY SOFT SKILLS LOG

This is a list of my soft skills. They are skills I use every day. They are important for work, school, and home. In a job interview, I can talk about my soft skills. I can give these examples from my life.

Unit 1: I'm friendly.

For example, _____

_____

_____

_____

Unit 2: I'm a good listener.

For example, _____

_____

_____

_____

Unit 3: I'm flexible.

For example, _____

_____

_____

_____

Unit 4: I separate work and home life.

For example, _____

_____

_____

_____

Unit 5: I'm professional.

For example, _____

_____

_____

_____

Unit 6: I'm good at finding information.

For example, _____

_____

_____

_____

MY SOFT SKILLS LOG

Unit 7: I'm a team player.

For example, _____

_____

_____

_____

Unit 8: I take action.

For example, _____

_____

_____

_____

Unit 9: I'm ready to learn new skills.

For example, _____

_____

_____

_____

Unit 10: I'm reliable.

For example, _____

_____

_____

_____

Unit 11: I make good decisions.

For example, _____

_____

_____

_____

Unit 12: I respond well to feedback.

For example, _____

_____

_____

_____

UNIT 1 GRAMMAR REVIEW

A Complete the sentences with the correct form of *be*. Use contractions where possible.

1. I _____'m_____ in Level 2. I _____'m not_____ in Level 1.
   (be)   (be/not)

2. The book _____ hard. It _____ easy.
   (be/not)   (be)

3. My teacher _____ from the U.S. He _____ from Canada.
   (be)   (be/not)

4. Paula and I _____ from Mexico. We _____ from El Salvador.
   (be)   (be/not)

5. I _____ in Level 1. I _____ in Level 2.
   (be/not)   (be)

6. My classmates _____ helpful. My class _____ hard.
   (be)   (be)

B PARTNERS. Look at the pictures. Complete the conversations. Use your own words.

1.

Hi. I'm Bill.

Hi. I'm Pia.
Nice to meet you.

2.

Where are you from?

_____

3.

Where's Dawit?

_____

4.

Where are they from?

I think
_____

C PARTNERS. Practice the conversations.

D ▶ DICTATION. Listen. Then listen again and complete the conversation.

Carla: This is Dinh and Mai. _____They're_____ from Vietnam.
                                        1.

Boris: Nice to _____ _____. _____ Boris Popov. Carla
                        2.   3.   4.

and I are students at the Greenville Adult School. _____ in Level 1.
                                                                5.

Mai: Nice to meet you, Boris. Where _____ you _____?
6.   7.

Boris: _____ _____ Russia.
8.   9.

Carla: Dinh and Mai _____ students at Greenville, too. _____ in
10.   11.

Level 5, and _____ in Level 6.
12.

Boris: Really? That's great.

E STEP 1. Complete the sentences. Choose the correct words.

1. My name _____ Boris Popov. I _____ from Russia.
(is / are)   (is / am)

2. Carla is my classmate. _____ _____ from Peru.
(They / She)   (is / are)

_____ are in Level 1.
(We / She)

3. Ms. Reed _____ the teacher. _____ _____ from
(is / are)   (He / She)   (are not / is not)

my country. _____ _____ from Canada.
(He / She)   (is / are)

STEP 2. Write two or three sentences about yourself, a classmate, or your teacher.
Use the sentences in Step 1 as examples.

_____

_____

_____

UNIT 2 GRAMMAR REVIEW

A Complete the conversation. Use the words in the box.

a   an   servers   is   Is   Is   work   work   works

A: _____Is_____ that Carlos?
1.

B: No. That's Pablo Gomez. He _____ with
2.

Maria and Helena Peres. They _____ at
3.

Rico's Diner.

A: Oh. What do they do?

B: They're _____.
4.

A: Really? I _____ at a restaurant, too.
5.

I'm _____ cook. What about you?
6.

What do you do?

B: I'm _____ electrician.
7.

A: How's your job? _____ it hard?
8.

B: Yes, it _____. But it's interesting, too.
9.

Name: Meg Brown
Job: Server
Place of work: Rico's Diner
Home: Queens, New York

B **STEP 1.** Read the information about Meg Brown. Answer these questions: What does Meg do? Where does she work? Where does she live?

Meg ___*is a server*___.

She _____.

She _____.

STEP 2. Answer the questions about yourself. What do you do? Where do you work? Where do you live? Write complete sentences.

_____

_____

_____

UNIT 3 GRAMMAR REVIEW

A Complete these instructions. Write the correct words.

OK, class. ___*Open*___ your books to page 10. _____ is a picture
1. (Open / Close)   2. (This / These)

story. Now work with a partner. _____ at the picture. Ask questions. For
3. (Look / Don't look)

example, "Is _____ a marker? Are _____ tablets?" Now look at
4. (that / those)   5. (that / those)

the picture on page 11. _____ about _____ with your partner.
6. (Talk / Don't talk)   7. (it / them)

Tell _____ or _____ about the picture. _____ four
8. (he / him)   9. (she / her)   10. (Write / Don't write)

sentences about it. Show _____ to your partner.
11. (they / them)

B **STEP 1. Complete the sentences. Use words from the box. Use** *Don't* **when necessary. Sometimes more than one answer is correct.**

Tips for Learning English

1. _Speak_ English in class
2. _____ your language in class.
3. _____ English books at home.
4. _____ TV in English.
5. _____ new words in a notebook.

ask
listen
practice
read
speak
use
study
watch
write

STEP 2. Write four more tips for learning English. Use words from the box in Step 1.

_____

_____

_____

_____

UNIT 4 GRAMMAR REVIEW

A **Complete the paragraph. Choose the correct words.**

_____My_____ name is Tina.
1. (Our / My)

_____ husband's name is Mike.
2. (My / Her)

We _____ both 53 years old, and
3. (are / have)

we're both tall and thin. _____
4. (Our / We)

have two children. _____ son's name is Chris, and our daughter's name is
5. (Your / Our)

Kate. Chris is married. _____ wife's name is Jennie. Chris and Jennie have
6. (His / Her)

a daughter. _____ name is Amanda. She _____ ten years old.
7. (Their / Her)   8. (has / is)

Amanda is _____ first granddaughter! She _____ tall, and she
9. (our / their)   10. (is / has)

_____ long hair. Amanda looks just like _____ Aunt Kate!
11. (is / has)   12. (my / her)

B STEP 1. Complete the paragraph about Mel. Use *my*, *their*, and the correct form of *be* or *have*.

_____*My*_____ name is Mel. I _____ 75 years old. I _____
   1.   **2.**   **3.**

tall, and I _____ a beard. _____ wife's name is Anna. She
          4.   **5.**

_____ tall, too, and she _____ short hair. We _____
   6.   **7.**   **8.**

two daughters. _____ names _____ Tina and Cindy.
           9.   **10.**

STEP 2. Write about yourself. Use the paragraph in Step 1 as an example.

My name is _____. *I . . .*

_____

_____

_____

UNIT 5 GRAMMAR REVIEW

A Complete the sentences. Use the verbs in parentheses.

A: Hi. I _____*need*_____ a gift for my friend.
      1. (need)

_____ you _____ this
                 2. (have)

shirt in white?

B: No, we _____. But we _____
           3.   **4. (have)**

it in yellow.

A: Hmm. My friend _____ yellow.
              5. (not/like)

B: _____ your friend _____ blue?
                     6. (like)

A: Yes, he _____. He _____ a large.
           7.   **8. (need)**

B: Oh, sorry. We _____ a large.
          9. (not/have)

B STEP 1. Complete the questions. Use words from the box or your own ideas.

Do you have _____*red shoes*_____?

red	white	pink		sweater	jacket
yellow	khaki	orange		jeans	shoes
blue	black	purple		pants	shirt

1. Do you have _____?
2. Do you want _____?
3. Do you need _____?
4. Do you like _____?

GRAMMAR REVIEW

STEP 2. PARTNERS. Take turns. Student A, ask a question from Step 1. Student B, answer the question. Then add information.

A: Do you have red shoes?
B: No, I don't. But I have pink shoes. Do you have . . . ?

STEP 3. Write sentences about your partner.

Mai has pink shoes.

1. _____
2. _____
3. _____

UNIT 6 GRAMMAR REVIEW

A Complete the conversation. Use *is there*, *there's*, *there's no*, and *there are no*.

A: This apartment is very nice. _____Is there_____ a laundry room in the building?
   1.

B: Yes, _____ a laundry room on the second floor.
   2.

A: Good. _____ a garage?
   3.

B: Yes, _____ a garage, too.
   4.

A: OK. One more thing. What about furniture? There's a table in the living room, but

   _____ sofa, and _____ chairs in the dining room.
   5.   6.

B: Well, _____ a furniture store in Riverside. Their furniture is good, and it's not
   7.

   expensive. And _____ a good sale on now.
   8.

B STEP 1. Look at the map. Complete the directions from the apartment to the furniture store.

Directions ___from___ Ana's apartment

_____ Ted's Furniture Store:

Go _____ on 1st Avenue _____

2nd Street. Turn _____ on 2nd Street.

Go _____ 3rd Avenue. Turn

_____ on 3rd Avenue. The store is

_____ 3rd Avenue between 2nd and

3rd Streets across from a small park.

STEP 2. Write directions from the Furniture Store to the Appliance Store.

_____

_____

_____

_____

UNIT 7 GRAMMAR REVIEW

A ▶ DICTATION. Listen. Then listen again and complete the conversation.

A: Hey, Brenda. You look great.

B: Thanks, Alan. I feel great! I think it's because I ride my bike a lot.

A: Oh? _____How_____ often _____ you ride your bike?
　　　　　　 1.　　　　　　　　　**2.**

B: Four or five _____ a week.
　　　　　　　　　　 3.

A: Really? _____?
　　　　　　　　 4.

B: I _____ ride before work, _____ 6:00 to 7:00, and I
　　　　 5.　　　　　　　　　　　　　　　**6.**

　　_____ ride on Saturdays from 9:00 to 10:00.
　　　 7.

A: Good for you!

B PARTNERS. Practice the conversation in Exercise A.

GRAMMAR REVIEW

C **STEP 1. PARTNERS. Talk about free-time activities.**

A: What do you do in your free time?
B: I play soccer.
A: Oh. How often do you play?
B: Once a week. I play on Thursdays from 5:00 to 7:00.

STEP 2. Write three sentences about your partner's free-time activities.

David plays soccer once a week. He plays on Thursdays. He plays from 5:00 to 7:00.

_____

_____

_____

_____

UNIT 8 GRAMMAR REVIEW

A ▶ **DICTATION. Two friends are talking about a recipe. Listen. Then listen again and complete the conversation.**

A: This omelet is really good. What's in it?

B: _____Eggs_____ and cheese. Oh, and there's
        1.

   _____, but not much.
        2.

A: Eggs? How _____ eggs?
                   3.

B: Three.

A: And how _____ cheese?
                4.

B: Just one slice.

A: What do you cook it in? Do you use butter _____ oil?
                                                      5.

B: I use _____, but it's good with _____, too.
            6.   **7.**

B **STEP 1. You are planning a meal. What do you want? Circle one food or drink in each pair.**

1. soup or salad   3. rice or potatoes   5. coffee or tea

2. meat or fish   4. carrots or green beans   6. ice cream or cake

STEP 2. GROUPS OF 5. Ask your classmates about their choices. Count the students. Write the number next to each food.

How many people want soup?

soup __2__ salad __3__

1. soup ____   salad ____
2. meat ____   fish ____
3. rice ____   potatoes ____

4. carrots ____   green beans ____
5. coffee ____   tea ____
6. ice cream ____   cake ____

STEP 3. Write six sentences about your group's choices.

Two students want soup, and three students want salad.

STEP 4. Tell the class about your group's meal.

Our group wants salad, fish, . . .

UNIT 9 GRAMMAR REVIEW

A ▶ **DICTATION. Listen. Then listen again and complete the conversation.**

A: Hi, Sandy. It's me, Gail. Are you at work?

B: _____, I _____ today. I'm home. There's a _____
         1.   2.   3.
bad snowstorm here. Schools are closed again.

A: Wow! So, what _____ the kids _____?
                            4.   5.

B: Well, Tony and Dino are outside in the snow. They _____ pictures.
                                                                  6.

A: That's nice. What about Maria? _____ she _____ in the snow?
                                             7.   8.

B: _____, she _____. She _____ computer games with
         9.   10.   11.
my dad.

A: And you?

B: Well, I _____. And my mom and I _____ laundry. I'm not at
                    12.   13.
work, but I'm _____ busy. And I'm _____ tired.
                    14.   15.

GRAMMAR REVIEW

B **STEP 1. PARTNERS. Look at the picture. What are the people doing?**

A: In Apartment 1, the man is sleeping.
B: Right. And in Apartment 2 ...

STEP 2. Choose six apartments. Write sentences about the people.

In Apartment 1, the man is sleeping.

_____

_____

_____

_____

_____

_____

UNIT 10 GRAMMAR REVIEW

A Complete the conversation. Cross out the incorrect words.

A: What ~~do you do~~ / **are you doing** tomorrow?
B: I **go** / **'m going** to the library in Greenville. I **go** / **'m going** every Friday.
A: Every Friday! **How** / **Where** do you get there?
B: Well, I always **take** / **am taking** the Number 2 bus. The library is on Oak **near** / **between** 7th and 8th Avenues. The bus stops **down** / **near** the block from the library.
A: Oh, really? **What** / **When** are you going?
B: At noon. Why?
A: I **go** / **'m going** to the DMV. It's right **around** / **between** the corner from the library. We can go together!

B **STEP 1. Think about your weekend plans. Fill in the "You" rows. Write two activities.**

	What?	When?	Who?
You	concert	Sat. afternoon	me, Amy, Joe
Your Partner			

STEP 2. PARTNERS. Talk about your plans. Complete the chart.

A: *What are you doing this weekend?*
B: *I'm going to a concert in the park.*
A: *Oh. When . . .*

STEP 3. Write two sentences about your plans and two sentences about your partner's plans.

I am going to a concert on Saturday afternoon. I am going with . . .

_____

_____

UNIT 11 GRAMMAR REVIEW

A Complete the conversation. Use the words in the box.

| does feels has have hurts should was was ~~weren't~~ |

A: You _____ weren't _____ here last week.
   1.

B: No, I _____ home. My son _____ sick with the flu.
        2.   **3.**

A: Oh, I'm so sorry to hear that. _____ he feel better now?
                                   4.

B: Not really. He still _____ a bad headache, and his throat _____.
                        5.   **6.**

A: Hmm. Maybe you _____ take him to the doctor.
                   7.

B: We _____ an appointment for tomorrow.
      8.

A: Well, I hope he _____ better soon.
                   9.

B STEP 1. GROUPS OF 3. Read the problems. Make suggestions.

Problem 1	**Problem 2**	**Problem 3**
Bobby, a 10-year-old boy, has a stomachache every morning before school. What should his parents do?	Sara has a backache. Her friend tells her to exercise. Is this a good suggestion? Sara isn't sure. What should she do?	Ted has a bad sore throat. He wants to go to work. His wife thinks he should stay home. What should he do?

A: *OK, Problem 1. What should Bobby's parents do?*
B: *Hmm. Maybe they should talk to his teacher. Maybe there's a problem at school.*
C: *Or, maybe they should take him to the doctor.*

STEP 2. Write one suggestion for each problem.

Problem 1. _____

Problem 2. _____

Problem 3. _____

UNIT 12 GRAMMAR REVIEW

A Complete the interview with *was*, *were*, *can*, and *can't*.

A: So, I see you _____ *were* _____ a sales assistant at Creative Clothing in Smithfield.
1.

How long _____ *were* _____ you there?
2.

B: Three years. I _____ there from 2013 to 2016. Then my family moved.
3.

A: _____ you speak Korean? We have a lot of Korean customers.
4.

B: Yes, I _____ speak Korean, English, and a little Spanish. I _____
5.   6.

a cashier in a Mexican restaurant for six months.

A: Our store is always busy on weekends. _____ you work weekends?
7.

B: Well, I can work Saturdays, but I _____ work Sundays.
8.

A: That's OK. When can you start?

B: I _____ start next weekend.
9.

B **STEP 1.** Complete the information about a job you or a friend had.

Company: _____

Job: _____   Dates Worked: From _____   To _____

The job was   ☐ full-time   ☐ part-time

C **STEP 2.** Write three sentences about the job in Step 1.

I was a sales assistant at Creative Clothing in Smithfield. I was there for three years.

The job was . . .

_____

_____

_____

GRAMMAR REFERENCE

Unit 2, Lesson 3, page 31

Some irregular plural nouns

child	**children**	person	**people**
man	**men**	foot	**feet**
woman	**women**	tooth	**teeth**

Unit 2, Lesson 9, page 42

Spelling rules for simple present tense: Third-person singular (*he, she, it*)

1. Add **-s** for most verbs: *work—work**s**   play—play**s***
2. Add **-es** for words that end in **-ch, -s, -sh, -x,** or **-z**: *watch—watch**es**   relax—relax**es***
3. Change the ***y*** to ***i*** and add **-es** when the base form ends in a consonant + ***y***: *study—stud**ies***
4. Add **-s** when the base form ends in a vowel + ***y***: *play—play**s**   enjoy—enjoy**s***
5. Some verbs have **irregular forms**: *do—**does**   have—**has**   go—**goes***

Unit 7, Lesson 3, page 130

Prepositions of time

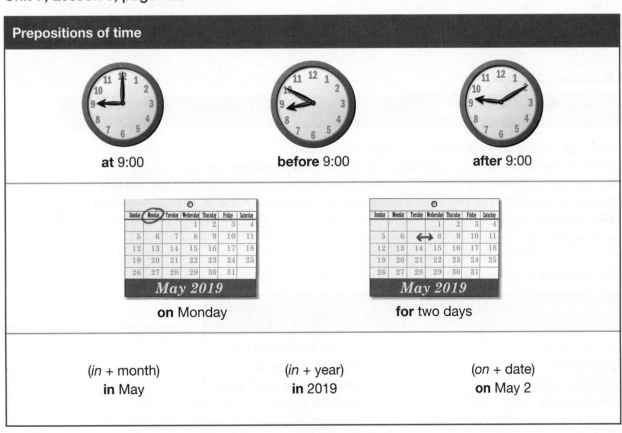

at 9:00   **before** 9:00   **after** 9:00

on Monday   **for** two days

(*in* + month)   (*in* + year)   (*on* + date)
in May   **in** 2019   **on** May 2

GRAMMAR REFERENCE

Unit 8, Lesson 3, page 150

Some common non-count nouns

Food: beef, bread, butter, cabbage, cake, cereal, chicken, chocolate, fish, ice cream, lettuce, oil, pizza, rice, salmon, shrimp, soup, yogurt
Drinks: coffee, juice, milk, soda, tea, water
School Subjects: art, English, history, math, music, science
Activities: basketball, homework, laundry, soccer
Others: air-conditioning, chalk, electricity, furniture, hair, information, luggage, money, news, paper, transportation, weather

Remember: Non-count nouns are singular. Example: *Pizza is my favorite food.*

Spelling rules for plural count nouns

Add **-s** to most nouns	book—book**s**	
Add **-es** to most nouns that end in **-ch, -s, -sh, -x,**	watch—watch**es**	box—box**es**
or a consonant + **o**.	guess—guess**es**	potato—potato**es**
	dish—dish**es**	
Change **y** to **i** and add **-es** to nouns that end in a consonant + **y**.	baby—bab**ies**	city—cit**ies**
Change **f** to **v** and add **-s** to nouns that end in **-fe**.	knife—kni**ves**	wife—wi**ves**
Change **f** to **v** and add **-es** to nouns that ends in **-f**.	loaf—loa**ves**	shelf shel**ves**

Unit 9, Lesson 3, page 170

Spelling rules for present continuous

1. Add **-ing** to the base form: cook—cook**ing**   eat—eat**ing**
2. For verbs that end in **e,** drop the final **e** and add **-ing**: take—tak**ing**   make—mak**ing**
3. For one-syllable verbs that end in a consonant, a vowel, and a consonant, double the final consonant and add **-ing**. Do not double the final consonant if it is a **w, x,** or **y**: get—get**ting** play—play**ing**

Unit 10, Lesson 3, page 190

Prepositions of place

in Los Angeles	**across from** the bank
on First Street	**around** the corner
at 231 First Street	**next to** the supermarket
down the block	**near** the corner
between First and Second Streets	**in/at** school

ABCs and Numbers

▶ The Alphabet

Aa	Bb	Cc	Dd	Ee	Ff	Gg	Hh	Ii	Jj	Kk	Ll	Mm
Nn	Oo	Pp	Qq	Rr	Ss	Tt	Uu	Vv	Ww	Xx	Yy	Zz

▶ Cardinal Numbers

1	2	3	4	5	6
one	two	three	four	five	six
7	8	9	10	11	12
seven	eight	nine	ten	eleven	twelve
13	14	15	16	17	18
thirteen	fourteen	fifteen	sixteen	seventeen	eighteen
19	20	21	22	23	24
nineteen	twenty	twenty-one	twenty-two	twenty-three	twenty-four
25	26	27	28	29	30
twenty-five	twenty-six	twenty-seven	twenty-eight	twenty-nine	thirty
40	50	60	70	80	90
forty	fifty	sixty	seventy	eighty	ninety
100					
hundred					

▶ Ordinal Numbers

1st	2nd	3rd	4th	5th	6th
first	second	third	fourth	fifth	sixth
7th	8th	9th	10th	11th	12th
seventh	eighth	ninth	tenth	eleventh	twelfth
13th	14th	15th	16th	17th	18th
thirteenth	fourteenth	fifteenth	sixteenth	seventeenth	eighteenth
19th	20th	21st	22nd	23rd	24th
nineteenth	twentieth	twenty-first	twenty-second	twenty-third	twenty-fourth
25th	26th	27th	28th	29th	30th
twenty-fifth	twenty-sixth	twenty-seventh	twenty-eighth	twenty-ninth	thirtieth
40th	50th	60th	70th	80th	90th
fortieth	fiftieth	sixtieth	seventieth	eightieth	ninetieth
100th					
hundredth					

WORD LIST

UNIT 1

Regions
Africa, 7
Asia, 7
Central America, 7
Europe, 7
Middle East (the), 7
North America, 7
South America, 7

Countries
Brazil, 7
Canada, 7
China, 7

Cuba, 7
El Salvador, 7
Ethiopia, 7
Iraq, 7
Mexico, 7
Peru, 7
Poland, 7
Russia, 7
Somalia, 7
South Korea, 7
Syria, 7
United State (the), 7
Vietnam, 7

absent, 12
boring, 18
bow, 8
class, 14
classmate, 12
countries, 7
easy, 16
first name, 10
friendly, 19
good, 18
great, 18
hard, 16
helpful, 19

hug, 8
Identification Card
 (ID Card), 15
immigrant, 16
interesting, 18
last name, 10
late, 12
regions, 7
shake hands, 8
smart, 19
regions, 7
student, 19
teacher, 19

UNIT 2

accountant, 27
assembly line worker, 41
caregiver, 41
carpenter, 41
cashier, 27
child-care worker, 27
CNA, 38
construction site, 27
cook, 27

custodian, 27
doctor, 27
driver, 27
electrician, 27
email address, 33
factory, 41
healthcare, 38
home, 27
homemaker, 27

hospital, 27
landscaper, 27
manager, 27
nurse, 27
nursing home, 38
office, 27
office assistant, 27
orderly, 38
painter, 27

phone number, 32
restaurant, 27
sales assistant, 27
server, 27
stock clerk, 41
store, 27
supermarket, 41

UNIT 3

across from, 59
backpack, 47
board, 47
book, 47
borrow, 48
cafeteria, 58
computer lab, 58
computer lab assistant, 60
custodian, 60
desk, 47
dictionary, 47

director, 60
director's office, 61
elevator, 58
eraser, 47
folder, 47
hall, 58
keyboard, 54
laptop, 47
librarian, 60
library, 58
marker, 47

mouse, 54
next to, 59
notebook, 47
office, 58
on the left, 59
on the right, 59
phone, 47
piece of paper, 47
printer, 54
projector, 47
put away, 48

restroom, 58
screen, 54
stairs, 58
sticky note, 47
tablet, 47
take out, 48
three-ring binder, 47
turn off, 48

UNIT 4

Months
January, 78
February, 78
March, 78
April, 78
May, 78
June 78
July, 78
August, 78
September, 78
October, 78
November, 78
December, 78

aunt, 69
average, 74
beard, 74
birthday, 79
blended family, 72
brother, 67
calendar, 78
children, 67
common, 73
cousin, 69
date, 78
daughter, 67
divorced, 72
family tree, 67
family, 68

father, 67
female, 67
grandfather, 67
grandmother, 67
height, 74
holiday, 78
husband, 67
look like, 68
male, 67
married, 72
month of the year, 78
mother, 67
mustache, 74
parents, 67
photo, 69

remarried, 73
short, 74
sister, 67
son, 67
step-brother, 72
step-father, 72
step-mother, 72
step-sister, 72
tall, 74
thin, 74
uncle, 69
weight, 74
wife, 67

UNIT 5

bank account, 99
bill, 98
black, 87
blouse, 87
blue, 87
brown, 87
cash, 98

clothes, 86
credit card, 98
debit card, 98
dime, 92
dress, 87
due date, 99
extra large, 94

extra small, 94
gray, 87
green, 87
handbag, 89
interest, 99
jacket, 87
jeans, 87

khaki, 87
large, 94
medium, 94
need, 88
nickel, 92
orange, 87
pants, 87

penny, 92
pink, 87
plastic, 98
price, 93
purple, 87
quarter, 92
receipt, 93

red, 87
return, 100
shirt, 87
shoes, 87
skirt, 87
small, 94
sneakers, 87

socks, 87
sweater, 87
T-shirt, 87
tax, 93
tight, 101
wallet, 89
want, 88

watch, 89
wear, 87
white, 87
yellow, 87
zipper, 100

UNIT 6

address, 118
air conditioning, 119
apartment, 110
appliances, 114
avenue, 118
bathroom, 107
bathtub, 107
bed, 107
bedroom, 107
boulevard, 118
cable, 119
ceiling, 112
chair, 107
closet, 107
coffee table, 107

dark, 108
dining room, 107
dresser, 107
drive, 118
east, 120
expensive, 108
fire, 113
floor lamp, 115
for rent, 108
furnished, 114
garage, 109
go off, 112
GPS, 120
heat, 119
inexpensive, 108

Internet, 19
kitchen, 107
lamp, 107
landlord, 112
laundry room, 109
living room, 107
map, 120
microwave, 107
north, 120
parking, 119
pet, 119
refrigerator, 107
renter, 112
road, 118
shower, 107

sink, 107
smoke alarm, 112
sofa, 107
south, 120
stove, 107
street, 118
studio, 115
sunny, 108
table, 107
toilet, 107
unfurnished, 114
west, 120
yard, 109

UNIT 7

Days
Monday, 132
Tuesday, 132
Wednesday, 132
Thursday, 132
Friday, 132
Saturday, 132
Sunday, 132

babysit, 129
chore, 138
clean, 134
communicate, 138
cook dinner, 127
days of the week, 132
do homework, 127
do puzzles, 140

do the laundry, 135
eat breakfast, 127
eat dinner, 127
employee, 133
exercise, 127
free time, 138
get dressed, 127
get home, 127
get up, 127
go dancing, 135
go running, 140
go swimming, 135
go to bed, 127
go to the beach, 135
go to the mall, 128
go to the movies, 128
go to the park, 128

go to work, 127
ID number, 133
knit, 140
listen to music, 140
on average, 138
play basketball, 135
play cards, 135
play soccer, 128
play sports, 139
play video games, 135
read, 135
relax, 138
ride a bike, 135
shop for food, 134
socialize, 138
spend time with
    someone, 134

stay home, 135
stressed, 141
take a (computer) class,
129
take a hot bath, 140
take a long walk, 140
take a shower, 127
time in, 133
time out, 133
time sheet, 133
visit someone, 129
wash a car, 135
wash the dishes, 127
watch TV, 127
work schedule, 132

UNIT 8

apple pie, 154
apples, 147
avocados, 161
baked potato, 154
bananas, 147
beans, 147
beef, 147
black bean taco, 155
bread, 147
butter, 147
cabbage, 147
cabinet, 152
calories, 158
canned foods, 153
carrots, 161
cereal, 147
cheese, 147
chicken, 147
coffee, 154
counter, 152
cucumbers, 161

dairy, 147
eggs, 147
fat, 158
fish, 147
freezer, 152
fresh, 152
fried, 160
fries, 154
frozen food, 153
fruit, 147
fruit cup, 154
grains, 147
gram (g), 159
green beans, 158
grilled, 160
hamburger, 148
ice cream, 154
iced tea, 154
lettuce, 147
mango, 161
milk, 147

milligram (mg), 159
net weight, 159
nuts, 161
oils, 147
onions, 147
orange juice, 155
oranges, 147
pancakes, 149
pasta, 149
pizza, 148
potatoes, 147
proteins, 147
red peppers, 161
refrigerator, 152
rice, 147
roast beef, 161
salad, 149
salmon, 161
scallions, 161
scrambled eggs, 149
sell-by date, 153

serving size, 159
shrimp, 161
soda, 154
sodium, 158
spinach, 161
steak, 149
steamed, 160
sugar, 158
taco, 148
tomatoes, 161
tomato soup, 154
turkey, 161
turkey sandwich, 154
use-by date, 153
vegetable oil, 147
vegetables, 147
watermelon, 161
wraps, 149
yogurt, 147

WORD LIST

UNIT 9

alarm system, 173
batteries, 174
boots, 180
cloudy, 167
cold, 167
cool, 167
earmuffs, 180
earthquake, 172
emergency, 172
emergency exit, 173
exit doors, 173
exit maps, 173
fall, 167
fire, 172

first aid kit, 174
flashlight, 174
flood, 172
foggy, 169
gloves, 180
hat, 180
hot, 167
humid, 169
hurricane, 172
hurricane warning, 178
hurricane watch, 178
landslide, 172
light clothes, 180
matches, 174

northeast, 178
northwest, 178
raincoat, 180
rainy, 167
scarf, 180
seasons, 167
shorts, 180
snowstorm, 172
snowy, 167
southeast, 178
southwest, 178
spring, 167
storm surges, 179
summer, 167

sunblock, 180
sunglasses, 180
sunny, 167
thunderstorm, 172
tornado, 172
umbrella, 180
warm, 167
weather, 167
wildfire, 172
winds, 179
windy, 169
winter, 167

UNIT 10

around the corner from, 190
ATM, 187
bank, 187
baseball game, 200
between, 190
bike, 191
bus, 191
bus schedule, 193
bus stop, 187
café, 187

car, 191
clothing store, 187
concert, 200
courthouse, 189
DMV, 189
down the street/ block, 190
drugstore, 187
due date, 198
e-book, 198
exact change, 194

fare, 194
farmers' market, 187
fire station, 187
gas station, 187
get off/on, 194
grand opening, 200
gym, 187
laundromat, 187
library card, 198
near, 190
on the corner of, 190

park, 187
police station, 187
post office, 187
salon, 187
subway, 191
supermarket, 187
taxi, 191
traffic signs, 192
train, 191
transportation, 191
yard sale, 200

UNIT 11

ankle, 207
antibiotics, 220
arm, 207
back, 207
chest, 207
clap, 207
cold, 209
cough, 209
doctor, 208
ear, 207
earache, 209
elbow, 207
energy, 218
eye, 207
face, 207
fever, 209
flu, 209

foot/feet, 207
get strong, 218
hand, 207
head, 207
headache, 208
health, 219
heart, 219
heating pad, 220
ice pack, 220
knee, 207
leg, 207
lie down, 212
look straight ahead, 212
lose weight, 218
make a fist, 212
mouth, 207
neck, 207

nod, 207
nose, 207
open your mouth, 212
operate machinery, 213
orally, 213
out of reach, 213
patient, 212
put heat on it, 220
roll up your sleeve, 212
shake, 207
shoulder, 207
sick, 208
sit on the table, 212
sore throat, 208
stay in bed, 220
step on the scale, 212
steps, 219

stomach, 207
stomachache, 208
stuffy nose, 209
tablet, 213
take a deep breath, 212
take a hot shower, 220
take antibiotics, 220
tooth/teeth, 207
toothache, 208
touch, 207
use a heating pad, 220
use an ice pack, 220
weight, 219
wrist, 207

UNIT 12

answer the phone, 227
apply for a job, 229
carpenter, 229
cashier, 241
create presentations, 230
customer, 234
drive a truck, 227
experience, 232
fix furniture, 229
fix things, 227

full-time, 232
hair stylist, 241
help customers, 227
help patients, 227
hotel, 235
in person, 232
job interview, 238
make cabinets, 229
make copies, 227
make food, 227

office assistant, 229
organize things, 230
part-time, 232
repair person, 234
résumé, 232
sales assistant, 229
salon, 241
serve food, 227
shift, 233
supervise workers, 227

take care of children, 227
take care of grounds, 227
take inventory, 229
take returns, 229
use a cash register, 227
use a computer, 227
work on buildings, 227
work with numbers, 230
write reports, 230

AUDIO SCRIPT

UNIT 1

Page 8, Exercises 2B and 2C

Carla: Hi, I'm Carla Cruz.
Boris: Hi, I'm Boris Popov.
Carla: Nice to meet you.
Boris: Nice to meet you, too.

Page 8, Exercise 2D

Carla: Hi, I'm Carla Cruz.
Boris: Hi, I'm Boris Popov.
Carla: Nice to meet you.
Boris: Nice to meet you, too.
Carla: Where are you from, Boris?
Boris: I'm from Russia. What about you?
Carla: I'm from Peru.

Page 11, Exercise 2D

1.
A: Your name, please?
B: Michael Chen.
A: Can you spell your first name, please?
B: Sure. M-I-C-H-A-E-L.
A: M-I-C-H-A-E-L. OK, Mr. Chen. You want to take English classes, right?
B: Right.
A: Thank you, Mr. Chen.

2.
A: Your name, please?
B: Vera Kotova.
A: Can you spell your last name, please?
B: Sure. K-O-T-O-V-A.
A: K-O-T-O-V-A. OK, Miss Kotova. You want to take English classes, right?
B: Right.
A: Thank you, Miss Kotova.

3.
A: Your name, please?
B: Ana Lopez.
A: Can you spell your last name, please?
B: Sure. L-O-P-E-Z.
A: L-O-P-E-Z. OK, Ms. Lopez. You want to take English classes, right?
B: Right.
A: Thank you, Ms. Lopez.

Page 12, Exercises 2B and 2C

Carla: Who's that?
Sen: That's Boris.
Carla: No, that's not Boris.
Sen: Oh, you're right. That's Max.
Carla: Max? Where's he from?
Sen: He's from Mexico.

Page 12, Exercise 2D

Carla: Who's that?
Sen: That's Boris.
Carla: No, that's not Boris.

Sen: Oh, you're right. That's Max.
Carla: Max? Where's he from?
Sen: He's from Mexico.
Carla: So, where's Boris?
Sen: I don't know. I guess he's absent.
Boris: I'm not absent. I'm here! Sorry I'm late.

Page 13, Exercise 3B

1. She's a student.
2. He's in Level 1.
3. He's late.
4. She's Sen.
5. She's not here.
6. He's from China.

Page 18, Exercises 2A and 2B

Min Jung: Hi. So, what class are you in?
Boris: We're in Level 1.
Min Jung: Oh. How is it?
Mimi: It's good. The teacher is great.
Min Jung: How are the students?
Boris: They're great, too.

Page 18, Exercise 2C

Min Jung: Hi. So, what class are you in?
Boris: We're in Level 1.
Min Jung: Oh. How is it?
Mimi: It's good. The teacher is great.
Min Jung: How are the students?
Boris: They're great, too. There's just one problem.
Min Jung: Oh? What's the problem?
Boris: English! It's hard.

Page 22, Exercise C

1. He's not in Level 3.
2. Level 3 isn't easy.
3. We're not late.
4. They're in my class.
5. They aren't absent.
6. The teachers are helpful.

UNIT 2

Page 28, Exercise 2A

Edgar: Omar, this is Rosa. Rosa, this is Omar.
Rosa: Hi, Omar. Nice to meet you.
Omar: Hi, Rosa. Nice to meet you, too.

Page 28, Exercises 2B and 2C;
Page 29, Exercise 4A

Rosa: So, what do you do?
Omar: I'm a landscaper. And I'm a student at Greenville Adult School.
Rosa: Really? I'm a student there, too. And I'm a sales assistant.
Omar: Oh, that's interesting.

Page 28, Exercise 2D

Rosa: So, what do you do?
Omar: I'm a landscaper. And I'm a student at Greenville Adult School.
Rosa: Really? I'm a student there, too. And I'm a sales assistant.
Omar: Oh, that's interesting. I think Emilio is a sales assistant, too.
Rosa: No, he's not. He's an office assistant, not a sales assistant.

Page 31, Show What You Know, Exercise 3

Which are the most common jobs in the U.S.?
Sales assistants are number 1.
Cashiers are number 2.
Food preparers and servers are number 3.
Office assistants are number 4.
Nurses are number 5.

Page 32, Exercise 1C

1. 412-960-5334
2. 619-464-2083
3. 305-576-1169
4. 323-835-4191
5. 214-847-3726
6. 773-399-2114

Page 32, Exercise 1D

1.
Hi, Ben. This is Mr. Fernandez at Center Hospital. I'm calling about the Landscaper job. Please call me back at 562-555-1349. That's 562-555-1349.

2.
Hi, Maya. This is Grace Simms at Grace's Office Supplies. I'm calling about the cashier job. Please call me back. My number is 408-555-7821. That's 408-555-7821.

3.
Hi, Nara. This is Jin Wu at Greenville Store. I'm calling about the sales assistant job. Please call me back at 773-555-9602. That's 773-555-9602.

4.
Hi, Juan. This is Ms. Rodriguez at Carla's Restaurant. I'm calling about the manager job. Please call me back at 339-555-8851. That's 339-555-8851.

Page 33, Exercise 2C

1. D-A-N dot S-I-L-V-E-R at cc mail dot edu
2. G dot Simms at h mail dot com
3. T Lopez 7-1-5 at go mail dot com
4. J-I-N dot W-U at new mail dot edu

Page 34, Exercises 2B and 2C

Marta: Who's that? Is she a teacher?
Boris: No, she's not. She's a student. And she's a cashier at Al's Restaurant.
Marta: Oh, that's interesting. And what do you do?
Boris: I'm a cook.

Page 34, Exercise 2D

Marta: Who's that? Is she a teacher?
Boris: No, she's not. She's a student. And she's a cashier at Al's Restaurant.
Marta: Oh, that's interesting. And what do you do?
Boris: I'm a cook.
Marta: A cook! I'm a cook, too.
Boris: Really?
Marta: Yes. I'm a cook, a server, a child-care worker, and a doctor.
Boris: Four jobs!
Marta: Yes. I'm a homemaker!

Page 35, Exercise 3B

1. Is she a teacher?
2. She's a student.
3. What do you do?
4. Are you a doctor?
5. Are they servers?
6. Where are you from?
7. Who's that?
8. you a cook?

Page 40, Exercises 2A and 2B

Dora: So, what do you do?
Sali: I'm a nurse.
Dora: Really? Where do you work?
Sali: I work at a school on Main Street. I'm a school nurse.
Dora: Oh. That's nice.

Page 40, Exercise 2C

Dora: So, what do you do?
Sali: I'm a nurse.
Dora: Really? Where do you work?
Sali: I work at a school on Main Street. I'm a school nurse.
Dora: Oh. That's nice. What about you, Omar?
Omar: I work at a school, too.
Dora: Are you a teacher?
Omar: No.
Dora: Are you an office assistant?
Omar: No. I'm a student.
Sali: That's not a job, Omar.
Omar: Oh, yes, it is. It's a hard job.

UNIT 3

Page 48, Exercises 2A and 2B

Ms. Reed: OK, everyone. Please put away your books. Take out a piece of paper.
Student 1: Can I borrow a pencil?
Student 2: Sure. Here you go.

Page 48, Exercise 2C

Ms. Reed: OK, everyone. Please put away your books. Take out a piece of paper.
Student 1: Can I borrow a pencil?
Student 2: Sure. Here you go.

Ms. Reed:	Uh-oh. Please turn off your phones.
Student 1:	Uhmm. Ms. Reed?
Ms. Reed:	Yes?
Student 1:	I think that's your phone.
Ms. Reed:	Oh!

Page 54, Exercises 2B and 2C

Carlos:	What's this called in English?
Mimi:	It's a mouse.
Carlos:	And these? What are these called?
Mimi:	They're printers.

Page 54, Exercise 2D

Carlos:	What's this called in English?
Mimi:	It's a mouse.
Carlos:	And these? What are these called?
Mimi:	They're printers.
Carlos:	Nope. You're wrong.
Mimi:	What? I'm not wrong. That's a mouse, and those are printers.
Carlos:	No, they're not. This is a picture of a mouse, and that's a picture of printers.
Mimi:	Very funny.

Page 55, Exercise 3B

1. ten
2. they
3. these

Page 60, Exercises 2B and 2C

Ken:	Excuse me. Is the computer lab open?
Berta:	Sorry. I don't know. Ask him.
Ken:	Oh, OK. But . . . Who is he?
Berta:	He's the computer lab assistant.

UNIT 4

Page 68, Exercises 2B and 2C

Kim:	That's a great photo. Who's that?
Gina:	My father.
Kim:	Oh, he looks nice.
Gina:	Thanks.

Page 68, Exercise 2D

Kim:	That's a great photo. Who's that?
Gina:	My father.
Kim:	Oh, he looks nice.
Gina:	Thanks.
Kim:	And is that your sister? She looks like you.
Gina:	Thanks, but that's not my sister. That's my daughter!

Page 74, Exercises 2A and 2B

Pam:	Is your family here in this country?
Leo:	My brother is here. He's a carpenter.
Pam:	Oh. What's he like?
Leo:	He's great. He's a lot of fun.
Pam:	Does he look like you?
Leo:	No. He's tall and thin and he has long hair.

Page 74, Exercise 2C

Pam:	Is your family here in this country?
Leo:	My brother is here. He's a carpenter.
Pam:	Oh. What's he like?
Leo:	He's great. He's a lot of fun.
Pam:	Does he look like you?
Leo:	No. He's tall and thin, and he has long hair. Here's a picture of him.
Pam:	Oh. He has a beard and a mustache, too.
Leo:	He has one more thing, too.
Pam:	Oh, yeah. What's that?
Leo:	He has a wife.
Pam:	Oh.

Page 78, Exercise 2B

1. January twenty-first
2. January fifth
3. January seventeenth
4. January eighth
5. January twenty-fourth
6. January eleventh
7. January thirtieth
8. January ninth

Page 79, Exercise 2E

1.
A:	What's your date of birth?
B:	It's March fourteenth, nineteen eighty-seven.

2.
A:	When was your son born?
B:	October second, two thousand eleven.

3.
A:	What's your sister's date of birth?
B:	It's May twenty-eighth, nineteen ninety-eight.

4.
A:	When was your daughter born?
B:	August thirty-first, two thousand five.

5.
A:	When was your father born?
B:	December seventeenth, nineteen sixty-nine.

6.
A:	What's your brother's date of birth?
B:	It's September second, nineteen seventy-two.

Page 80, Exercises 2B and 2C

Kofi:	Hi, Ellen. Where are you?
Ellen:	I'm at my friend's house. I'm babysitting for her kids.
Kofi:	Oh. How old are they?
Ellen:	Well, her son is in the fifth grade. I think he's eleven. And her daughter is six. She's in the first grade.

Page 80, Exercise 2D

Kofi:	Hi, Ellen. Where are you?
Ellen:	I'm at my friend's house. I'm babysitting for her kids.

Kofi: Oh. How old are they?

Ellen: Well, her son is in the fifth grade. I think he's eleven. And her daughter is six. She's in the first grade.

Kofi: What are they like?

Ellen: Well, the boy is great. His name is Ken.

Kofi: Oh. And what about the girl?

Ellen: Terry? She's really friendly, but my friend says she's Terry the terrible.

Kofi: Why?

Ellen: I really don't know.

UNIT 5

Page 88, Exercises 2A and 2B

Meg: I need a gift for my brother. It's his birthday next week.

Carlos: How about clothes?

Meg: Well, he needs clothes, but he wants a backpack.

Page 88, Exercise 2C

Meg: I need a gift for my brother. It's his birthday next week.

Carlos: How about clothes?

Meg: Well, he needs clothes, but he wants a backpack.

Carlos: So get two backpacks.

Meg: Two backpacks? Why two, Carlos?

Carlos: My birthday is next month, and I want a backpack!

Page 93, Exercise 2B

1.

Customer: Excuse me. How much is this blouse?

Assistant: It's $11.95.

2.

Customer: Excuse me. How much are these shoes?

Assistant: They're $34.99.

3.

Customer: Excuse me. How much is this watch?

Assistant: It's $23.50.

4.

Customer: Excuse me. How much are these pants?

Assistant: They're $13.49.

Page 94, Exercises 2B and 2C

Kofi: Do you have this sweater in a large?

Assistant: No, I'm sorry. We don't.

Kofi: Too bad. It's for my sister, and she needs a large.

Page 94, Exercise 2D

Kofi: Do you have this sweater in a large?

Assistant: No, I'm sorry. We don't.

Kofi: Too bad. It's for my sister, and she needs a large.

Assistant: What about this sweater? Does she like blue?

Kofi: Yes, she does.

Assistant: Well, here you go.

Kofi: Great. Thanks.

Page 100, Exercises 2A and 2B

Assistant: May I help you?

Customer 1: Yes. I need to return these pants.

Assistant: OK. What's the problem?

Customer 1: They don't fit. They're too big.

Assistant: Do you have your receipt?

Customer 1: Yes, I do. It's here somewhere! . . . Oh, here it is.

Assistant: Thank you. And here's your money . . . Next. May I help you?

Customer 2: Yes. I'd like to return this jacket.

Assistant: OK. What's the problem?

Customer 2: The zipper is broken.

Assistant: Do you have your receipt?

Customer 2: Uh, no.

Assistant: We can only give you store credit.

Customer 2: That's OK. I always shop here.

Assistant: Well, here you go.

Customer 2: Thank you.

UNIT 6

Page 108, Exercises 2B and 2C

Dan: Oh, wow! This house looks great!

Emily: Really?

Dan: Yes. There are two bedrooms and a large kitchen.

Emily: What about a dining room?

Dan: Well, no. There's no dining room.

Page 108, Exercise 2D

Dan: Oh, wow! This house looks great!

Emily: Really?

Dan: Yes. There are two bedrooms and a large kitchen.

Emily: What about a dining room?

Dan: Well, no. There's no dining room.

Emily: That's OK. The kitchen's large. How's the rent?

Dan: Not bad. It's pretty inexpensive. There is one problem, though.

Emily: Oh? What's that?

Dan: It's not in the United States. It's in Canada!

Page 114, Exercises 2B and 2C

Amy: Excuse me. Is there an apartment for rent in this building?

Manager: Yes, there is. There's a one-bedroom apartment on the second floor.

Amy: Oh, great. Is it furnished?

Manager: Well, yes and no. There's a dresser, but no beds.

Lei: Oh. Well, are there appliances?

Manager:	Uh, yes and no. There's a stove, but no refrigerator.

Page 114, Exercise 2D

Amy:	Excuse me. Is there an apartment for rent in this building?
Manager:	Yes, there is. There's a one-bedroom apartment on the second floor.
Amy:	Oh, great. Is it furnished?
Manager:	Well, yes and no. There's a dresser, but no beds.
Lei:	Oh. Well, are there appliances?
Manager:	Uh, yes and no. There's a stove, but no refrigerator. So? Are you interested?
Amy:	Well, yes.
Lei:	And no.

Page 120, Exercises 2A and 2B

Woman:	How do we get to Joe's Furniture Store?
Man:	Let me check on my phone. OK. First, go north on Route 1 for three miles.
Woman:	North?
Man:	Uh-huh. Then turn left on Fifth Avenue. Continue for one block. It's on the left, across from a park.
Woman:	That sounds easy.

Page 120, Exercise 2C.

Woman:	How do we get to Joe's Furniture Store?
Man:	Let me check on my phone. OK. First, go north on Route 1 for three miles.
Woman:	North?
Man:	Uh-huh. Then turn left on Fifth Avenue. Continue for one block. It's on the left, across from a park.
Woman:	That sounds easy.
Man:	So, let's go!
Woman:	Wait a second. Today is Sunday, and it's 3:30. Is Joe's open?
Man:	Good question. Let me check. They're open Monday to Saturday from 10:00 AM to 7:00 PM, and Sunday from 10:00 AM to 5:00 PM.
Woman:	OK. Let's hurry. They close soon.

UNIT 7

Page 128, Exercises 2B and 2C

Sue:	Are you free tomorrow? How about a movie?
Mia:	Sorry, I'm busy. I work on Saturdays.
Sue:	Oh. Well, when do you get home?
Mia:	At 8:00.

Page 128, Exercise 2D

Sue:	Are you free tomorrow? How about a movie?
Mia:	Sorry, I'm busy. I work on Saturdays.
Sue:	Oh. Well, when do you get home?
Mia:	At 8:00. [eight o'clock]
Sue:	That's not a problem.

Mia:	No? What time is the movie?
Sue:	What do you mean?
Mia:	What time does the movie start?
Sue:	It starts when we want. I have lots of movies at home.

Page 129, Exercise 3B

1. What do you do in your free time?
2. When do you have English class?
3. What time do you go to work?
4. Where do you exercise?

Page 134, Exercises 2A and 2B

Ling:	Gee, I'm so glad it's Friday.
Tony:	Me, too. What do you usually do on the weekend?
Ling:	Well, I always clean the house on Saturdays, and I always spend time with my family on Sundays. What about you?
Tony:	I usually shop for food on Saturdays, and I sometimes go to the park on Sundays.

Page 134, Exercise 2C

Ling:	Gee, I'm so glad it's Friday.
Tony:	Me, too. What do you usually do on the weekend?
Ling:	Well, I always clean the house on Saturdays, and I always spend time with my family on Sundays. What about you?
Tony:	I usually shop for food on Saturdays, and I sometimes go to the park on Sundays.
Ling:	I love the weekend.
Tony:	Yeah, especially Sunday.
Ling:	Right. Saturday is for cleaning and shopping, and Sunday is for fun.
Tony:	Exactly. In our house, we call Sunday "fun day."

Page 140, Exercises 2A and 2B

Hello. This is Dr. Sue Miller with Life Styles. Our podcast today is about relaxing.

Many people say, "Relax? I never relax." What about you? Do you relax? How often do you relax?

How often do you take a long hot bath?
How often do you go running?
How often do you listen to music?
How often do you take a long walk?

Sometimes? Never? That's not good.

We're all busy, but we all need to relax—and not just sometimes. We need to relax every day.

It helps us be better students, workers, friends, and family members.

Remember: You'll do more if you relax. So, take a bath, go for a run, listen to music, take a long walk. Thank you for listening to Life Styles. This is Dr. Sue Miller saying good-bye and relax!

UNIT 8

Page 148, Exercises 2A and 2B

Mark: Wow, I'm hungry!
Rosa: Yeah, me too. What do you want for lunch?
Mark: Pizza! I love pizza! What about you?
Rosa: I don't really like pizza, but I love tacos!

Page 148, Exercise 2C

Mark: Wow, I'm hungry!
Rosa: Yeah, me too. What do you want for lunch?
Mark: Pizza! I love pizza! What about you?
Rosa: I don't really like pizza, but I love tacos! And look! There's a taco place over there!
Mark: Sounds good! And there's a pizza place, too. But wait a minute. It's not time for lunch!
Rosa: No?
Mark: No. It's only 10:30!
Rosa: So, forget about lunch. Let's have pizza and tacos for breakfast.

Page 154, Exercises 2A and 2B

Server: Can I help you?
Greg: Yes, I'd like a hamburger and a soda.
Server: Is that a large soda or a small soda?
Greg: Large, please.
Server: OK, a large soda . . . Anything else?
Greg: Yes. A small order of fries.

Page 154, Exercise 2C

Server: Can I help you?
Greg: Yes, I'd like a hamburger and a soda.
Server: Is that a large soda or a small soda?
Greg: Large, please.
Server: OK, a large soda . . . Anything else?
Greg: Yes. A small order of fries.
Liz: A hamburger, fries, and a soda? You know, that's not very healthy! What about vegetables?
Greg: Well, there's lettuce on the hamburger.
Liz: OK . . . And what about fruit?
Greg: You're right! I need fruit. I know . . . I'll have a piece of apple pie, too.

Page 157, Exercise 1B

1.
A: How much is the chicken?
B: It's three twenty-nine a pound.

2.
A: How much are the bananas?
B: They're ninety-nine cents a pound.

3.
A: How much is the yogurt?
B: It's three eighty-five.

4.
A: How much are the apples?
B: They're one ninety-nine a pound.

5.
A: How much are the onions?
B: They're eighty-nine cents a pound.

6.
A: How much is the bread?
B: It's two fifty-nine.

Page 160, Exercises 2A and 2B

Hannah: Good morning. This is Hannah Charles with Greenville News Radio. You're listening to The Food Show. Do you have questions about food? Well, call and ask. Now here's our first caller . . .
Greg: Hi Hannah. I'm Greg Johnson. My wife says that I don't eat healthy food. She says, "Eat more fruit and vegetables." But I'm a meat and potatoes man.
Hannah: OK, Mr. Meat and Potatoes. Tell me, do you like chicken?
Greg: Sure. I eat a lot of chicken.
Hannah: And do you like grilled chicken or fried chicken?
Greg: I like grilled chicken and fried chicken.
Hannah: OK. Now let me ask you a question. How many calories are there in a piece of fried chicken?
Greg: Hmm. I don't know.
Hannah: 250 calories.
Greg: 250 calories!
Hannah: That's right, but in a piece of grilled chicken there are only about 100 calories. So, the choice is easy. The next time you have chicken, eat grilled chicken, not fried.
Greg: OK. That's not so hard.
Hannah: Now another question. This is about potatoes. How much fat is there in an order of fries? Do you know?
Greg: A lot?
Hanna: You're right. There are 15 grams of fat in a small order of fries. But there's no fat in a plain baked potato. That's 15 grams in the fries and no grams in the baked! But remember, no butter! So the next time you have potatoes, think baked, not fried.
Greg: Wow. I don't believe it!
Hannah: Yes. And one more thing, listen to your wife! She's right. Those vegetables and fruit are good for you. Thanks a lot for calling The Food Show. We have time for one more call.

UNIT 9

Page 168, Exercises 2A and 2B

David: Hello?
Laura: Hi! It's me. How are you doing?
David: I'm fine, thanks. Where are you?
Laura: I'm in Tampa. I'm visiting family, but they're at work now.

David: Tampa! That's great! How's the weather there?

Laura: Well, it's cold and rainy.

Page 168, Exercise 2C

David: Hello?

Laura: Hi! It's me. How are you doing?

David: I'm fine, thanks. Where are you?

Laura: I'm in Tampa. I'm visiting family, but they're at work now.

David: Tampa! That's great! How's the weather there?

Laura: Well, it's cold and rainy.

David: Oh, that's too bad. It's beautiful here in Green Bay. It's not warm, but it's sunny.

Laura: Don't tell me that! Here I am in Tampa, and I'm just sitting in the living room and watching the rain!

Page 174, Exercises 2A and 2B

Ron: Are you watching the news?

Emma: No, I'm not. I'm doing the laundry.

Ron: Turn on the TV. A big storm is coming.

Emma: Really?

Ron: Yes. I'm coming home early. I'm at the supermarket now.

Page 174, Exercise 2C

Ron: Are you watching the news?

Emma: No, I'm not. I'm doing the laundry.

Ron: Turn on the TV. A big storm is coming.

Emma: Really?

Ron: Yes. I'm coming home early. I'm at the supermarket now.

Emma: Oh, good. Are you getting water?

Ron: Yes. I'm getting water, food, and a lot of batteries.

Emma: Great. Get matches, too.

Ron: OK. Do we need anything else?

Emma: Yes. We need good weather!

Page 181, Exercises 2A and 2B

Good morning. This is Weather Watch on Greenville News Radio.

Here's the weather report for cities across the country.

It's cloudy and very hot in Los Angeles. The temperature is already 90 degrees. Wear light clothes and drink lots of water if you go outside.

It's a beautiful day in Atlanta! It's warm and very sunny now with a temperature of 75 degrees So, go outside, take your sunglasses, and enjoy the nice weather.

It's raining in New York City, and the temperature is 62 degrees. Take your umbrella if you go out.

It's very windy in Chicago. The temperature is only 38 degrees. So, don't forget your scarf and gloves. It's pretty cold out there.

UNIT 10

Page 188, Exercises 2A and 2B

Woman: Excuse me. Can you help me? I'm looking for Foodsmart.

Man: Sure. It's on Seventh between Hill and Oak.

Woman: Sorry?

Man: It's on Seventh Avenue between Hill Street and Oak Street.

Woman: Thanks.

Page 188, Exercise 2C

Woman: Excuse me. Can you help me? I'm looking for Foodsmart.

Man: Sure. It's on Seventh between Hill and Oak.

Woman: Sorry?

Man: It's on Seventh Avenue between Hill Street and Oak Street.

Woman: Thanks. Uh . . . is that near here?

Man: Yes. It's just around the corner.

Woman: They're having a grand opening. I guess there are a lot of people there.

Man: No, not really. Only one or two workers.

Woman: Really? I don't understand.

Man: Today is October 7. The grand opening is tomorrow, October 8!

Page 192, Exercise 2B

Conversation 1

A: Don't turn left here.

B: Oh, thanks. I'll turn at the next street.

Conversation 2

A: Be careful. There's a school near here.

B: You're right. I'll drive slowly. A lot of kids cross here.

Conversation 3

A: Be careful. There's a railroad crossing.

B: I know. Do you see a train?

A: Not right now, but be careful anyway.

Page 193, Exercise 3B

Bus 36 leaves 39th Avenue at 8:06 A.M.

Bus 47 leaves Park Avenue at 8:34 A.M.

Bus 51 leaves Pine Street at 8:36 A.M.

Page 194, Exercises 2B and 2C

Tina: Excuse me. How do you get to Adams College?

Officer: Take the Number 4 bus, and get off at Second Street. It's not far from there.

Tina: Thanks. Oh, and how much does the bus cost?

Officer: Two dollars, but you need exact change.

Page 194, Exercise 2D

Driver: Second Street.

Matt:	OK. Here we are at Second Street. Now what?
Tina:	There's a woman. Let's ask her.
Matt:	Excuse me. We want to go to Adams College. How do we get there?
Woman:	It's easy! Study, study, study.

Pages 200–201, Exercise 2A and 2B

Welcome back to Greenville News Radio. It's time for our Weekend Watch.

What are your plans for this weekend? Are you looking for something to do? Well, here's what's happening in our community.

Foodsmart is having its grand opening on Saturday, October 8. They're giving away samples at 3:00. There'll be lots of food and drinks at this free event. Saturday night, Greenville's very own Zeebees are singing at the community college. The concert begins at 8:00. Tickets are on sale now for five dollars.

There's a baseball game Sunday afternoon at one o'clock. Greenville High is playing Lincoln High in Greenville Park. Free with a student ID.

And also on Sunday there's a community yard sale at the Community Center across from the fire station. People are selling old toys, furniture, and clothes. The sale is from 10 A.M. to 4 P.M. Get there early. It doesn't cost just to look!

This is Simon Chan. Have a great weekend!

UNIT 11

Page 207, Show What You Know, Exercise 2

1. Touch your nose.
2. Clap your hands.
3. Close your eyes.
4. Shake your head.
5. Touch your arm.
6. Point to your chest.
7. Nod your head.
8. Point to your knee.

Page 208, Exercises 2B and 2C

Assistant:	Good morning. Greenville Elementary.
Mrs. Lee:	Hello. This is Terry Lee. I'm calling about my son Alex.
Assistant:	Is that Alex Lee?
Mrs. Lee:	Yes. He's sick today. He has a sore throat and a headache.
Assistant:	I'm sorry to hear that. What class is he in?
Mrs. Lee:	He's in Ms. Wong's class.

Page 208, Exercise 2D

Assistant:	Good morning. Greenville Elementary.
Mrs. Lee:	Hello. This is Terry Lee. I'm calling about my son Alex.
Assistant:	Is that Alex Lee?

Mrs. Lee:	Yes. He's sick today. He has a sore throat and a headache.
Assistant:	I'm sorry to hear that. What class is he in?
Mrs. Lee:	He's in Ms. Wong's class.
Assistant:	OK. Thank you for calling. I'll tell Ms. Wong. I hope he feels better soon.
Daughter 1:	Mom, my throat hurts!
Son:	Mom, my head hurts!
Daughter 2:	Mommy, my stomach hurts!
Mrs. Lee:	Uh-oh. Can I call you back?

Page 213, Exercise 2C

Cold Away!
Pain Reliever. Antihistamine.

Directions:
Take 2 tablets orally every 6 hours.

Warnings:
• Do not take more than 8 tablets per day.
• Take with food or milk.
• Do not drive or operate machinery.
• Do not give to children under 12.
• Keep out of reach of children.

Page 214, Exercises 2A and 2B

Tuan:	You weren't here yesterday.
Luisa:	I know. My daughter was home sick. She had a bad cold.
Tuan:	Oh, too bad. How is she now?
Luisa:	A lot better, thanks. She's back at school.

Page 214, Exercise 2C

Tuan:	You weren't here yesterday.
Luisa:	I know. My daughter was home sick. She had a bad cold.
Tuan:	Oh, too bad. How is she now?
Luisa:	A lot better thanks. She's back at school.
Tuan:	Great. And what about your other kids?
Luisa:	Well, they were sick last week, but they're OK now.
Tuan:	That's good. Well, take care, Luisa, and have a good day.
Luisa:	Oh, thanks, Tuan. I'll try.

Page 215, Exercise 3B

1. Marie wasn't here yesterday morning.
2. The students were in class.
3. The teacher was absent.
4. We weren't at work.
5. She was in school.
6. They weren't sick.

Pages 220–221, Exercises 2A and 2B

Dr. Garcia:	Good evening. This is Dr. Elias Garcia. You're listening to Ask the Doctor. I'm here to answer your health questions. Our first question is from Carl Gold. Carl?

Carl:	Yes. Hello, Dr. Garcia. Here's my problem. I exercise. I know it's good to exercise, but I get these terrible backaches. What should I do? Should I use an ice pack?
Dr. Garcia:	Yes, ice is good if your backache is from exercising. But only at first. Later, heat is better. And take a long hot shower.
Carl:	A hot shower?
Dr. Garcia:	Yes. You should use a heating pad, too.
Carl:	OK, great. Thank you, Dr. Garcia.
Dr. Garcia:	You're welcome. Hello, this is Ask the Doctor. Who's speaking?
Jon:	Hello, Dr. Garcia. My name is Jon Kerins. I have a terrible toothache. What should I do? Should I put heat on it?
Dr. Garcia:	No. You shouldn't. Heat feels good, but it isn't good for you. Here's what you should do. Eat a piece of onion.
Jon:	A piece of onion?
Dr. Garcia:	Yes! An onion helps the pain. Also, you should drink lime juice regularly—it helps prevent toothaches.
Jon:	Wow. Lime juice. OK, thank you, Dr. Garcia.
Dr. Garcia:	Thanks for calling. . . . Hello?
Dana:	Hi, I'm Dana Jones. My whole family has the flu. What should we do?
Dr. Garcia:	Gee, I'm really sorry to hear that. There's not much you can do. Stay in bed and drink a lot of fluids.
Dana:	You mean, like water?
Dr. Garcia:	Yes, water, or tea, or even juice. You should drink as much as you can.
Dana:	What about antibiotics?
Dr. Garcia:	No, Antibiotics don't help the flu. You shouldn't take them.
Dana:	OK. Well, thanks.
Dr. Garcia:	I hope you all feel better soon. And that's all the time we have for today . . .

UNIT 12

Page 228, Exercises 2A and 2B

Kofi:	I noticed the Help Wanted sign. I'd like to apply for a job.
Dino:	OK. Which job?
Kofi:	Well, I'm a cook. I can make great hamburgers.
Dino:	Can you make pizza?
Kofi:	No, I can't make pizza, but I can learn.

Page 228, Exercise 2C

Kofi:	I noticed the Help Wanted sign. I'd like to apply for a job.
Dino:	OK. Which job?
Kofi:	Well, I'm a cook. I can make great hamburgers.
Dino:	Can you make pizza?

Kofi:	No, I can't make pizza, but I can learn.
Dino:	Good. As you can see, this place is really busy. The phone never stops.
Kofi:	Well, I can answer the phone, too.
Dino:	Great. Can you start now? Can you answer the phone?
Kofi:	Sure. Dino's Diner. Can I help you?

Page 229, Exercise 3B

1. He can't drive.
2. He can use a computer.
3. She can fix things.
4. She can't cook.
5. I can't lift boxes.
6. I can answer phones.

Page 233, Exercise 1E

A:	Hey, you're looking for a job, right?
B:	That's right. Why?
A:	Well, here's an online job posting. It says you don't need experience.
B:	Really? What's the schedule?
A:	Well, it's only part-time, but you can work any shift.
B:	Oh, that's great. And how much is the pay?
A:	Twelve dollars an hour.
B:	Hmmmm. That's not bad. How can I apply?

Page 234, Exercises 2A and 2B

Dana:	Hi, I'm Dana.
Sam:	Hi, I'm Sam. Wow. This store is really busy.
Dana:	I know. Listen, I need a favor. Can you work this Saturday?
Sam:	Uh, well, yes, I can.
Dana:	Oh, great, thanks, because I can't. Can you work from 2:00 to 7:00?
Sam:	Um, yes. I guess so.

Page 234, Exercise 2C

Dana:	Hi, I'm Dana.
Sam:	Hi, I'm Sam. Wow. This store is really busy.
Dana:	I know. Listen, I need a favor. Can you work this Saturday?
Sam:	Uh, well, yes, I can.
Dana:	Oh, great, thanks, because I can't. Can you work from 2:00 to 7:00?
Sam:	Um, yes. I guess so . . . but, I don't understand. Why are you asking me all these questions?
Dana:	Well, you're the new sales assistant, right?
Sam:	No . . . I'm the elevator repair guy. I'm here to fix the elevator.

Page 240, Exercises 2A, 2B, and 2C.

Tina:	Good afternoon. This is Tina Martins. You're listening to Meet Your Neighbors. Today, I'm in Saigon, Greenville's first Vietnamese restaurant, and I'm talking with Dinh Tran and Mai Lam. Hello. And congratulations! Your restaurant looks great.

Mai: Thank you.

Dinh: Thanks, Tina.

Tina: So, Dinh, is this your first restaurant?

Dinh: Yes, it is. But I worked in a restaurant before.

Tina: Oh. Was that here it Greenville?

Dinh: Yes. The Greenville Café.

Tina: How long were you there?

Dinh: Eight years.

Tina: And what did you do? Were you a cook?

Dinh: Oh, I did a lot of things. I was a cashier, a server, and a cook.

Tina: Wow. So, you really know the restaurant business.

Dinh: Yes, I think so.

Tina: Mai, were you in the restaurant business, too?

Mai: No. I worked in people's homes. I took care of children and I cooked for the families.

Tina: That's interesting. When did you come to this country?

Mai: Twelve years ago.

Tina: Well, your English is great.

Mai: Thanks. We were students at the Greenville Adult School. We also cooked at the school!

Tina: Really!?

Dinh: Yes, we cooked for class parties.

Mai: Right. As our first teacher, Emily Reed, says, we were good students, but we were great cooks!

Dinh: That's right! She says our class parties were always wonderful because of our food.

Mai: Actually, Dinh and I always loved to cook. And now we can cook for everyone here in Greenville. We want everyone here to visit us.

Dinh: Yes. We're right across the street from the new Foodsmart. And we're open every day from noon to 11 P.M.

Tina: Well, it's almost noon now, and people are waiting for the doors to open. So business looks good, and the food smells delicious. For those of you listening today, make a reservation for Saigon at 213-555-8775. And thank you for listening to Meet your Neighbors.

Page 247, Exercise D

Carla: This is Dinh and Mai. They're from Vietnam.

Boris: Nice to meet you. I'm Boris Popov. Carla and I are students at the Greenville Adult School. We're in Level 1.

Mai: Nice to meet you, Boris. Where are you from?

Boris: I'm from Russia.

Carla: Dinh and Mai are students at Greenville, too. He's in Level 5, and she's in Level 6.

Boris: Really? That's great.

Page 253, Exercise A

A: Hey, Brenda. You look great.

B: Thanks, Alan. I feel great! I think it's because I ride my bike a lot.

A: Oh? How often do you ride your bike?

B: Four or five times a week.

A: Really? When?

B: I usually ride before work, from 6:00 to 7:00, and I always ride on Saturdays from 9:00 to 10:00.

A: Good for you!

Page 254, Exercise A

A: This omelet is really good. What's in it?

B: Eggs and cheese. Oh, and there's salt, but not much.

A: Eggs? How many eggs?

B: Three.

A: And how much cheese?

B: Just one slice.

A: What do you cook it in? Do you use butter or oil?

B: I use oil, but it's good with butter, too.

Page 255, Exercise A

A: Hi, Sandy. It's me, Gail. Are you at work?

B: No, I'm not working today. I'm home. There's a really bad snowstorm here. Schools are closed again.

A: Wow! So, what are the kids doing?

B: Well, Tony and Dino are outside in the snow. They're taking pictures.

A: That's nice. What about Maria? Is she playing in the snow?

B: No, she isn't. She's playing computer games with my dad.

A: And you?

B: Well, I'm cooking. And my mom and I are doing laundry. I'm not at work, but I'm pretty busy. And I'm very tired.

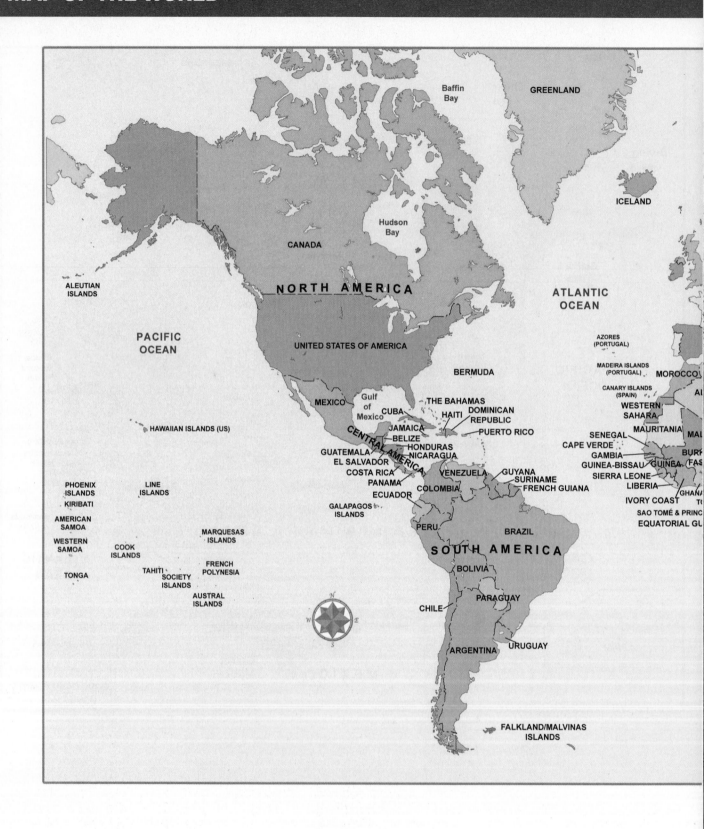

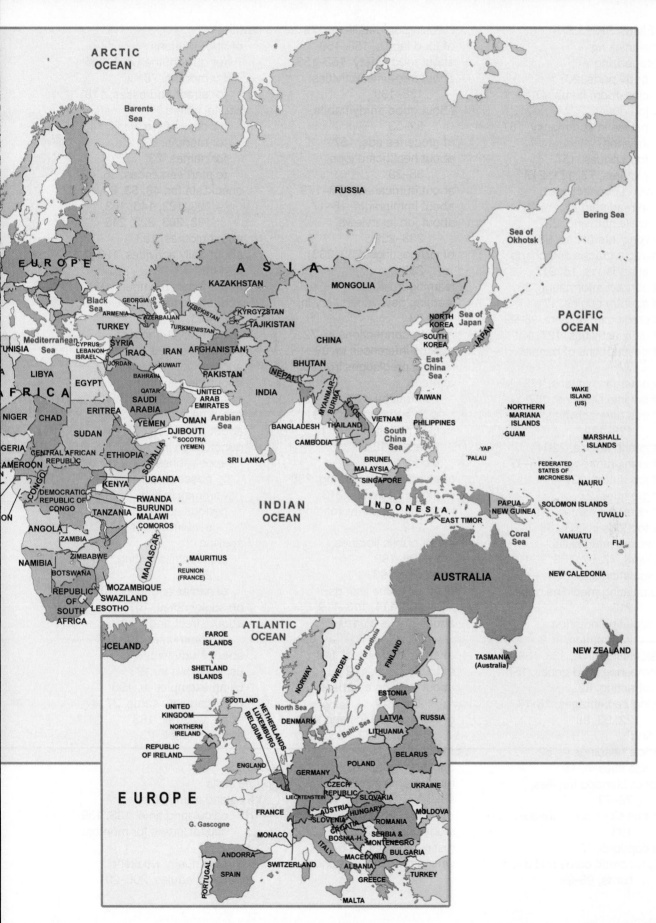

INDEX

GRAMMAR

As soft skill at work, 44
To weather reports, 180–181
About weekend activities,
134–135
About weekend plans,
200–201
About work experience,
240–241
About work hours, 234–235

SPEAKING

About bus routes and costs,
194–195
About child's age and grade,
80–81
About classroom instructions,
48–49
About classroom items, 54–55
About contact information,
32–33
About dates, 78–79
Describing people, 74–75
About directions, 120–121,
188–189
About emergencies, activities
during, 174–175
To explain absence, 208–209
About family, 68–69
About food likes and dislikes,
148–149
About health advice, 220–221
About health problems,
214–215
About hours you can work,
234–235
Identifying people, 12–13
Intonation in
of choice questions with or,
155
falling, 29
rising, 35
Introducing others, 28
Introducing yourself, 8–9
About jobs, 28–29, 40–41
About money and prices,
92–93
About needed and wanted
things, 88–89
To order food in restaurants,
154–155
About people at school, 60–61
About people's jobs, 34–35
About places at school, 58–61

About places in community,
188–189
Pronunciation in
of compound nouns, 115
of consonant sounds
a before, 30
at end of words,
pronouncing, 81
of -es endings, 141
of he's and she's,
linking words together in, 81
of possessive 's, 71
stress in
on can/can't, 229, 235
in compound nouns, 115
on important words, 95
lack of, 195, 215
sound of,
on syllables, 61, 189
on was/wasn't, were/
weren't, 215
syllables in
counting, 187
definition of, 61
with -es endings, 141
stress on, 61, 189
of th, 55
of vowel sounds
an before, 30
at start of words,
pronouncing, 81
About relaxing activities,
140–141
About rental houses, 108–109,
114–117
About school, 18–19
About sizes and colors of
clothes, 94–95
About transportation, 191–193
About weather and activities,
168–169
About weekend activities,
134–137, 200–201
About where people are from,
12–13
About work experience,
240–241

WORK SKILLS

Career awareness
identifying titles of jobs, 27
identifying types of jobs,
26–27

speaking about jobs, 28–29,
34–35, 40–41
types of healthcare jobs,
38–39
Employability skills
job searches, 225–244
body language in
interviews in, 238–239
identifying duties in,
226–227
identifying skills in,
230–231
reading about interviews
in, 238–239
reading job postings in,
232–233, 237
responding to help-wanted
signs in, 228–229
speaking about
experience in, 240–241
speaking about hours in,
234–235
writing about skills in, 243
Workplace skills
being team player, 144
calling to explain absence,
208–209
exchanging contact
information, 32–33
finding information, 124
flexibility, 64
friendliness, 24
learning new, 184
listening, 44
log of, 245–246
making good decisions, 224
professionalism, 104
reading and completing
time sheets, 133
reading work schedules,
132–133
reliability, 204
responding well to
feedback, 244
separating work and home
life, 84
taking action, 164

CREDITS

Photos:

T = top, B = bottom, L = left, C = center, R = right

Front cover: Juanmonino/Getty Images (C); Dave & Les Jacobs/Blend Images/Getty Images (L); Hill Street Studios/Blend Images/Getty Images (R).

Frontmatter

Page vi (front cover inages): Juanmonino/E+/Getty Images; Dave & Les Jacobs/Blend Images/Getty Images; Hill Street Studios/Blend Images/Getty Images; vi (MyEnglishLab screenshot): Pearson Education, Inc.; vi (ActiveTeach screenshot): Pearson Education Inc.; vi (photo in ActiveTeach screenshot): Viacheslav Iakobchuk/Alamy Stock Photo; vi (CCRS page, top, right): Illustration Forest/Shutterstock; vi (CCRS page, bottom, left): Wavebreakmedia/Shutterstock; vii: Sirtravelalot/Shutterstock; viii (1): Suhendri/Shutterstock; viii (2): Wavebreakmedia/Shutterstock; viii (3): Wavebreakmedia/Shutterstock; viii (4): Stephen Simpson/The Image Bank/Getty Images; viii (5): Auremar/123RF; viii (6): Dmitry Kalinovsky/Shutterstock; viii (7): Xinhua/Alamy Stock Photo; viii (8): Dmitry Kalinovsky/123RF; viii (9): Kali9/iStock/Getty Images; viii (10): GogaTao/Getty Images; viii (11): Drazen/ E+/Getty Images; viii (12): Dmitry Kalinovsky/123RF; viii (13): Dmitry Kalinovsky/123RF; viii (14): PR Image Factory/Shutterstock; viii (15): Ingram Publishing/Getty Images; viii (16): Welcomia/123RF;ix (Left page: T): David Mager/Pearson Education, Inc.; ix (Left page: BL): FotoAndalucia/Shutterstock; ix (Left page: TL): PR Image Factory/Shutterstock; ix (Right page: TL): Real Deal Photo/Shutterstock; ix (Right page: TL): Medioimages/Photodisc/Getty Images; ix (Right page: CL): Medioimages/Photodisc/Getty Images; ix (Right page: BL): Andersen Ross/Photodisc/Getty Images; ix (Right page: B): Kali9/iStock/Getty Images; x (Left page: T): RedChopsticks Batch 3/Glow Asia RF/Alamy Stock Photo; x (Left page: B): Hero Images/Getty Images; xi (Left page: T): Denys Semenchenko/123RF; xi (Right page: C): Andrew Poplavsky/123RF; xii (Left page: L): Medioimages/Photodisc/Getty Images; xii (Left page: C): Blue Jean Images/Alamy Stock Photo; xii (Left page: R): Kzenon/Shutterstock; xiii (Right page: T): Sirtravelalot/Shutterstock; xxii (T): Courtesy of Sarah Lynn; xxii (C): Courtesy of Ronna Magy; xxii (B): Courtesy of Federico SalasIsnardi.

Unit 1

Page 5: Steve Debenport/E+/Getty Images; 8 (CR): David Mager/Pearson Education, Inc.; 8 (TL): Sirtravelalot/Shutterstock; 8 (TC): Jennifer Lam/Shutterstock; 8 (TR): Betsie Van der Meer/DigitalVision/Getty Images; 8 (CC): David Mager/Pearson Education, Inc.; 8 (CCC): David Mager/Pearson Education, Inc.; 8 (CL): David Mager/Pearson Education, Inc.; 10: Tyler Olson/Shutterstock; 11 (TL): David Mager/Pearson Education, Inc.; 11 (TR): David Mager/Pearson Education, Inc.; 11 (TR): Ghislain & Marie David de Lossy/DigitalVision/Getty Images; 11 (BL): Ryan McVay/Photodisc/Getty Images; 11 (BR): Jhorrocks/E+/Getty Images; 12 (C): David Mager/Pearson Education, Inc.; 12 (BL): David Mager/Pearson Education, Inc.; 12 (BC): David Mager/Pearson Education, Inc.; 13 (T): Funglochpan/Shutterstock; 13 (C): Don Mason/Blend Images/Getty Images; 13 (B): Karen Struthers/Shutterstock; 14 (all photos): David Mager/Pearson Education, Inc.; 15 (L): David Mager/Pearson Education, Inc.; 15 (R): David Mager/Pearson Education, Inc.; 16 (TL): Andersen Ros/Blend Images/Getty Images; 16 (TC): Sakala/Shutterstock; 16 (TR): Arne Pastoor/Stock4BRF/Getty Images; 18: David Mager/Pearson Education, Inc.; 20: Dragon Images/Shutterstock; 24: Vstock/UpperCut Images/Getty Images.

Unit 2

Page 25: Sirtravelalot/Shutterstock; 26 (1): Suhendri/Shutterstock; 26 (2): Wavebreakmedia/Shutterstock; 26 (3): Wavebreakmedia/Shutterstock; 26 (4): Stephen Simpson/The Image Bank/Getty Images; 26 (5): Auremar/123RF; 26 (6): Dmitry Kalinovsky/Shutterstock; 26 (7): Xinhua/Alamy Stock Photo; 26 (8): Dmitry Kalinovsky/123RF; 26 (9): Kali9/E+/Getty Images; 26 (10): GogaTao/Getty Images; 26 (11): Drazen/E+/Getty Images; 26 (12): Dmitry Kalinovsky/123RF; 26 (13): Dmitry Kalinovsky/123RF; 26 (14): PR Image Factory/Shutterstock; 26 (15): Ingram Publishing/Getty Images; 26 (16): Welcomia/123RF; 28 (T): David Mager/Pearson Education, Inc.; 28 (BL): FotoAndalucia/Shutterstock; 28 (BR): Dmitry Kalinovsky/123RF; 29 (TL): PR Image Factory/Shutterstock; 29 (TR): Real Deal Photo/Shutterstock; 29 (CL): Wavebreakmedia/Photodisc/Getty Images; 29 (BL): Andersen Ross/Blend Images/Getty Images; 29 (BR): Kali9/iStock/Getty Images; 30 (T): RedChopsticks Batch 3/Glow Asia RF/Alamy Stock Photo; 30 (B): Andersen Ross/Photodisc/Getty Images; 32: Denys Semenchenko/123RF; 33: Andrew Poplavsky/123RF; 34 (TL): Erwinova/Shutterstock; 34 (TCL): Andres/E+/Getty Images; 34 (TCR): Evgeny Atamanenko/Shutterstock; 34 (TR): Kjetil Kolbjornsrud/Shutterstock; 34 (CR): David Mager/Pearson Education, Inc.; 38 (T): Hero Images/Getty Images; 38 (C): Blue Jean Images/Alamy Stock Photo; 38 (B): Kzenon/Shutterstock; 40 (TR): PhotosIndia.com RM 11/Alamy Stock Photo; 40 (CL): Steven Frame/Alamy Stock Photo; 40 (CR): David Mager/Pearson Education, Inc.; 41 (TL): Stephen Coburn/Shutterstock; 041 (TR): Africa Studio/Shutterstock; 40 (BL): Blend Images/Andersen Ross/Brand X Pictures/Getty Images; 41 (BL): Dmitry Kalinovsky/Shutterstock; 41 (BR): Hongqi Zhang/123RF; 42 (T): Ariwasabi/123RF; 42 (C): Syda Productions/Shutterstock; 42 (B): Pressmaster/Shutterstock; 44: Sirtravelalot/Shutterstock.

Unit 3

Page 45: Goodluz/Shutterstock; 46 (1): Svetlana Happyland/Shutterstock; 46 (2): Gt29/Shutterstock; 46(3): Igor Zakharevich/123RF; 46 (4): Skoda/Shutterstock; 46 (5): Aigars Reinholds/123RF; 46 (6): Andrey_Kuzmin/Shutterstock; 46 (7): Alexander Kharchenko/123RF; 46 (8): Valentin Agapov/Shutterstock; 46 (9): Coleman Yuen/Pearson Education Asia Ltd.; 46 (10): Tobkatrina/Shutterstock; 46 (11): Ed Phillips/Shutterstock; 46 (12): Suradech Prapairat/Shutterstock; 46 (13): Yurakp/123RF; 46 (14): Natalya Erofeeva/Shutterstock; 46 (15): Shtanzman/123RF; 46 (16): J. Helgason/Shutterstock; 48: David Mager/Pearson Education, Inc.; 49 (TL): Suradech Prapairat/Shutterstock; 49 (TC): You Touch Pix of EuToch/Shutterstock; 49 (TR): Tobkatrina/Shutterstock; 49 (BL): David Mager/Pearson Education, Inc.; 49 (BC): Julia Ivantsova/Shutterstock; 49 (BR): Yurakp/123RF; 52: Viacheslav Iakobchuk/Alamy Stock Photo; 54 (TL): Anton Samsonov/123RF; 54 (TR): Adisa/Shutterstock; 54 (CR): David Mager/Pearson Education, Inc.; 55 (TL): Christophe Testi/Shutterstock; 55 (TC): Igor Zakharevich/123RF; 55 (TR): Aigars Reinholds/123RF; 55 (BL): Stillfx/Shutterstock; 55 (BC): Dan Bucko/Shutterstock; 55 (BR): Akekokomshutter/Shutterstock; 59: Hill Street Studios/Sarah Golonka/Blend Images/Alamy Stock Photo; 60 (TL): Kurhan/Shutterstock; 60 (TCL): Radius Images/Alamy Stock Photo; 60 (TCR): Andersen Ross/Blend Images/Getty Images; 60 (TR): Radius Images/Alamy Stock Photo; 60 (BR): David Mager/Pearson Education, Inc.; 61 (L): ColorBlind Images/Blend Images/Getty Images; 61 (R): Cheryl Savan/Shutterstock; 64: Maroke/Shutterstock.

Unit 4

Page 65: Hill Street Studios/Blend Images/Alamy Stock Photo; 68 (TL): Priscilla Grant/Everett Collection; 68 (TR): Rehan Qureshi/Shutterstock; 68 (BR): Caiaimage/Tom Merton/OJO+/Getty Images; 69: Frederic Cirou/PhotoAlto Agency RF Collections/Getty Images; 71 (Ross): Iofoto/Shutterstock; 71 (Mary): Absolut/Shutterstock; 71 (Ryan): SteveLuker/Shutterstock; 71 (Eva): Kurhan/Shutterstock; 71 (Tess): Fullvalue/E+/Getty Images; 71 (Ed): Jacob Wackerhausen/iStock/Getty Images; 71 (Pat): Alberto Zornetta/Shutterstock; 71 (Alex): Lisa F. Young/Shutterstock; 71 (Meg): Iofoto/Shutterstock; 71 (Jake): Dogachov/123RF; 74: Deborah Suarez/Shutterstock; 76 (TL): Joseph/Shutterstock; 76 (TC): Pkchai/Shutterstock; 76 (TR): Art Vandalay/DigitalVision/Getty Images; 76 (BL): Brosa/Getty Images; 76 (BC): Ariel Skelley/DigitalVision/Getty Images; 76 (BR): Ebtikar/Shutterstock; 79: Volt Collection/Shutterstock; 80 (CR): David Mager/Pearson Education, Inc.; 80 (BR): David Mager/Pearson Education, Inc.; 81 (T): Fuse/Corbis/Getty Images; 81 (C): Design Pics/Con Tanasiuk/Getty Images; 81 (B): Alexkatkov/Shutterstock; 82 (1): RPM Pictures/The Image Bank/Getty Images; 82 (2): Sylva Villerot/Photononstop/Alamy Stock Photo; 82 (3): ESB Basic/Shutterstock; 82 (4): Bill Bachmann/Alamy Stock Photo; 82 (5): Fuse/Corbis/Getty Images; 82 (BL): Euan Cherry/Retna/Photoshot/Everett Collection; 82 (BCL): Photoshot/Everett Collection; 82 (BCR): ZUMA Press, Inc./Alamy Stock Photo; 82 (BR): Kristin Callahan/Everett Collection; 84: Andy Chadwick/Alamy Stock Photo.

Unit 5

Page 85: Shutterstock; 86 (1): Tarzhanova/Shutterstock; 86 (2): Elnur/Shutterstock; 86 (3): Magdalena Wielobob/Shutterstock; 86 (4): Sagir/Shutterstock; 86 (5): Karkas/Shutterstock; 86 (6): Sripfoto/Shutterstock; 86 (7): Elenovsky/Shutterstock; 86 (8): Dmitry Zimin/Shutterstock; 86 (9): Mstudio/Shutterstock; 86 (10): Rj Ierich/Shutterstock; 86 (11): Suradech Prapairat/Shutterstock; 86 (12): DR Travel Photo and Video/Shutterstock; 88 (TL): Pathdoc/Shutterstock; 88 (TR): Mila Supinskaya Glashchenko/Shutterstock; 88 (CR): David Mager/Pearson Education, Inc.; 88 (BL): Lepas/Shutterstock; 88 (BC): J. Helgason/Shutterstock; 88 (BR): Elnur/Shutterstock; 89 (TR): Comstock/Stockbyte/Getty Images; 89 (TL): Theerasak/Shutterstock; 89 (TR): Shutterstock; 89 (BL): Bogdan Florea/Shutterstock; 89 (BC): Karkas/Shutterstock; 89 (CR): Olga Popova/Shutterstock; 89 (T): Nivek Neslo/Stone/Getty Images; 90 (T [inset]): Elnur/Shutterstock; 90 (B): Leungchopan/Shutterstock; 90 (B [insest]): Maxstockphoto/Shutterstock; 92 ($1): Nimon/Shutterstock; 92 ($5): Robynrg/Shutterstock; 92 ($10): Reiulf Grønnevik/Shutterstock; 92 ($20): Robynrg/Shutterstock; 92 (penny): Vladimir Wrangel/Shutterstock; 92 (nickel): Bennyartist/Shutterstock; 92 (dime): Pearson Education, Inc.; 92 (quarter): Jackhollingsworth.com/Shutterstock; 92 (quarter, dime, nickel): Jackhollingsworth.com/Shutterstock, Pearson Education, Inc.; Bennyartist/Shutterstock; 92 (dime, nickel, penny quarter,): Pearson Education, Inc., Bennyartist/Shutterstock, Vladimir Wrangel/Shutterstock, Jackhollingsworth.com/Shutterstock; 92 ($10, $1, nickel, penny): Reiulf Grønnevik/Shutterstock, Nimon/Shutterstock, Bennyartist/Shutterstock, Vladimir Wrangel/Shutterstock; 92($5, dime, penny): Robynrg/Shutterstock, Pearson Education, Inc., Vladimir Wrangel/Shutterstock; 94 (BR): David Mager/Pearson Education, Inc.; 94 (green sweater): Elnur/Shutterstock; 94 (red sweater): Elnur/Shutterstock; 94 (blue sweater): Elnur/Shutterstock; 95 (BL): Sagir/Shutterstock; 95 (BC): Karkas/Shutterstock; 95 (BR): Maxstockphoto/Shutterstock; 96: Goncharov Artem/Shutterstock; 98 (TL): Africa Studio/Shutterstock; 98 (TC): Jeramey Lende/Alamy Stock Photo; 98 (TR): Seeme/Shutterstock; 100 (TL): Himchenko.E/Shutterstock; 100 (TCL): Image Source/Getty Images; 100 (TCR [jeans]): Elenovsky/Shutterstock; 100 (TCR [shirt]): Bonetta/iStock/Getty Images; 100 (TR): Stanley45/iStock/Getty Images; 101 (T): Alexandr Makarov/Shutterstock; 101 (C): Nina Buday/Shutterstock; 101 (B): Aleksandar Mijatovic/123RF; 104: Odua Images/Shutterstock.

Unit 6

Page 105: Shutterstock; 106 (TL): Whitestar1955/123RF; 106 (TR): Breadmaker/Shutterstock; 106 (CL): Interior Design/Shutterstock; 106 (CR): Gaf_Lila/Shutterstock; 106 (BL): Diane Uhley/Shutterstock; 108 (TL): LuckyPhoto/Shutterstock; 108 (TR): Artazum/Shutterstock; 108 (TCR): Robert Kneschke/Shutterstock; 108 (TR): Abd/Shutterstock; 108 (BL): AnnaTamila/Shutterstock; 108 (BCL): Pavel L Photo and Video/Shutterstock; 108 (BR): Wavebreakmedia/Shutterstock; 112 (TL): TerryM/Shutterstock; 112 (TR): Thanatos Media/Shutterstock; 112 (TR): Goodluz/Shutterstock; 114: David Mager/Pearson Education, Inc.; 115: Iofoto/Shutterstock; 116 (TR): Gaf_Lila/Shutterstock; 116 (BR): Interior Design/Shutterstock; 119 (CL): Vadim Ovchinnikov/Shutterstock; 119 (CR): Artazum and Iriana Shiyan/Shutterstock; 120 (TL): Scanrail/123RF; 120 (CL): Andrew Michael/Alamy Stock Photo; 120 (CR): T.W. Van Urk/123RF; 121: Gareth Boden/Pearson Education Ltd; 124: Praet/Shutterstock.

Unit 7

Page 125: Tyler Olson/Shutterstock; 126 (1): PeopleImages/DigitalVision/Getty Images; 126 (2): ESB Professional/Shutterstock; 126 (3): BJI/Blue Jean Images/Shutterstock; 126 (4): Rido/Shutterstock; 126 (5):

PaylessImages/123RF; 126 (6): Shutterstock; 126 (7): Antoniodiaz/Shutterstock; 126 (8): Périg Morisse/123RF; 126 (9): Iakov Filimonov/Shutterstock; 126 (10): Maskot/Getty Images; 126 (11): Elnur/Shutterstock; 126 (12): Africa Studio/Shutterstock; 126 (13): Rommel Canlas/Shutterstock; 128 (TL): Syda Productions/Shutterstock; 128 (TCL): Shutterstock; 128 (TCR): Wavebreak Media Ltd/123RF; 128 (TR): Goran Bogicevic/Shutterstock; 128 (CR): William Perugini/Shutterstock; 128 (BL): Syda Productions/Shutterstock; 128 (BR): Andriy Popov/123RF; 129 (T): Nick White/Getty Images; 129 (C): Gpointstudio/Shutterstock; 129 (B): Elyse Lewin/The Image Bank/Getty Images; 130: David Mager/Pearson Education, Inc.; 134 (TL): BE&W agencja fotograficzna Sp. z o.o./Alamy Stock Photo; 134 (TC): Tom Stewart/Corbis/Getty Images; 134 (TR): William Stall/Shutterstock; 134 (BR): David Mager/Pearson Education, Inc.; 135 (cook): David Tothill/Photofusion Picture Library/Alamy Stock Photo; 135 (bike): CandyBox Images/Shutterstock; 135 (stay home): Peathegee Inc/Blend Images/Getty Images; 135 (basketball): David Buffington/Blend Images/Alamy Stock Photo; 135 (read): Mira/Alamy Stock Photo; 135 (laundry): Pressmaster/Shutterstock; 135 (laundry): Adam Crowley/Photodisc/Getty Images; 135 (beach): Robert Warren/The Image Bank/Getty Images; 135 (wash car): Katarzyna Bialasiewicz/123RF; 135 (play cards): JGI/Blend Images/Alamy Stock Photo; 135 (video games): Phillip Jarrell Photographer/The Image Bank/Getty Images; 135 (swimming): Wavebreak Media Ltd/123RF; 138 (T): Dolgachov/123RF; 138 (TC): Dinis Tolipov/123RF; 138 (BC): Todd Arena/123RF; 138 (B): Image Source/Getty Images; 140 (TL): Blend Images/Shutterstock; 140 (TC): Asia Images Group/Shutterstock; 140 (TR): Tyler Olson/Shutterstock; 140 (BL): Mel Yates/Getty Images; 140 (BR): Fuse/Corbis/Getty Images; 140 (BR): EdBockStock/Shutterstock; 141: Wavebreak Media Ltd/123RF; 144: Lightpoet/123RF.

Unit 8

Page 145: Andresr/E+/Getty Images; 146 (1): Peter Jochems/Shutterstock; 146 (2): Ingvald Kaldhussater/Shutterstock; 146 (3): Baloncici/Shutterstock; 146 (4): Norman Chan/Shutterstock; 146 (5): Frances L Fruit/Shutterstock; 146 (6): Chernyanskiy Vladimir Alexandrovich/Shutterstock; 146 (7): Lisa F. Young/Shutterstock; 146 (8): Robert Milek/Shutterstock; 146 (9): Marlee/Shutterstock; 146 (10): Mikeledray/Shutterstock; 146 (11): MaraZe/Shutterstock; 146 (12): Nataliya Peregudova/Shutterstock; 146 (13): Cokemomo/123RF; 146 (14): Feng Yu/Shutterstock; 146 (15): Elena Elisseeva/Shutterstock; 146 (16): Pixelrobot/123RF; 146 (17): Kamenetskiy Konstantin/Shutterstock; 146 (18): Africa Studio/Shutterstock; 146 (19): You Touch Pix of EuToch/Shutterstock; 146 (20): Trinacria Photo/Shutterstock; 148 (TL): Feverpitched/123RF; 148 (TCL): Hurst Photo/Shutterstock; 148 (TCR): Sergey Peterman/Shutterstock; 148 (TR): Yeko Photo Studio/Shutterstock; 148 (BR): David Mager/Pearson Education, Inc.; 149 (TL): Viktor1/Shutterstock; 149 (TR): Michael C. Gray/Shutterstock; 149 (CL): Siamionau pavel/Shutterstock; 149 (CR): Foodiepics/Shutterstock; 149 (BL): Emil Vasilev Iliev/Shutterstock; 149 (BR): Khz/Shutterstock; 151 (T): Frances L Fruit/Shutterstock; 151 (TC): Feng Yu/Shutterstock; 151 (BC): Trinacria Photo/Shutterstock; 151 (B): Mikeledray/Shutterstock; 152 (TL): Didecs/123RF; 152 (TCL): ASuruwataRi/Shutterstock; 152 (TCR): ND700/Shutterstock; 152 (TR): Didecs/Shutterstock; 152 (BL): Corbis/VCG/Getty Images; 152 (BR): Planet5D LLC/Shutterstock; 154 (tomato soup): MichaelJohn Wolfe/Shutterstock; 154 (coffee): Stocksnapper/Shutterstock; 154 (turkey sandwich): SoleilC/Shutterstock; 154 (fries): Gabriela Trojanowska/Shutterstock; 154 (soda): Africa Studio/Shutterstock; 154 (potato): Joe Gough/Shutterstock; 154 (hamburger): Sergey Peterman/Shutterstock; 154 (iced tea): Rob Byron/Shutterstock; 154 (salad): Bochkarev Photography/Shutterstock; 154 (fruit): Muhammad Kamran Akhlaq/Shutterstock; 154 (apple pie): Marjanneke de Jong/Shutterstock; 154 (ice cream): M. Unal Ozmen/Shutterstock; 154 (BR): Dmac/Alamy Stock Photo; 156: Wavebreakmedia/Shutterstock; 158 (top row, left): Thomas M Perkins/Shutterstock; 158 (top row, center left): Danny Smythe/Shutterstock; 158 (top row, center): Sergei Gorin/123RF; 158 (top row, center right): Matka_Wariatka/Shutterstock; 158 (top row, right): Sukharevskyy Dmytro (nevodka)/Shutterstock; 158 (center row, left): Emil Vasilev Iliev/Shutterstock; 158 (center row, center left): Michael C. Gray/Shutterstock; 158 (center row, center): Olga Lyubkin/Shutterstock; 158 (center row, right): Cameramannz/Shutterstock; 158 (bottom row, left): Pogonici/Shutterstock; 158 (bottom row, center left): Gabriela Trojanowska/Shutterstock; 158 (bottom row, center right): Evgeny Karandaev/Shutterstock; 158 (bottom row, center right): Lisa F. Young/Shutterstock; 160 (salad): Bochkarev Photography/Shutterstock; 160 (potato): Joe Gough/Shutterstock; 160 (fried chicken): Unpict/Shutterstock; 160 (grilled chicken): Andrey Starostin/Shutterstock; 160 (apples): Frances L Fruit/Shutterstock; 160 (milk): Lana Langlois/Shutterstock; 160 (rice): Mikeledray/Shutterstock; 160 (cake): Helen bird/Shutterstock; 160 (fruit): April Turner/Shutterstock; 160 (hamburger): Sergey Peterman/Shutterstock; 160 (green beans): Cameramannz/Shutterstock; 160 (4) (shrimp): Magdanatka/Shutterstock; 161 (tomatoes): Monika Olszewska/Shutterstock; 161 (turkey): Paul Cowan/Shutterstock; 161 (peppers): Fredrednat/Shutterstock; 161 (salmon): Brian Senic/Shutterstock; 161 (cucumbers): Viktar Malyshchyts/Shutterstock; 161 (roast beef): Margouillat photo/Shutterstock; 161 (avocados): Workmans Photos/Shutterstock; 161 (mango): Svetlana Kuznetsova/Shutterstock; 161 (nuts): Oksana2010/Shutterstock; 161 (spinach): Reika/Shutterstock; 161 (carrots): Goncharuk/Shutterstock; 161 (scallions): Binh Thanh Bui/Shutterstock; 161 (watermelon): Tatiana Popova/123RF; 164: Wavebreakmedia/Shutterstock.

Unit 9

Page 165: David Grossman/Alamy Stock Photo; 166 (TL): Evgenii Emelianov/Shutterstock; 166 (TR): Suzanne Tucker/Shutterstock; 166 (BL): Steve Dunwell/Photolibrary/Getty Images; 166 (BR): Smicholi/123RF; 168 (T): Vgstockstudio/Shutterstock; 168 (B): Sam74100/123RF; 169 (L): Robert Kneschke/Shutterstock; 169 (C): Pavels/Shutterstock; 169 (R): Robert Hoetink/Shutterstock; 172 (1): Trekandshoot/Shutterstock; 172 (2): Playalife2006/123RF; 172 (3): Minerva Studio/Shutterstock; 172 (4): JellevdWolf/Shutterstock; 172 (5): Mishoo/123RF;172 (6): Adrian Sherratt/Alamy Stock Photo; 172 (7): Dainis Derics/Shutterstock; 172 (8): Fotostory/Shutterstock; 173: Elizabeth Leyden/Alamy Stock Photo; 174: David Mager/Pearson Education, Inc.; 175 (L): Tyler Olson/Shutterstock; 175 (C): Montgomery Martin/Alamy Stock Photo; 175 (R): David Mager/Pearson Education, Inc.; 177: EpicStockMedia/Shutterstock; 180 (1 [shirt]): Africa Studio/Shutterstock; 180 (1 [trousers]): Gogoiso/Shutterstock; 180 (2): Tudor Photography/Pearson Education Ltd; 180 (3): Dainis/Shutterstock; 180 (4): Iver/Shutterstock; 180 (5): Gvictoria/Shutterstock; 180 (6): John Nairne/Shutterstock; 180 (7): Bjphotographs/Shutterstock; 180 (8): Mega Pixel/Shutterstock; 180 (9): Ingvald Kaldhussater/Shutterstock; 180 (10): Yuyangc/Shutterstock; 180 (11): Sasha Davas/Shutterstock; 180 (12): Coprid/Shutterstock; 181 (CR): Avid_creative/iStock/Getty Images; 184: Sergei Denisov/Shutterstock.

Unit 10

Page 185: Tzido Sun/Shutterstock; 186 (1): Kinn Deacon/Alamy Stock Photo; 186 (2): RaksyBH/Shutterstock; 186 (3): James R. Martin/Shutterstock; 186 (4): David R. Frazier Photolibrary, Inc./Alamy Stock Photo; 186 (5): 06photo/Shutterstock; 186 (6): Mangostock/Shutterstock; 186 (7): Whitestar1955/123RF; 186 (8): Maifly/123RF; 186 (9): Auremar/123RF; 186 (10): Annkozar/Shutterstock; 186 (11): Inga Spence/Alamy Stock Photo; 186 (12): Tyler Olson/123RF; 186 (13): Skydive Erick/Shutterstock; 186 (14): Fiphoto/Shutterstock; 186 (15): Wavebreakmedia/Shutterstock; 186 (16): Iakov Filimonov/123RF; 188 (CL): Olyniteowl/iStock/Getty Images; 189 (TR): Nick Ut/AP Images; 189 (BL): Wavebreakmedia/Shutterstock; 189 (BR): RichLegg/E+/Getty Images; 191 (L): Isaak/Shutterstock; 191 (TC): Kickstand/E+/Getty Images; 191 (TR): Diego Silvestre/Shutterstock; 191 (BL): Andrus Ciprian/Shutterstock; 191 (BC): Anthony Hall/Shutterstock; 191 (BR): Laura Ashley/Alamy Stock Photo; 192 (1): Dcwcreations/Shutterstock; 192 (2): Zoart Studio/Shutterstock; 192 (3): Robert J. Beyers II/Shutterstock; 192 (4): Idea.s/Shutterstock; 192 (5): Vitezslav Valka/Shutterstock; 192 (6): Mr. Alien/Shutterstock; 192 (7): Paul Brennan/Shutterstock; 192 (8): Thitipong Chotwicha/Shutterstock; 192 (9): Shah Rohani/Shutterstock; 194: David Mager/Pearson Education, Inc.; 195 (park): Destinyweddingstudio/Shutterstock; 195 (bus 15): Milkovasa/Shutterstock; 195 (Green's store): Fiphoto/Shutterstock; 195 (bus 16): Milkovasa/Shutterstock; 195 (post office): Andrewasternsky/Shutterstock; 195 (bus 8): Milkovasa/Shutterstock; 197 (TR): Martindm/E+/Getty Images; 197 (chocolate): Lemonpink Images/Shutterstock; 197 (tissues): Graham Stewart/Shutterstock; 197 (milk): Hurst Photo/Shutterstock; 197 (pens): Nattika/Shutterstock; 198 (TL): Todd Strand/Independent Picture Service/Alamy Stock Photo; 198 (TC): Ronnie McMillan/Alamy Stock Photo; 198 (TR): Robnroll/Shutterstock; 198 (BR): Wavebreakmediamicro/123RF; 202: David Mager/Pearson Education, Inc.; 204: Antonio Diaz/123RF.

Unit 11

Page 205: AVAVA/Shutterstock; 206 (L): Michal and Yossi Rotem/Shutterstock; 206 (inset): Michal and Yossi Rotem/Shutterstock; 206 (R): Dolgachov/123RF; 208 (CR): David Mager/Pearson Education, Inc.; 206 (1): Narikan/Shutterstock; 208 (2): Philippe Renaud/123RF; 208 (3): Lucidio Studio Inc/Corbis/Getty Images; 208 (4): Ben Gingell/123RF; 214 (CR): David Mager/Pearson Education, Inc.; 218: PaylessImages/123RF; 221 (woman): Katarzyna Bialasiewicz/123RF; 221 (man): Imtmphoto/123RF; 221 (inset, tea): Anmbph/123RF; 221 (inset, honey): Dustin Dennis/Shutterstock; 224: Shutterpix/Shutterstock.

Unit 12

Page 225: Shutterstock; 226 (1): Elnur/Shutterstock; 226 (2): Fuse/Corbis/Getty Images; 226 (3): Andriy Popov/123RF; 226 (4): Wavebreakmedia/Shutterstock; 226 (5): Top Photo Corporation/Top Photo Group/Getty Images; 226 (6): Solomiya Malovana/Shutterstock; 226 (7): Barros & Barros/Photographer's Choice RF/Getty Images; 226 (8): Monty Rakusen/Cultura/Getty Images; 226 (9): Herjua/123RF; 226 (10): Kadmy/123RF; 226 (11): Andrew Woodley/Alamy Stock Photo; 226 (12): Radius Images/Getty Images; 226 (13): Akurtz/E+/Getty Images; 226 (14): Ernest R. Prim/Shutterstock; 228 (CR): David Mager/Pearson Education, Inc.; 228 (1a): Suhendri/Shutterstock; 228 (1b): Gstockstudio/Shutterstock; 228 (1c): Wavebreakmedia/Shutterstock; 228 (2a): Chris Bence/Shutterstock; 228 (2b): Sergey Peterman/Shutterstock; 228 (2c): Dustin Dennis/Shutterstock; 230: Dotshock/123RF; 233: Andriy Popov/123RF; 234 (BR): David Mager/Pearson Education, Inc.; 237 (L): Leung Cho Pan/123RF; 237 (R [inset]): Chatuporn Sornlampoo/123RF; 238 (B): Tanya Constantine/Blend Images/Getty Images; 240: Dragon Images/Shutterstock; 241 (TR): Fuse/Corbis/Getty Images; 241 (salon): TheDesignTrade/Shutterstock; 241 (stylist): Antoniodiaz/Shutterstock; 241 (grocery store): Montgomery Martin/Alamy Stock Photo; 241 (cashier): Ariel Skelley/Blend Images/Alamy Stock Photo; 241 (clothing store): Fiphoto/Shutterstock; 241 (sales assistant): Sirtravelalot/Shutterstock; 244: Buddit Nidsornkul/Shutterstock.

Backmatter

Page 248: Fuse/Corbis/Getty Images; 249: Daniel M Ernst/Shutterstock; 251: Digital Vision/Photodisc/Getty Images; 254 (T): Wavebreak Media Ltd/123RF; 254 (B): Designs by Jack/Shutterstock.

Illustrations: Steve Attoe, pp. 97, 101; Kenneth Bateman, pp. 111, 253; Luis Briseno, pp. 18, 52, 91, 93, 109, 150, 160, 193; Laurie Conley, pp. 12, 31, 51, 55, 74, 194, 196, 212–213 (top), 218, 250; Deborah Crowle, pp. 6, 168, 181; Len Ebert represented by Ann Remen-Willis, pp. 2 (top); ElectraGraphics, Inc., pp. 24, 37, 44, 48, 50, 58, 64, 72, 78, 79, 84, 104, 114, 119, 124, 131, 132, 133, 136, 138, 142, 146–147, 144, 164, 172, 173, 176, 178, 184, 187, 204, 213 (bottom), 214, 217 (top), 224, 234, 244, 275–277; Brian Hughes, pp. 94, 112, 117, 120, 122, 157, 162, 188–190, 228, 259; Steve MacEachern, pp. 15; André Labrie, pp. 182, 210, 217 (bottom), 231, 236, 238; Luis Montiel, pp. 67, 72 (bottom); Alan Moon, pp. 69, 71, 72, 214; Michel Rabagliati, pp. 3, 36, 62, 216; Roberto Sadi, pp. 77; John Schreiner/Wolfe LTD, pp. 159; Steve Schulman, pp. 3, 76, 137, 174; David Silva, pp. 18–19, 209, 229; Neil Stewart/NSV Productions, pp. 42; Anna Veltfort, pp. 2 (bottom six), 20, 21, 56–57, 80, 102, 170–171, 200–201, 206, 220, 247, 256; Rose Zgodzinski, pp. 166, 222.